Interpreting Historic
House Museums

ABOUT THE SERIES
The American Association for State and Local History Book Series publishes technical and professional information for those who practice and support history, and addresses issues critical to the field of state and local history. To submit a proposal or manuscript to the series, please request proposal guidelines from AASLH headquarters: AASLH Book Series, 1717 Church St., Nashville, Tennessee 37203. Telephone: (615) 320-3203. Fax: (615) 327-9013. Web site: www.aaslh.org.

ABOUT THE ORGANIZATION
The American Association for State and Local History (AASLH) is a nonprofit educational organization dedicated to advancing knowledge, understanding, and appreciation of local history in the United States and Canada. In addition to sponsorship of this book series, the Association publishes the periodical *History News*, a newsletter, technical leaflets and reports, and other materials; confers prizes and awards in recognition of outstanding achievement in the field; and supports a broad education program and other activities designed to help members work more effectively. To join the organization, contact: Membership Director, AASLH, 1717 Church St., Nashville, Tennessee 37203.

Interpreting Historic House Museums

Edited by
Jessica Foy Donnelly

PRESS

A Division of Rowman and Littlefield Publishers, Inc.
Walnut Creek • Lanham • New York • Oxford

ALTAMIRA PRESS
A Division of Rowman & Littlefield Publishers, Inc.
1630 North Main Street, #367
Walnut Creek, CA 94596
www.altamirapress.com

Rowman & Littlefield Publishers, Inc.
A Member of the Rowman & Littlefield Publishing Group
4720 Boston Way
Lanham, MD 20706

PO Box 317
Oxford
OX2 9RU, UK

British Library Cataloguing in Publication Information Available

Library of Congress Cataloging-in-Publication Data

Donnelly, Jessica Foy, 1960–
    Interpreting historic house museums / Jessica Foy Donnelly.
        p. cm.—(American Association for State and Local History book series)
    Includes bibliographical references and index.
    ISBN 0-7591-0250-3 (alk. paper)—ISBN 0-7591-0251-1 (pbk. : alk. paper)
    1. Historical museums—United States—Management.   2. Historic buildings—
Conservation and restoration—United States.   3. Dwellings—Conservation and
restoration—United States.   4. Historic Sites—Interpretive programs—United
States.   5. United States—History, Local.   6. Public history—United States.   7.
United States—Cultural policy.   I. Title.   II. Series.
    E159 .D66   2002
    973'.07473—dc21   2002001963

    Printed in the United States of America

♾ ™The paper used in this publication meets the minimum requirements of American
National Standard for Information Sciences—Permanence of Paper for Printed Library
Materials, ANSI/NISO Z39.48–1992.

CONTENTS

CONTENTS

ACKNOWLEDGMENTS

Interpreting history goes on every day in thousands of house museums across the United States. Even in places where the closest large, well-heeled museum is miles away, a historic house museum usually can be found, valiantly going about its business of preserving and communicating some aspect of the past. The people who staff and support these institutions believe that sharing the past through the context of a site, a structure, its furnishings, the landscape, a family or other residents—famous or not—and their personal possessions is important. They are correct, because house museums are natural settings for teaching and learning history and can be among the most effective environments for successfully carrying out these tasks.

Involved in this effort since the mid-1980s, the Mamie McFaddin Ward Heritage Foundation has given generous grants to the house museum it oversees—the McFaddin-Ward House in Beaumont, Texas—to seek and share information on how best to interpret the site. It provided funding for the two conferences hosted by the museum that served as the basis for this collection of essays. Gary Smith, Bradley Brooks, and Matthew White, the three museum directors whose successive tenures spanned the years from the earlier conference in 1995 to the release of this publication, contributed significantly to the book's development. I am grateful to each for his advice, support, and confidence; to Arlene Troutman for her assistance with a number of details; and to the McFaddin-Ward House board of directors for believing this project was worthwhile and for allowing me to have a hand in it.

Of course, the willingness of the authors to turn their conference presentations into book chapters was paramount. They did so diligently, and without compensation. It has been a great privilege and pleasure to work with this group of dedicated professionals. Their standards are high, and they have vast reservoirs of patience, good nature, and knowledge about their topics. I deeply appreciate their efforts.

ACKNOWLEDGMENTS

The arrival of John Henry in the midst of this project added immensely to the challenge and adventure for me. He has already enlivened the stories that could be told of life in our house. Consequently, my heartfelt thanks go to my husband, John, who not only offered cogent editorial advice but also was instrumental in helping me find time and energy to continue my work despite the major adjustments required by our changed lives. Welcoming our son into the world and shepherding him through his first year have been joyful experiences. Indeed, this book will be forever linked in my mind to this happiest of times.

J. F. D.

The McFaddin-Ward House (built 1905–1906), a historic house museum in Beaumont, Texas. Photograph by Hal Conroy. Courtesy of McFaddin-Ward House.

INTRODUCTION

Jessica Foy Donnelly

Historic house interpretation can be exciting and invigorating or lacklus-ter and just plain boring. Too often, the latter holds true, despite the diligence of a house museum's volunteers and paid staff. I have spent my career working in the historic house and historic site arena, but often find myself lukewarm to the notion of taking a house tour. I enjoy the challenges and opportunities of my professional life and believe strongly in the value of historic house preservation and education. But at some point, I subconsciously became disenchanted with my favorite historical institutions' chief educational offering to the public—the house tour.

Reasons for my restlessness during many of these tours have as much to do with content as presentation style. For instance, tours that a large number of visi-tors probably consider tedious and dull routinely result from interpretations that lack balance. Not only have house museums tended to concentrate heavily on the lives of the rich and famous, and consequently the heads of households, they have also traditionally subjected visitors to an overweighted emphasis on facts about objects. Professionals in the field have recognized the failures of these types of tours, and interpretive emphases have begun to change.

It is tempting to say that house museums have long been confused about their value to the field of history and about the interests of most of their potential audiences. But this criticism is probably too harsh, because views of what is important for them to showcase and teach (and for historians to study) have changed over the years. In light of current thinking, however, house museums that disproportionately interpret the heads of their historical households do so at the expense of the other people, activities, and relationships that also distinguish their sites' histories. They jeopardize their own credibility and public appeal, as well.

Much the same can be said of historic house museums that feature objects as the be-all and end-all of their interpretations.[1] The original domestic environ-ment was, after all, less often a place simply to view things than a place for work-

1

ing, playing, and carrying out all of the activities of life at home. In too many cases, house museums (not established as art museums) that devote their tours exclusively to discussions of objects are also inclined to present their collections strictly as decorative arts. By doing so, they often ignore the homeowners' reasons for acquiring and owning the objects, neglect the artifacts' primary uses in the house, and discriminate against the host of nondecorative items that were equally essential to the particular home environment.[2] Such an approach may also deter learning if visitors consider the objects ugly or the historical resident's aesthetic tastes lacking. And if visitors don't care whether a chair exhibits characteristics of the work of New York craftsmen or Midwest manufacturers or of the Renaissance revival or the rococo style and so on, much of the information shared is meaningless and irrelevant.

Indeed, facts about things mean little to people who aren't interested in them or who have no context within which to place the information. Many times a guide will single out an object simply because someone has unearthed a bit of information about where it was made or what it is made of, when instead the object's greatest interpretive contribution is as a piece of the puzzle that, when assembled, presents settings and suggests meanings. Objects, taken collectively, give context and structure to the realities of domestic living. House museums are likely to overlook this potential when a larger framework within which to place and sort fragments of information is absent.

The object collection is neither the sole nor the supreme element, but a coequal component of historic house interpretation. It is integral. Objects should not be downplayed or overplayed, but—like all other pertinent historical elements—incorporated into the interpretive agenda with balance and discernment. The study of material culture is fascinating and sheds a bright light on our understanding of the past. House museums should take advantage of this discipline and use it to uncover and understand the relationships between the tangible and intangible aspects of their sites' histories.

In some cases, a focus on things has satisfied those visiting the home of a famous historical figure. Just seeing the possessions of a revered person, like George Washington or even Elvis, has been exactly what the visitor wanted. There's nothing wrong with that, but any site can offer a much more complex vision of its past through multilayered and multisensory experiences that expand interpretive choices and create connections. In doing so, it will ultimately appeal to more people. The staff at Mount Vernon has found this to be true, and many other house museums have made or are beginning to make the same discovery.[3]

Happily, an awareness of the opportunities missed by merely interpreting objects and famous people has begun to take hold in recent years. Making the

2

transition, however, will not happen overnight. Deliberate planning and research to develop a site's story into a carefully thought-out and implemented interpretation requires time and commitment from all areas of the museum. This book offers recommendations on how to go about this task. The authors were speakers at conferences organized and hosted in the 1990s by the McFaddin-Ward House Museum in Beaumont, Texas. These symposia featured practical discussions of issues and operations pertinent to house museums of all sizes, types, periods, and financial conditions, with special consideration for the small, understaffed, and underfunded ones. The articles included here are based on conference presentations about topics related to interpretation.[4] This volume, therefore, is not intended to be a comprehensive study of house museum interpretation, but it attempts to lay out some of the most important elements of discovering, organizing, and telling the historic house story.

The House Museum Advantage

While the authors primarily focus their attention on historic houses, much of what they share here is applicable to interpretation at other historic places, as well. Still, a historic dwelling provides a compact and holistic environment for offering lessons in history. No matter what its age, size, or style, or what life inside and outside was like, a *residence* is a universally understood place. Every visitor starts with the benefit of understanding this fundamental relationship— the greatest advantage of interpreting the past through historic houses.

Good interpretation builds on such connections. That *people* actually lived in the structure extends the basic connection, for people are interested in and can relate in basic ways to others, even those of a different time. Within the home, people eat, play, work, sleep, entertain, clean, cook, and carry out many of the same activities that they have since time began. Although those who lived and worked in the historic house may be long gone, it is not a great stretch for visitors to imagine life within it, for they have their own experiences as a base of knowledge within which to understand, compare, and compartmentalize interpreted information.

At one time or another, people actually experienced life in these historic structures. Without having to contrive settings or unrelated activities, house museums can construct *experiences* through which their visitors can actively learn about the past and engage in the re-created past in believable ways. Replicating ambient conditions, as authentically and appropriately as possible, and allowing visitors to participate in activities of the past can tap emotions and senses. Applying this approach to sharing the past, rather than just telling about it, is a fitting way to enrich understanding about domestic life in years gone by.[5]

This approach also enhances the telling of a site's *stories*. Domestic life is rich with stories, and they, not simply their constituent parts (the facts), should form the center of historic house interpretation. Professor David Lowenthal reminds us, after all, that facts "woven together as stories" make the past intelligible.[6] Stories link people, events, things, places, problems, solutions, conversations, ideas, situations, and any number of activities. The interesting ones have plots, variously accented with drama, intrigue, adventure, scandal, romance, and humor. No two sites have the same story to tell, although time periods, geographic locations, house styles, and the like may be common elements. The site's mission and history are the most important parameters, and within these any number of stories may spring forth. Effective interpretation demands judicious choices as to which stories are most important and how to narrow the number to a manageable few, or even just one.

Historic houses also are places where objects can be displayed and stories told in their original *contexts*. House museum director George McDaniel describes the historic building as the "'skin' on the abstraction of time past."[7] The settings for the artifacts are real. The visitor's imagination is freed from wondering what and where to contemplating how the items were used, who used them, when, and why. In this way, the house and its collection are not the whole story but the surviving tangible parts that supply critical information, add color and dimension, and serve as springboards for discovering life as it was at that particular place and time.

Interior and exterior spaces at the house are also part of the context. The placement of public rooms in relation to private rooms and service areas is readily apparent. Visitors can see or trace how far the cooking area was from the eating area, or how far the bathroom (or outhouse) was from the sleeping areas. They are able to see the dwelling's spatial relationships. Unless the structure has been moved from its original location, at least some of the historical exterior features are also extant. A yard, outbuildings or neighboring structures, landscape features—a tree, a creek, a vista uninterrupted by modern elements—anything with roots in the building's historical era provide some context, however limited or expansive, for viewing the placement of the house in relation to the world outside. Even if such elements are long gone, they existed at one time and need to be rediscovered. Providing a context for learning is essential for successful interpretation, and house museums often have an inherent head start in this aspect of teaching the past.

4

The authors of the chapters that follow expand on these and other issues. Additionally, they acknowledge the drawbacks and challenges intrinsic to house museum interpretation. As anyone who has ever worked at one of these sites understands, the houses were not intended to serve as public buildings for dozens of people to traipse through every day. The difficulties of access and the need to adapt interpretive narratives to fixed sets or sequences of spaces present other hurdles.

Furthermore, interpretation generally has to take place within the setting as it is. Collections don't change much and space for installing supplemental exhibits is usually not available. As a result, historic house interpretation can remain static for years, even decades. Other typical reasons for unchanging exhibits include understaffing, inadequate resources, and indifference. However, with creativity, energy, and an eye toward new research and interpretive strategies, historic house museums can refresh and enliven the telling of their stories, all the while preserving authenticity, staying true to their sites' missions, and illuminating the many engaging aspects of home life in the past.

Scholarship and Perspective

As all of the authors here point out, house museum interpretation must be based on historical evidence and good scholarship. When people visit house museums, or any other museum for that matter, they probably expect to learn something. They have many other ways to get historical information, so when they choose a house museum as a venue not only for entertainment, but for learning, they have every right to expect that what they see, hear, and experience is accurate and true. In fact, most people would consider a house museum to be a credible, even expert, source for information about home life in the past.[8] One way a site can severely damage its reputation is to fail to present good history that is based on thorough and up-to-date research. Letting visitors down in this manner is unnecessary and irresponsible, and often irreparable.

Developing an interpretation is not easy, in part because knowing the past and deciding which or whose past to interpret are not simple matters. Even a snippet of the past—such as the story of a particular house and its residents at a particular time—contains an immense amount of data with many aspects, many perspectives, many historical truths. Accepting this reality and confronting it head on are essential to house museum interpretation in the twenty-first century.

In analyzing research and developing interpretations, house museum planners must understand that features of their site's past hold—and held—different meanings to different people, including those who constitute the museum's audience. The same past may arouse pride or fond sentiment in some, while causing resentment, indifference, or consternation in others. It may trigger feelings of joy or pain, happiness or discontentment, interest or disgust. Indeed, daily life in a particular home will have meant something entirely different to the parent, the child, and the housekeeper. Different people would probably describe the personality of the homeowner in different terms. A slave would remember plantation life differently than would the slave's owner. The landscape setting for the interpreted house will have undergone change in ways that the historic structure would not have, and vice versa. The farmer, his wife, children, buyers, and neighbors would prize his crops differently. The chauffeur or carriage driver would view his vehicle and work through a much different lens than would those who paid for his services. Historical truths are, therefore, numerous and varied. This fact can be inconvenient for historic house interpretation, for it precludes simple, and simplistic, depictions of life in the past.

Before the end of the twentieth century, the house museum movement faced criticism for interpreting almost exclusively the history of famous men, most of whom were wealthy and white. Critics accurately pointed out that, by doing so, historic house museums were neglecting a huge chunk of history. In the 1960s and 1970s, historians increasingly devoted their efforts to researching the rest of the population, and their successors have followed suit. As a result, American society has gained historical insight into a much broader cross section of its population, at the same time exposing the narrowness of the traditional house museum approach. More historical truths continue to be exposed, and house museum interpretation has begun to respond.

Obviously, the house museum that tries to be all things to all people and all histories will fail. Discipline and judgment as to what not to interpret are as important as defining and fleshing out the main story. While these institutions cannot effectively interpret every aspect of their pasts, they can and should convey the historical stories they choose to interpret in light of as many contexts and points of view as is feasible. The home of a wealthy merchant, for example, was not just a setting for unbridled consumption, leisure, and rich people; it was a center of significant daily activity by craftsmen, domestic servants, yardmen, schoolchildren, husbands and fathers, wives and mothers. The homes of laborers, immigrants, slaves, tenants, and other less-studied groups are equally valid, interesting, and complex settings for learning history.

In terms of house museum interpretation, the statement "This is the way it was" should be true of as much of the past as possible. *Balance*, shaped by informed judgment, is key. The solution does not lie in excluding the houses and histories of famous white men, for therein lie historical truths, too. Some historians have cautioned that giving uncritical attention to previously neglected groups "can wind up producing the same sort of celebratory history found in traditional great-man" interpretations.[9] But incorporating other histories and views and expanding and focusing on those that have long been untold or understated will bring greater accuracy and enrichment to any historic house interpretation. Everyone has a history that contains positive and negative elements. The successful house museum will do its best to acknowledge all that enhances the meaning of the main story.

While the stories of people are essential to interpretive inclusiveness, so is the story of the site's exterior setting. The house existed at a place, on a square of land or on vast acreage sometimes dotted with one or more outbuildings. Interpreting the context of the main structure stimulates greater understanding of the way life actually happened. Was the family isolated from neighbors, businesses, and town centers? Did the landscape reflect the decorative qualities of the house, and thus the aesthetic taste and financial status of the owners? Was it used to contribute to the family's self-sufficiency or as a place where household activities and entertainment moved outdoors? Did children play there? Did changes in the landscape's living features make any difference to life inside? As trees grew, was the house's interior climate in the summer more comfortable for residents? Historic houses are much more than self-contained buildings. They represent whole places, and they will benefit from a holistic approach to interpretation—a consideration of all perspectives, features, and activities within the context of all others.

With this in mind, it is vital that historic house researchers and interpretive planners not limit their investigations. A widerange of resources and research strategies will expose what one or two historical accounts cannot: a complex picture seen within the broader contexts of what was relatively a mere moment in time. This picture becomes clearer and nearer to authenticity with each additional source consulted and analyzed.

A number of published sources provide ideas and guidelines for conducting some of the fundamental research required of house museum specialists. *Recreating the Historic House Interior* by William Seale and *Underfoot: An Everyday Guide to Exploring the American Past* by David Weitzman are examples of books that describe resources for basic house and family research. Sherry Butcher-Younghans also outlines some methods, questions, and resources for research in her book *Historic House Museums: A Practical Handbook for Their Care, Preservation, and Management*. In *American Farms: Exploring their History*, R. Douglas Hurt provides practical tips for researching farms and farm families.[10] The "Nearby History Series," a project of the American Association of State and Local History, features titles such as *Houses and Homes: Exploring Their History* and *Nearby History: Exploring the Past around You*, both valuable sources for the historic house researcher. For understanding local and domestic history issues within a social history context, *Ordinary People and Everyday Life: Perspectives on the New Social History*, an anthology edited by James Gardner and G. Rollie Adams, is a good place to start.

Readers will discover numerous other guides and reference materials mentioned in the chapters and chapter notes that follow. The authors reiterate some strategies and considerations outlined in the books listed above and offer others. Oral history, archaeology, public and private records, material culture, academicians and local historians, and of course libraries and archives can all reveal useful information. Preparing a Historic Structures Report is one of the most important steps that historic house researchers can take in the research process. Consultation with historians and staff at other sites of the same time period can also produce a treasure trove of pertinent information. Specialists in areas appropriate to the research effort can provide valuable perspective on the merits and applicability of the information gathered. They can also be guides to the latest scholarship on a given topic.

No data uncovered, however, should be considered in isolation. Before applying it to the interpretation under development, researchers must analyze it carefully and critically. For information gathered from primary sources, they should ask numerous questions. What was the purpose and general degree of accuracy of its source? What is its relationship to similar evidence from other sources? Does its credibility hold up within the context of other data?

One of the largest primary sources at a historic house museum is the building itself, and—if the staff is fortunate—an intact collection of furnishings, personal belongings, and family papers. Museum personnel must carefully scrutinize and assess physical evidence within the context of the era interpreted; earlier and later changes, alterations, and arrangements; the family's lifestyles and habits; and other examples within the collection, neighborhood, and town—and beyond. Sites with collections intact also can be valuable sources of information for staff at other museums representing the same historical, social, or economic stratum. Seeking out and consulting these institutions is time well spent.

In the case of secondary sources, researchers need to consider the perspective, values, and approach of the author or analyst; whether the author's conclusions are based on good evidence; the quality of the research; and how the conclusions compare with those of other scholars. All in all, interpretive planners cannot look at too many sources. Certainly, planning eventually has to proceed toward implementation, but the wise and effective house museum will realize that its research will never be done and will pursue it relentlessly and use it judiciously.

Various forces within an institution may hinder this goal, so an institution-wide dedication to making priorities of research and good history is necessary. Small staffs may be especially constrained, but volunteers, students (especially if there is a college or university nearby), even consultants—if the institution has the resources—can all assist. The strength of the museum's founding philosophy may also hinder expanding research and, for that matter, making any changes to the original interpretation.[11] This sort of dilemma requires care and discretion, but the museum's reputation and success depend upon its integrating accurate and up-to-date research into its efforts. If descendants of the homeowners are interested or involved in the museum in any way, staff members ought to respect their concerns and cultivate them as valuable resources for research. It is possible to be sensitive to their strong opinions and still interpret the site accurately. In general, high ethical standards demand that staff extend their creativity to dealing with these situations with integrity, sensitivity, and balance.

Places to Learn

To be effective places to learn something about history, house museums must reflect in their interpretations not only knowledge of historical facts, but also knowledge of their audiences—who visits, what they expect, why they come, how they learn, what they think about their experience, and who doesn't come and why. Historic house museums traditionally have not devoted a lot of energy to this kind of study. An individual, group, or governmental body once thought the site important enough to preserve and restore so it could be shared with the public. It, therefore, continues to exist for the purpose of serving the public interest. The effectiveness of people or places that serve others depends on their care and skill in attending to or addressing someone else's interests and needs. House museums must do the same for their visitors and potential audiences or risk wasting their interpretive energies on themselves.

Connecting the present with the domestic past, house museums exist today but represent life way back when. Part of their challenge lies in figuring out how to help visitors comprehend the past. The people, the lives they lived, and the era are all gone and no historical account or piece of evidence, even when combined with all of the others, can ever recapture that past. We can know various facets of it, but those particulars that we ultimately learn and understand generally pertain to subjects that we already *care* about in some way.[12] A primary goal of historic house interpretation, then, should be creating experiences and telling stories within the context of the lives represented by the house and its collection and about things that mean something to visitors—things that they care about and that bear some relation to their own interests and lives.

Many in the house museum field are concerned that these institutions will lose audiences if they lag in incorporating new technologies into their interpretive strategies. House museums have been slow to use and participate in shaping the latest innovations to help tell their stories. Today's technology-friendly society is accustomed to dealing with high-tech devices in most areas of life. It is tricky, however, to incorporate them into the historic house setting without intruding on the historical environment. For the many underfunded sites, doing so may not even be practical, because maintenance and keeping up with the ever-changing nature of the technology might require more resources than they can allocate. Creative uses and adaptations of new technologies in house interpretation lie waiting to be explored and experimented with—and they need to be—but they are not *the* answer to the dilemma of developing an interpretation that appeals to the general public. Such considerations are impractical until a house museum turns its efforts toward making what it says interesting and relevant to the people it serves.

In addition to tapping visitor interests for interpretive purposes, museums must factor in visitor expectations. Fortune smiles on hardworking interpretation planners who want to share knowledge, because many museum visitors probably arrive motivated, at least to some degree, to learn. House museum staffs need to spend time studying how people learn and what influences those processes. Published resources geared specifically to museums can be invaluable to this effort.[13] Successful approaches at other sites can be equally instructive if investigators understand fully the reasons *why* those programs and interpretive methods work. On the other hand, motivations for visiting museums may have nothing to do with learning. Advisory groups, visitor research, and program evaluation can all help planners pinpoint the multifarious expectations and then decide how to address them best.

Visitors also anticipate seeing or experiencing something akin to what they have been told by publicity materials or other people. In explaining the intense controversy surrounding the slave auction reenacted at Colonial Williamsburg in 1994, Christy Coleman Matthews, the program's director, notes that the institution's overall marketing efforts had not prepared visitors for the reality that "complex history was a part of its offerings." As a result, many potential visitors did not know what to expect or that the institution had extensive experience dealing with African-American history.[14] Marketing and publicity efforts play an important role in portraying a museum's interpretive image and cultivating the expectations of those who have yet to visit. As house museums travel the road toward increasingly complex interpretive experiences, all of their personnel must be along for the ride to garner an effective, consistent image.

10

As trends develop and diverge and as people continue to have even greater access to historical information, especially through the Internet and its successors, what the public expects and wants to learn from historic houses will change. Historic house museums cannot afford to wait around to see what those new interests will be. Time marches on. With each day comes a new past, as well as new perspectives on more distant pasts. We constantly learn more about the results of the events, conditions, and discoveries of bygone eras. We know, for example, how harnessing electricity modernized homes. We know that slavery in America ended. Our forebears could not see what the future, near or far, held for them; but we know their futures—and how their lives changed or would have changed—because we can look into the past.

By the same token, general attitudes shift and new understandings emerge about what has been overemphasized, underemphasized, or ignored in historical interpretation. Consequently, plans developed by and for house museums must remain fluid, especially with regard to interpretation. They must respond to what visitors want, to how they learn, and to the ever-expanding body of historical research. What we know and need to know about that past increases daily; therefore institutions of history, in particular historic house museums, must stay abreast, constantly reevaluate and update what they're doing and how they are sharing their messages, and apply fresh knowledge of the past as expeditiously as possible. There is usually more than one good way to do things, and creativity and well-reasoned experimentation with different interpretive tools and methods can strengthen the undertakings of house museums well into the twenty-first century.

Steps to Take

In the following chapters, the authors address all of these issues and many others as they present practical information and advice on how to go about the business of interpreting historic houses. Providing useful context, Patrick H. Butler III begins by tracing the history of the American house museum movement. The types of houses preserved and ideas about what sort of information they should convey have evolved since the historic house preservation movement began in the mid-1800s. Butler is concerned, however, that too many historic houses have not kept up with the times and are locked into an image of a "fussy, dusty place" with little or no relevance to the present. As the number of house museums has increased, especially since World War II, the challenges facing them have intensified. Funding issues remain, but new and rapidly changing technologies, the changing character and diversity of the American population, and the fundamental question of survival all push house museum stewards toward reevaluation and perhaps even a reconfiguration of their institutions' relevance and purpose.

At the center of this search for significance is interpretation, which, Butler asserts, should convey the "complexity of life in the past and the relationship of that complexity to our present and to our future." Effectively presenting such a complex story requires careful planning. Barbara Abramoff Levy provides a step-by-step method for developing an interpretive plan that can be useful to all aspects of the museum's operations for years to come. Hers is not a quick and easy process, but it is one that any site can use. Following it will invigorate the staff and provide a base of information and a strategy for making all sorts of interpretation-related decisions. She describes the value of presenting information according to a small number of themes, and she emphasizes building interpretive programs that correspond to the ways people learn best. Noting that the educational value of any interpretation depends on "the quality of the history on which it is based," Levy supplies an organized approach to identifying the site's most important stories, its audiences and their needs and interests with regard to the museum, and the best means for communicating the interpretation to the public.

Rex M. Ellis stresses the need for historic house museums to interpret the variety of perspectives their sites represent. He notes that, as institutions of history, house museums have lagged in teaching the latest historical scholarship. This has put them behind the rest of the history field and even much of the public. High levels of access to information in this technological age have elevated the standards of historical accuracy and inclusion, and house museums are often not keeping up. Reminding us that there is "no one true window through which to view the past," Ellis lays out considerations and strategies for achieving inclusiveness in historical interpretation. Good research, informed interpreters, good presentation techniques, preparing for and handling controversy, making connections, and telling good stories are all issues pertinent to amplifying previously unheard voices with effectiveness and meaning.

Debra A. Reid, too, thinks that no voice associated with a historic house should be left silent. Her emphasis is, however, on gender roles, which house museums have been prone to misinterpret. This is partly a result of preconceived notions about the responsibilities that men and women historically assumed with regard to home and family. It can also be traced to the particular ways many museum founders sought to portray the historical characters associated with their preservation efforts. Although research in women's studies has produced more secondary information about the domestic lives of women than is available on the same topic for men, Reid advocates balance in interpreting male and female perspectives in the historical home. She continues the mantra that interpretation planning and good research are essential, and that with these solid fundamentals, museum staffs can launch into an exploration and inventory of gender issues and then incorporate them into the site's chosen interpretive themes.

Human perspectives aren't the only elements often missing from house museum interpretation. Significant features of the site itself have also been overlooked. To promote full understanding of the history of a house, its interpretation must consider the context of the entire site. Catherine Howett maintains that, from the standpoint of our forebears, the development of the landscape was at least as important as the development of the residence and related structures. Present-day perspectives have led us to neglect the historical significance to homeowners of the land. As does the built environment, landscapes carry "meaning and value across generations," and Howett believes that historic house museums must heighten their respect and scholarly attention toward them if they want to convey a true sense of place to their visitors. Museums face interesting challenges with regard to landscape interpretation, primarily because of the transience and constant change of living things. With a realistic understanding of the extent to which we can really know the past and within the boundaries of careful research, the story of the landscape, combined with all other elements of domestic living, helps complete the larger story house museums are obliged to tell.

Much of this storytelling is done within a dwelling—one that in most cases is furnished. Building on the theme that furnished settings must correspond in authenticity to the stories a site tells, Bradley C. Brooks explains what is involved in developing a comprehensive furnishings plan. Although it sometimes seems as though house museums are being advised to plan themselves to death, the resulting tools are important to an institution's success. The furnishings plan, Brooks points out, "exists so that the interpretive plan may be realized." Because this plan responds to interpretive needs, the responsible historic house staff will not leave it unchanged but will consult it regularly and alter it as necessary to address newly found information and evolving interpretive requirements. The author offers a definition and guidelines for accurately re-creating "a complex material culture vignette" in light of an array of interpretive, curatorial, and operational concerns.

Objects displayed must correspond to and illustrate the stories told or any meaning may be lost on the visitor, especially the many visual learners who carry away strong mental images but little of what was said. Nancy E. Villa Bryk describes how to use objects to tell stories, to evoke historical "moments in time." The resulting settings suggest believable images of real life, unlike the pristine period room settings that house museums have traditionally presented. They reveal personalities, habits, and activities and can effectively tap emotions and create connections between visitors and the historical figures through the "heart as well as the head." As in all interpretive efforts, careful research is of foremost importance, but investigating domestic lives often still leaves numerous gaps in information. Bryk suggests sharpening one's "disciplined imagination" to judiciously march ahead, although she notes that the moment-in-time furnishing method she sets forth is appropriate neither to every house museum nor to the faint-hearted curator. Under the right circumstances, however, it is an effective way to help visitors know and relate to the lives a museum interprets.

Before visitors can experience interpreted settings and learn about the lives associated with them, they must have access. Unless the historic house is accessible to visitors, its interpretation and planning will be meaningless. This issue may be complicated for structures dedicated to strict standards of preservation. In reality, is it possible to achieve access while maintaining historical and architectural integrity? Valerie Coons McAllister emphatically says yes. She refers to the Historic Preservation Act and the Americans with Disabilities Act to outline a process for compliance and for identifying appropriate accessibility options and solutions. Entry to the building and its interior and exterior spaces are not the only concerns. Accessible interpretation methods and programs contribute to making the site's story available to everyone. McAllister shakes her head at the limited vision of historic houses that address access issues only for the sake of obeying the law. The benefits in overall visitor satisfaction, community support, and audience development make the greater effort more than worthwhile. After all, people with disabilities (broadly defined) constitute what is perhaps our country's largest minority group, and it is one that any nonmember can join without a moment's notice. It's hard to imagine why access planning wouldn't be integral to all historic house operations.

The tour is arguably the educational experience most people associate with historic house museums. Deciding on the best way for visitors to access the site's story through tours is yet another important challenge. Barbara Abramoff Levy refers to the tour as "a method of storytelling." While noting that tour implementations vary widely, she focuses on the primary types—third-person, self-guided, recorded, and first-person—describing the strengths and weaknesses of each and citing specific examples of their effective use. She also shows that successful tours all share common characteristics: thematic organization, good evidence, people stories, historical context, and a carefully planned visitor experience.

Sandra Mackenzie Lloyd takes the discussion of tours a step further. She correlates her four-step process for developing memorable tours to the type of interpretation planning Levy describes in chapter 2. Lloyd maintains that as tour developers embark on their journey, they must set aside assumptions and preconceived ideas and turn the house "upside down and inside out" to uncover facts.

Then they must concentrate on creating strategies that will connect the site's stories with the public's interests and expectations in a captivating fashion. Presenting tours from the perspectives of various family members turned out to be an effective angle for the house museum she discusses. Choosing the specific eyes through which visitors will see a historic house is an aspect of tour development that is easily overlooked as museums attempt to present composite pictures of complex historical stories. Present-day biases will inevitably color any view that tours convey, but by focusing engagingly and accurately on the perspectives of individual characters in the historical story, such tours can enliven the public's understanding of the past in a personal way.

Indeed, the manner in which an interpreter communicates the site's story can make or break the effectiveness of the learning experience. Studies have shown that even more than the specifics of a museum's story, visitors remember their guides.[15] If interpreters have engaged visitors in the experience and demonstrated an interest in them, Margaret Piatt believes the memories will be positive and the essence of the interpretation will more likely be absorbed. Part of communicating well is using appropriate methods. Because of the prevalence of the house tour, interpretation at house museums most often relies on individual interpreters as the channel of communication. Piatt notes that their personal attitudes and outlooks influence the information they share in the same way that those of their visitors affect what they learn. Issues of perspective affect interpretation in almost every way. However, clear and meaningful messages, efficient organization of the interpretation, and good interpreter training that teaches effective presentation techniques can bring some degree of consistency to the storytelling and help create positive learning environments.

To assist interpreters in their significant responsibility, house museums must stay attuned to their needs just as they must care about visitors and their interests. Because interpreters are central to house museum interpretation, they require and deserve extensive attention and training from the museum. Meggett B. Lavin offers ideas for nurturing these staff members, who, more than anything or anyone else, represent and even embody the site for visitors. Preparing interpreters for their work and finding ways to help them enjoy it and feel comfortable will further the interpretive effort that the museum has spent so many resources to develop.

In addition to the tour, house museums that have developed their interpretive goals have the foundation for creating an endless array of other mission-related, research-based educational programs. Jamie Credle suggests a process for developing these programs, reminding us that creativity is essential. But without careful planning, knowledge of audiences and subject matter, as well as advice from others, efforts will likely fall short of their potential. She encourages museum educators to strive to make their programs opportunities for "critical thinking and active learning," keeping in mind that good education programs, skillfully presented, evoke the "special character of the place." All house museums, she argues, can achieve positive results.

But how do museums with small staffs and limited resources produce good programming? Patricia L. Kahle brings an end to this collection of essays by answering from the standpoint of Shadows-on-the-Teche, a National Trust for Historic Preservation property in Louisiana. Carefully conceived programs can reach people of all backgrounds, but sustaining them requires a staff committed to history education. With the help of dedicated volunteers and staff and an involved community, even small museums can succeed in presenting quality learning opportunities. Awareness of the needs of the audience keeps the interested parties engaged, and adherence to the site's mission holds the museum on its intended course. Kahle explains how sensitivity to these factors, as well as to the need to reflect up-to-date thinking, have led to successful changes in long-standing school programs at the Shadows. Hence, this small but energetic site represents the way patterns of house museum interpretation evolve, and will continue to do so, just as they have—as Patrick Butler showed in the very first chapter—throughout the history of the house museum movement.

To survive in the coming years, house museums must, among other things, be open to change in all of their interpretive efforts. Balanced considerations of the place, the objects, the people—their activities, relationships, and points of view—will be necessary. None is more or less important than any of the others when it comes to interpreting a historic house's story. The public will demand it, and with good scholarship, careful planning, and engaging presentations, these institutions will be able to meet with vigor the interpretive challenges that lie ahead.

Notes

1. Object-focused tours are appropriate for historic houses established as decorative arts museums. These museums often display in period room settings the impressive collections of a previous homeowner. They contribute immensely to our collective knowledge of fine and decorative arts. This book concentrates on house museums that primarily interpret the structure's history as a residence.

2. For more information on decorative arts interpretation in museums in general, see Nancy Bryk, "The Question of Decorative Arts," in *Old Collections, New Audiences: Deco-*

rative Arts and Visitor Experience for the Twenty-first Century (Dearborn, Mich.: Henry Ford Museum & Greenfield Village, 2000), 1–4.

3. James C. Rees, "Forever the Same, Forever Changing: The Dilemma Facing Historic Houses" (paper presented at *American House Museums*, an Athenæum of Philadelphia symposium, held 4–5 December 1998). Mr. Rees described the changes in interpretive strategies implemented at Mount Vernon during the late 1980s and the 1990s.

4. The two conferences, *Historic House Museums: Issues and Operations* and *Historic House Museums: Issues and Operations II*, were held 2–4 November 1995 and 5–7 November 1998, respectively. The chapter in this volume by Debra A. Reid is a departure from the topic—a more general discussion of interpretation—she presented at the 1995 conference.

5. For more on interpreting experiences in museums, see Harold Skramstad, "An Agenda for American Museums in the Twenty-First Century," *Dædalus* 128 (Summer 1999): 121–23.

6. David Lowenthal, *The Past Is a Foreign Country* (Cambridge: Cambridge University Press, 1985), 218. In this book, Lowenthal sets forth a number of cogent ideas regarding understanding the past. Consideration of these would benefit the work of anyone involved in historic site interpretation.

7. George W. McDaniel, "The Practice of Public History at Historic Houses and Buildings: Connecting Past, Present, and Future," in *Public History: Essays from the Field*, ed. James B. Gardner and Peter S. LaPaglia (Malabar, Fla.: Krieger Publishing Co., 1999), 234.

8. John H. Falk and Lynn D. Dierking, *Learning from Museums: Visitor Experiences and the Making of Meaning* (Walnut Creek, Calif.: AltaMira Press, 2000), 177, 232. (Falk and Dierking make these points about museums in general.) This is a good resource for information on "free-choice learning" and on how visitors learn at museums.

9. Warren Leon and Roy Rosenzweig, eds., *History Museums in the United States: A Critical Assessment* (Urbana: University of Illinois Press, 1989), xviii.

10. Debra A. Reid, who brought this book to my attention, points out that many houses operated as museums were originally farm or plantation houses.

11. For discussions of the influence of founding philosophies on house museums, see Patricia West, *Domesticating History: The Political Origins of America's House Museums* (Washington, D.C.: Smithsonian Institution Press, 1999), and John A. Herbst, "Historic Houses," in *History Museums in the United States*, 98–114.

12. Lowenthal, xxiii.

13. The following two books by John H. Falk and Lynn D. Dierking are excellent places to start: *The Museum Experience* (Washington, D.C.: Whalesback Books, 1992) and *Learning from Museums: Visitor Experiences and the Making of Meaning* (Walnut Creek, Calif.: AltaMira Press, 2000).

14. Christy Coleman Matthews, "Twenty Years Interpreting African American History: A Colonial Williamsburg Revolution," *History News* 54 (Spring 1999): 10.

15. See, for example, Nancy Carlisle, "SPNEA Takes a New Approach to an Old Building," in *Old Collections, New Audiences*, 78–79.

CHAPTER ONE

PAST, PRESENT, AND FUTURE:
THE PLACE OF THE HOUSE MUSEUM
IN THE MUSEUM COMMUNITY

Patrick H. Butler III

The house museum holds a particular and special place for many American museum professionals.[1] It is also a very popular institution with the public—since 1960, more than 6,000 new house museums joined the museum community. The development of the house museum as an institution crosses many traditional cultural, intellectual, and institutional boundaries. It encompasses issues in the traditional history and decorative arts museum; the historic preservation movement; the development of formal museum training programs; the role of government in museums and society; concepts of popular education for children and for general audiences; gender roles among museum volunteers and professionals; the role of volunteerism and, in particular, "patriotic" organizations in society; and the place of collectors and antique dealers in establishing and maintaining these institutions. In the century and a half since Mount Vernon opened its doors—and especially since World War II—the house museum field has grown and changed dramatically, although the forces that led to the creation of Mount Vernon continue as important elements of the historic house museum's enduring place in American life.[2]

Just what is a historic house museum? It is a museum, subscribing to the general definition of museums offered by the American Association of Museums, that centers on the maintenance, care, and interpretation of either a single, historic residential structure or a complex of structures associated with and including a single residence that serves as the primary focus. The interpretive emphasis of a historic house museum is primarily the residential structure itself and the lives of individuals related to the structure. In some instances, the emphasis may be on a collection of decorative arts or on a representative group of the individuals

18

associated with the house. In addition to individual residential house museums, other types of historic structures and complexes of open-air museums, such as Colonial Williamsburg, have contributed in many ways to the development of the idea of the historic house.

Mount Vernon and the Mid-Nineteenth Century

The mid-nineteenth century saw the earliest formal efforts to preserve historic residences in the United States. Although museums in what became the United States had existed since the 1770s, Americans had paid little attention to preserving the built environment associated with the colonial period or with the American Revolution. Many structures important to the image of the colonial era and the Revolution in particular had either been torn down or, as in the instance of Independence Hall, substantially altered.

The first formal effort to preserve a historic residential structure began in 1847 when the residents of Deerfield, Massachusetts, attempted to save the Hoyt or "Indian" House, the last surviving structure associated with the Deerfield Massacre of 1704. This effort failed, although the community preserved the door of the house and, much later, re-created the structure. The event provided the impetus for preservation in Deerfield, leading to the creation of the Pocumtuck Valley Historical Association and then to Historic Deerfield.

Preservation of the Hasbrouck House in Newburgh, New York, the first successful preservation effort, appears to have been serendipitous. The structure, a headquarters for George Washington, survived only because the owner, Jonathan Hasbrouck, could not repay a government loan and put the house on the market to pay his debt. One of the loan program commissioners, Andrew Caldwell, led efforts to save the structure. While appealing to local residents, Caldwell found support from the state in New York governor Hamilton Fish, whose 1850 rationale for saving the structure remains current in the early twenty-first century. (Note the use of the phrases "above dollars and cents" and "the illustrious man," which indicate an appeal to higher values, an important tool in a preservationist's strategy then and now):

> I respectfully submit that there are associations connected with this venerable edifice which are above the consideration of dollars and cents. . . . It is perhaps the last relic within the boundaries of the State [New York], under the control of the Legislature connected with the history of the illustrious man.[3]

Fish and Caldwell succeeded. In 1850, the New York legislature appropriated $2,391 to pay off the loan and acquire the property, plus another $6,000 to protect it with additional land.[4] On July 4, 1850, General Winfield Scott visited Newburgh to raise the flag over the first dedicated house museum in the United States. In this instance, the state of New York served as the agency of preservation, although the effort was driven by individual citizens.

In 1856, the state of Tennessee acquired the Hermitage although the modern organization to maintain it appeared only in 1888. The Carpenter's Company of Philadelphia chose to preserve its ancient headquarters in 1857. Individuals and groups made other efforts over the next few decades, some successful and others, including the attempt to save the John Hancock House in Boston, failures.

All of the structures, those saved and those destroyed, played a part in the nation's sense of identity. Different agencies, both groups of private citizens and public institutions, usually state governments, acted to preserve major historic sites. The furnishings used in these sites were often simple, although the saviors frequently sought to re-create the character of the interiors, usually through collections associated with the original owners and the house.

Ann Pamela Cunningham's work to make Mount Vernon a public museum remains the landmark effort in the field of house museums. Certainly the most important single effort prior to the Civil War, the creation of Mount Vernon as a museum—and with it the Mount Vernon Ladies Association as the owner—may be the primary model for historic preservation efforts over the last century and a half. John Augustine Washington, a collateral descendant of George Washington, owned the mansion in the 1850s. Although Washington could not afford to keep up the estate, as was reported by Ann Pamela Cunningham's mother in a letter to her daughter of 1853, he did not want to sell the house to speculators, hoping to see it converted into a shrine.

The letter Mrs. Louisa Bird Cunningham wrote to her daughter, then undergoing medical treatment in Philadelphia, became the spark for a national campaign to save the old mansion. In the letter, Mrs. Cunningham suggested that the ladies of the United States should act to save the old house. Her daughter, despite a history of infirmities, decided to take up the challenge and initiated the project. She wrote a series of letters, signed "a Southern Matron," to the *Charleston Mercury* in late 1853 and 1854, calling for the women of the South to organize and save Mount Vernon. These first efforts made it apparent that, to save the Washington home, the ladies faced several equally important tasks: establishing a legal entity to assure permanence for the project, developing a sense of confidence in it by John Augustine Washington, and managing a fund-raising program to bring the project to fruition.

Miss Cunningham expanded her effort by appealing to ladies across the nation for support of the effort. She developed a system of state regents that would be invaluable in creating the appropriate network for financial development and continuing support. While the original intent of the group had been to create an organization that would support the state of Virginia in managing the estate, the Virginia legislature could not come to terms with John Washington. By happy coincidence, a delay in sailing home after a visit to Mount Vernon provided the opportunity for Miss Cunningham to deal directly with Washington. She convinced him of the dedication of her group to Mount Vernon and, in the end, the Mount Vernon Ladies Association took direct title to the property in 1858, leaving Virginia out of the picture.

Support for the project came from across the nation, with Edward Everett, the great orator of the day, raising more than $60,000 toward the purchase price of $200,000.[5] While men played a significant role in saving Mount Vernon, women led the cause, better able to appeal to all parts of the nation and remain neutral at a time of increasing sectional tension that would lead in 1861 to civil war. The effort to save Mount Vernon became one of the last vehicles, albeit unsuccessful, for national reconciliation.

Fund-raising activities to pay off the purchase price and establish an endowment for Mount Vernon included speeches by Everett, tableaux and suppers, fancy dress balls, and a demonstration of the new telegraph and other activities often held on Washington's birthday or on the Fourth of July. Individuals and firms contributed to the cause, including Barber, Palmer, and Company of New York, the manufacturers of Mount Vernon Fine Cut Chewing Tobacco, who gave $100 to the cause. The ladies involved children, with appeals coming from many sources. For example, Susan Fenimore Cooper, daughter of the novelist James Fenimore Cooper, wrote to the "Children of America" asking for a donation, a dime or a penny, to be given "feelingly—as a simple act of love and respect for the memory of the great man."[6] Her words are reminiscent of those of Governor Hamilton Fish.

The money came pouring in and by November of 1859, all but $6,666 had been paid, with another $32,000 committed. To provide $20,000 for necessary repair of the mansion, the association delayed the final payment. Miss Cunningham estimated that an endowment of $125,000 to $150,000 was needed in addition to the annual expenditure of $8,000 to $10,000 for operations. She calculated that admissions would bring in between $1,500 and $2,000. In dollar amounts corresponding to the years 1995 to 2000, the annual operating budget would be about $360,000 while the endowment would be a bit more than $5.2 million.[7] The first staff included two professional positions and slaves for maintenance. Utilities were limited to firewood, candles, and lamp oil. No collections management or conservation staff existed.

During the Civil War, Mount Vernon became neutral ground, visited by Union soldiers at twenty-five cents a head, administered by superintendent Colonel Upton H. Herbert and Miss Cunningham's secretary, Sarah C. Tracy.[8] They maintained the property without Miss Cunningham, who was confined to her home in South Carolina for the duration of the war. A small group of regents in 1864 proposed to turn the property over to the federal government, which had recently acquired Arlington House by confiscation, but the regents rejected the proposal at their annual meeting.

In 1866, Miss Cunningham returned to Mount Vernon to lead the reorganization of the association. She served as a regent until her death on May 1, 1875. Despite health problems that kept her from attending the Regents' Council meeting in 1874, she forwarded a last address with the following admonition:

> Ladies, the home of Washington is in your charge. See to it that you keep it the home of Washington! Let no irreverent hand change it; no vandal hands desecrate it with the fingers of *progress*. Those who go to the home in which he lived and died, wish to see in what he lived and died! Let one spot in this grand country of ours be saved from "change!" Upon you rests this duty.[9]

The establishment of Mount Vernon is worth considering in some detail because it became the pattern for the development of many historic house museums, particularly by volunteer groups, and it is also an early example of a major national effort carried out primarily by women, again duplicated many times at different house museums and historic sites. Mount Vernon provides the present with other precedents as well. The approach to the preservation of Mount Vernon as saving the home of Washington, rather than as creating a gallery shrine with statues or as tearing down the structure to re-create it in ceramic, is one that has become the model for the operation of the preservation and historic house museum community over the years. This approach is now the standard for new house museums and focuses thinking about strategies for interpretation.

Concern for developing an endowment, as well as recognition that admissions could support only a small part of the operating budget, is an important precedent. Miss Cunningham recognized that the initial efforts, necessary to acquire the property and make the first repairs, were only the beginning of the continuing demand for funds necessary for the continued preservation and operation of Mount Vernon. Too often today, those who restore a house and establish a museum cease their efforts when the door opens, just as the need for a continuing funding source becomes apparent.

Although knowledge of preservation and restoration reflected standards of the 1850s, the philosophy of delay, research, and study that the original administration of Mount Vernon followed has proven to be a sound precedent in requiring that the best available knowledge drive the program of the museum. In essence, those responsible for the mansion did little that could not be undone, and they attempted, within the limits of the time, to carry out research on the house before making changes. In this, they established a pattern for careful research that remains at the heart of any good historic house museum. For example, Miss Cunningham peeled back layers of wallpaper in search of the wall treatment that existed during the Washington era, but while doing so, left samples of all the types of wall covering so visitors could see the layers.

When John Augustine Washington left Mount Vernon, he took his furnishings with him—including many items associated with George Washington—leaving an empty house. Gradually, the Ladies Association began to acquire collections to furnish the house. In the beginning, only a few Washington pieces, including the harpsichord given to Nelly Custis by Washington, returned to the house. To fill the gaps, regents took on the task of furnishing individual rooms, which they did by mixing antiques and contemporary pieces. As time passed, more Washington-associated pieces appeared. Only in the twentieth century did the association develop an overall collections plan. At the same time, the association expanded its research on Washington and Mount Vernon to support an improving interpretation of the man and the house.

Perhaps the most important legacy of the Cunningham years remains her vision for the house, given final voice in her statement of 1874. For many who have sought to save historic structures, a critical element of the rationale has been the almost mystical experience of and connection with the past developed through the experience of a historic object. Miss Cunningham was among the first to voice this motive.

Over the generations, Mount Vernon has benefited in many ways from the philosophy and practices established during the first years of the association. It is the most visited nonprofit house museum in the United States and often has covered its operating expenses with admission fees. Yet, as for many museums, the number of visitors has fluctuated at times, suggesting that the traditional approach to interpretation, focusing on Washington through the experience of going through his rooms and seeing his furnishings, may no longer be sufficient. The museum has made changes, including a more active interpretation in the house and elsewhere on the property, but further developments may be necessary to reattract visitors in an era of dramatic media technology.[10] This may well be more true for those many house museums lacking the significance of association with a truly national figure such as Washington.

The Late-Nineteenth and Early-Twentieth Centuries

In the late-nineteenth and early-twentieth centuries, the number of house museums established in the United States, particularly in the Northeast and the upper South, slowly grew. In many parts of the country, what would later be perceived as historic structures were still in use. For many such houses, the significant historic associations that would lead to their preservation and operation as museums had not yet appeared. Moreover, the Founding Fathers, particularly in terms of inculcating American virtues, remained the focus for preservation and interpretation. In this period, the growth of historic preservation and the development of the house museum became almost synonymous.

At the same time, Americans became interested in the artifacts of their past, first given focus through exhibits such as the Brooklyn "Sanitary Fair" of 1864. The Philadelphia Centennial Exposition of 1876—a celebration of the virtues of 1776 and 1876, the material progress made by the United States in the first century, and the reconciliation between North and South—did little to directly encourage interest in American antiques or historical exhibits, such as house museums. The exposition created only two interiors. The New England Kitchen, a quaint facility displayed in the Women's Pavilion, served to demonstrate how life had improved in the home rather than to foster nostalgia about the virtues of the "good old days." Atmosphere, not accuracy, was the important characteristic of the exhibit. At the same time Americans on the East Coast sought to re-create their historic past, those in the West continued to battle for new homesteads. Just as the fair opened in 1876, George Custer and his troops died at the Little Bighorn.

During the 1880s and 1890s, perhaps because of a growing interest in the past stimulated by America's Centennial, awareness of early American decorative arts and material culture expanded as individuals sought to identify and collect pieces that would remind them of the past. For the most part, this interest grew first in the northeastern United States, but a pattern for collecting and researching the decorative arts had appeared that would serve historic house museums nationwide by providing insight into what was truly appropriate rather than what was simply quaint and old. At the same time, furniture manufacturers and interior decorators responded to the new interest by creating reproductions of antique forms in what became the colonial revival style. By the end of the century, the colonial taste had reached the point that Sears, Roebuck and Co. mass marketed simple variants of the colonial revival through its catalogues.

While private collectors studied and preserved antiques, an associated development threatened many historic structures. Collectors and decorators sought fragments of historic buildings, particularly the interiors, for use as backgrounds or settings for their antiques. Museums, led by the Metropolitan Museum of Art, gave a legitimacy to this activity when they acquired interior elements for use in their exhibits. On occasion—at Gadsby's Tavern in Alexandria, Virginia, for example—the removal of an interior provided the impetus for local groups to organize to preserve and develop their own historic structures to prevent them from being removed by outsiders. In many cases, the structures gutted were to be demolished under any circumstance and the efforts of museums and collectors, such as Henry Francis du Pont and Henry Ford, resulted in saving much that otherwise would have been lost.

As individual interest in the past grew, so did efforts to expand and use this interest through the creation of preservation and museum organizations. Perhaps the most notable organization of the period was the Society for the Preservation of New England Antiquities (SPNEA), led by Bostonian William Sumner Appleton, who began his career by participating in the effort to preserve and restore the Paul Revere House in 1905. Appleton's education, European travel, and experience with the Revere House convinced him of the importance of the preservation and restoration of the built environment in New England. During the struggle to preserve the Harrington House on Lexington Green, Appleton determined that he would form an agency, similar in some ways to the existing Association for the Preservation of Virginia Antiquities, to save historic structures in New England. The Massachusetts Legislature granted SPNEA, established in 1910, the right to own property tax free. Although some local history groups feared absorption by the new regional agency, it survived the early opposition because of its efforts to work with local groups throughout New England. Its development benefited from the relatively small geographic area of New England and the large number of historic structures and sites marked for preservation, either by SPNEA or a related local agency.

Across the country, similar groups appeared, sometimes with the assistance of patriotic or genealogical organizations such as the Colonial Dames and the Daughters of the American Revolution. These groups shared the belief that patriotism and an appreciation of American virtues could be developed through the experience of historic structures. At the same time, they shared in the growing nativist sentiment at the end of the century that was a reaction to increasing immigration, particularly from Eastern Europe. They hoped that by preserving historic sites, they would be able to defend traditional values and inculcate these values in their own children, as well as among the newly arrived immigrants.

While state governments had become involved in the development of historic house museums during the 1850s, the federal government did not. It became directly involved in the process only with the development of new national parks. In 1872, the government created Yellowstone National Park and in 1899 Casa Grande in Arizona became a national monument, the first park site established specifically for historic value. Congress acted in 1907 to protect nationally important historic, natural, and scientific resources by passing the Antiquities Act. In 1916, the National Park Service (NPS) became a bureau of the Department of the Interior, gradually acquiring historic sites administered by other governmental agencies, particularly the War and Agriculture Departments. The NPS would serve as the mechanism for the expanded role of the federal government in the development of house museums during the middle years of the twentieth century.

The Depression and World War II

Efforts in the 1930s to combat the depression through the expanded role of the federal government in the New Deal included preservation and development of historic sites and house museums. In 1935, Congress passed the Historic Sites Act, establishing new research and inventory programs and providing for the continuation of the Historic American Buildings Survey established in 1933. Most important, it empowered the Secretary of the Interior to purchase privately owned historic sites; to execute corporate agreements with private owners; to preserve, maintain, and operate sites and buildings for the benefit of the public; and to initiate public education programs. It also gave the NPS the authority to create technical advisory committees. By this act, the federal government committed itself to historic preservation and the development of historic sites as a national goal.

At the same time, research programs initiated under the New Deal laid the foundation for additional programs after World War II. The Historic Records Survey began to catalogue local records. In the Index of American Design, artists provided renderings of examples of arts and handicrafts from all elements of American culture. The Federal Writers' Project supported local history research eventually published in the Works Progress Administration (WPA) state guides. These guides were, and remain, of particular value. They included historic sites and museums, providing directions and information to the public that, with the new automobile, now had access to these sites. Despite the depression, tourism expanded thanks to the automobile and the construction of highways. The Historic Sites Survey and the Historic American Buildings Survey identified and documented many historic sites and structures for the first time, providing an inventory that would be of great value after World War II. The coming of World

War II ended many of these programs, but they provided a precedent for further federal government involvement after 1945. More important, the work led to the creation of a research base of information and to the creation of a cadre of professionals, given employment by these projects, who would provide direction for the expansion of historic sites and house museums in the years after World War II.

Private activity also increased during the 1930s. Organizations exemplified by the San Antonio Conservation Society, established in 1924, began to grow. Historic districts appeared in Charleston, New Orleans, and Monterey, California, during the 1930s. In Mississippi, the Natchez Garden Club initiated a garden pilgrimage that became a source of economic support for the historic plantation houses of the community. Local governments, notably in Alexandria and Williamsburg, Virginia, and in Winston-Salem, North Carolina, enacted preservation legislation to support these groups.

Paralleling developments in the National Park Service, state parks departments began to create historical programs at some of their sites in the 1920s and 1930s. The Indiana state parks system, led by Colonel Richard Lieber, may have been one of the most notable, restoring Spring Mill Pioneer Village at Mitchell, Indiana. In California, the state purchased historic sites to establish parks at La Purisima Mission, San Juan Bautista, and the Vallejo Home in Sonoma. Pennsylvania re-created Pennsbury Manor in the late 1930s, and other states also developed historic sites. Many of these state programs benefited from resources provided by the federal programs of the 1930s.

Colonial Williamsburg became perhaps the single most important private preservation, historic site, historic house museum project of the era. Established by John D. Rockefeller Jr. in the late 1920s and the 1930s, Colonial Williamsburg served as both model and resource for the development of historic structures and historic house museums. The level and complexity of the research program implemented by Colonial Williamsburg reached beyond any previous effort. Involving architects, historians, scientists, archaeologists, and local historians, the research program redefined the standards for the research and interpretation of historic structures. Although now dated from a contemporary perspective, the interiors and interpretation of the 1930s and 1940s at Williamsburg were vital and far more "correct" than anything that predated the work.

The newly created interiors and programs at Williamsburg impressed visitors with the intensity and complexity of the research that combined archaeological, architectural, and artifactual research with exciting new documentary work. Many of the scholars involved with Williamsburg had never participated in local history research, because academic scholars often felt that exploration of the ancient world or European history represented the only research that truly merited advanced academic training. Williamsburg played an important role in the appreciation and application of academic research techniques to the study of the American past. Moreover, by creating a staff that developed the new strategies of research at Williamsburg and then, in the 1930s and after World War II, moving on to other projects, Williamsburg contributed much to the development of historic house museums in the decades after 1945.

World War II marked a turning point for the development of historic house museums in the United States. By the 1930s, there were about five hundred house museums in operation. Lawrence Vail Coleman recognized the development of the type with a volume on the management of house museums published by the American Association of Museums in 1931.[11] World War II ended the efforts to develop historic house museums that had taken shape in the 1920s and 1930s. Yet the end of the war, which had halted so much work, led to a renewal of interest in and growth of house museums that continued through the remainder of the century.

Post–World War II

The rapid growth of the historic house museum community in the United States in the years since 1945 is a result of many factors. Returning soldiers had developed an awareness of historic buildings, particularly in Europe, and began to examine their home communities with renewed interest and appreciation. As the economy shifted from war to peace, many individuals had both leisure and resources permitting them to take advantage of the automobile and the growing highway system to travel in search of entertainment and education. With the baby boom, demand for educational and cultural activities of all types rapidly increased, with American history being particularly valued. As the United States faced the Cold War, many educators and volunteer groups, all across the political spectrum, placed great value on the actual experience of historic places in shaping a perception of America's beliefs and traditions, thus becoming better prepared to participate in the struggle. My memories of growing up in Alexandria, Virginia, in the 1950s include countless field trips by school, church, camp, and Boy Scout groups, as well as family, to historic houses, battlefields, and museums. History had importance and museums became, for many, a good vehicle for instilling values in children, a continuation of the tradition of Ann Pamela Cunningham.

Public and private resources supported this interest in history, contributing to dramatic growth in the number of historic house museums. Between the end of World War II and the year 2000, well over 6,000 historic house museums were developed. This means that on average a new house museum opened somewhere in the United States every three days during the period. That number represents substantial accomplishment. It also documents a trust that has been assumed for the future. The responsibilities of caring for so many individual institutions are substantial and require a heavy investment in resources.

During those decades, many aspects of American society contributed to the environment that engendered the creation of so many institutions. The federal government took steps, beginning in the late 1940s, to carry on the mission of preservation and education established during the depression. Policy makers recognized that the scope of the task of preservation and interpretation of the historic built environment was beyond the capacity of the federal government in its existing programs, particularly those of the National Park Service. Also, as has always been true in the American experience, many private volunteer-managed groups (the Harris County Heritage Society in Houston, Texas, for instance) already worked in the field and demanded a place.

To facilitate the development of preservation and historic site programs, delegates from different museum and preservation organizations met at the National Gallery of Art in 1947 to plan for a national private agency that would bridge the gap between government and private interests. Two entities came from this meeting: the National Council for Historic Sites and Buildings and the National Trust for Historic Preservation. The former agency sought to encourage interest in preservation while the latter operated historic properties. Congress chartered the Trust in 1949. Within a few years, the functions of the two entities became confused and intertwined, leading to the 1953 merger of the Council with the Trust.

Historic preservation and historic sites became involved in the larger definition of the good environment. In 1954, the Supreme Court affirmed the environmental "right to be beautiful" in *Berman v. Parker*. William O. Douglas wrote, for the majority, that "the concept of public welfare is broad and inclusive. The values it represents are spiritual as well as physical, aesthetic as well as monetary. It is within the power of the legislature to determine that a community should be beautiful as well as healthy, spacious as well as clean."[12]

During the 1960s, Congress passed additional legislation having a significant impact on the development of historic house museums and related preservation activities. The 1964 *Report of the Commission on the Humanities* encouraged the creation of an entity within the federal government to provide support for the humanities with a special emphasis on programs in local history and preservation. This led to the National Arts and Cultural Development Act of 1964 and the National Foundation on the Arts and Humanities Act of 1965. Following this legislation, Congress established the National Endowment for the Arts (NEA) and the National Endowment for the Humanities (NEH) with support from Republicans (particularly President Richard Nixon) and Democrats for the next thirty years.

The endowments, particularly the NEH, provided important support for local history museums, including historic houses. Federal funding became available, always to be matched with funding raised in the community, to support research, public programs, and publications. The early years of the NEH saw a particular emphasis on local history. Financial support for scholarly work in local history research and methodology became extensive, accompanied by support for publications and interpretive programs from local history agencies, including historic house museums. The structure of the grant process encouraged the growth of the relationship between the academic community and the museum community by requiring academic participation in grant-funded programs. NEH funding underwrote a variety of exhibits, lectures, videos, school programs, and other activities that expanded the intellectual and creative range of local history museums.

The Johnson administration also supported the expansion and improvement of the care of the environment, including additional preservation and museum programs. Johnson called for a "new conservation" to be a creative conservation program of restoration and innovation. Reflecting the spirit of the 1954 William O. Douglas opinion, Johnson observed, "Its concern is not with nature alone, but with the total relation between man and the world around him. Its object is not just man's welfare, but the dignity of man's spirit."[13]

In 1966, a special committee of the U.S. Conference of Mayors published *With Heritage So Rich*, calling for additional support and funding for preservation and museum programs. This, in turn, led to the National Historic Preservation Act of 1966, which supported the expansion of historic districts, sites, buildings, and so forth, as well as a new National Register of Historic Places to accompany the National Historic Landmarks program established in 1960.

Congress passed other legislation in 1966 to contribute to the development of historic preservation efforts and historic house museums through the redefinition of the Federal-Aid Highway Act of 1956. The Transportation Act of 1966 established the Department of Transportation, which had in its mandate the duty to preserve natural and historic sites affected by new highway construction. Archaeological exploration of federal highway routes had been a part of the original legislation in 1956, but all other projects were left to the discretion of the states. The 1966 Act expanded the role of the federal government in historical archaeology projects along new federal highway routes.

The development of the interstate highway system had a twofold impact on museums. First, the mandate to preserve historic structures caused many communities to examine their historic resources and make efforts to preserve historic structures threatened by highway construction. The moving of the San Felipe Cottage, threatened by the construction of I-35, to Houston's Sam Houston Park is an example of the impact of this philosophy, although the funding for the move was private rather than public. At the same time, the growing highway system made it possible for more people to travel to more places, thus expanding the market for historic museums and sites. New privately produced publications supplemented the guidebooks developed by the WPA in the 1930s and early 1940s. While sometimes destructive of the historic environment, the new interstate highway system, combined with the increased use of the automobile as the primary transportation device, facilitated the development of the audience for historic house museums and sites.

The Demonstration Cities and Metropolitan Development Act of 1966, authorizing the Model Cities program under the Department of Housing and Urban Development (HUD), included the recommendation that development of urban areas should not come at the cost of historic sites and structures. Following the principles enunciated by Douglas in 1954, Congress made it clear that museums and historic districts had been recognized as important to the development of communities.

State and local government programs paralleled federal activity. These programs supported research, development of state historic sites and structures, and state preservation programs. Together with federal and private efforts, these state programs expanded the character and range of historic sites.

On another level, private programs initiated in the 1930s also came of age in the 1950s to benefit the historic house museum. Individual collectors such as Henry Francis du Pont, Stephen Clark, and Henry and Helen Flynt had assembled complexes of historic architecture and antiques. Their collections documented the past through the decorative arts and historic buildings. These individuals recognized that, to achieve lasting importance, the collections needed to be studied and used for educational purposes. They turned their private holdings into public museums in the 1940s and 1950s.

One of these individuals, Henry Francis du Pont, also recognized the need for an expanded cadre of professionals to carry out research on and interpretation of historic collections. In 1951, the Winterthur Program in Early American Culture began. Given direction by the late Charles F. Montgomery, a collector and dealer turned museum professional, the Winterthur Program became the first post–World War II graduate program to offer professional training for individuals interested in careers in historic administration and historic house museums.

While its emphasis was on the decorative arts of the Northeast in the period from 1640 through 1840, its graduates took the strategies developed in the Winterthur Program and applied them to the study of material culture and the decorative arts in all regions of the United States, including the history of material culture from the first Spanish settlement in Florida in 1585 to the recent past. Du Pont's example led to the creation of other programs. The Cooperstown Graduate Program, established in 1964, emphasized folk and popular culture, as well as administrative techniques. The Deerfield Summer Program, created in 1961, served to attract future professionals while in their undergraduate years. For those already working in historic sites and houses, the National Trust developed the Woodlawn Seminar and the Seminar for Historical Administration (held at Colonial Williamsburg) to provide short courses for active professionals. In the 1970s and 1980s, the number of academic programs continued to expand, with degrees in museum studies or historic administration granted by Texas Tech University, Baylor University, the University of Michigan, Syracuse University, George Washington University, and the University of Delaware, among others. State agencies also developed training seminars, such as Texas's Winedale Seminar for Historical Administration, to serve working museum professionals. Through an increasing sophistication in administration and a greater concern for advanced research to support programs in furnishing and interpretation, the impact of a trained cadre of professionals on house museums has been substantial. Board members and other volunteer leaders also benefited from these programs as well as other training devoted to board members and presented by AAM, the American Association for State and Local History (AASLH), the National Trust, and many state and regional agencies.

At the same time, the professional organizations that supported historic house museums expanded rapidly, both in membership and in programs and publications. The AASLH became particularly active, initiating a series called *Technical Leaflets* that dealt with a wide range of topics in the care, research, and management of historic structures. The AASLH, through its annual meetings and a variety of educational programs, seminars, and correspondence courses, served the profession by supporting additional research and by boosting access to current information about proper management of historical collections. For a time, the association also provided consultant services to historic houses on a limited basis.

The American Association of Museums, while serving all museums, also developed technical support information for house museums and published appropriate articles in its monthly magazine, *Museum News*. More importantly, in the Museum Assessment Program (MAP) and in the Accreditation Program, which includes a special component for historic sites, there are opportunities for the administrators, staff, and boards of house museums to judge their institution against the standards of the entire profession.

By the late 1950s, publications directed toward house museums expanded in number and improved in quality. Freeman Tilden provided a coherent theory of interpretation of historic sites in his 1957 book, *Interpreting Our Heritage*, which was revised in 1967 and 1977. In 1975, recognizing the evolution of the historic site and the changing character of audience for the sites, William T. Alderson and Shirley Payne Low published *Interpretation of Historic Sites*. These two books, along with many articles on interpretation in museums, influenced the development of public interpretation at historic house museums.

The level of information about collections, including research and use, also improved and expanded throughout the second half of the twentieth century. Of particular note is William Seale's *Recreating the Historic House Interior*.[14] In it, Seale provides a manual that may be applied to any historic structure for research on, analysis of, and preparation of historic rooms. Accompanied by a vast and growing literature on all aspects of the history of material culture, this book is required reading for anyone approaching the restoration and development of historic interiors. Seale's mix of anthropological insight and careful research reflects the impact of the new social history techniques of the era on the house museum in the 1970s and 1980s. In its grants and programs, the NEH had been encouraging this application of new social history methods to research and interpretation strategies for historic house museums.

During the 1960s and 1970s, volunteer support for house museum development also expanded as more individuals became involved in saving neighborhoods and historic structures in communities of all types and sizes. This growth in numbers accompanied the expansion of leisure time, particularly among women, that occurred during the period. In the late 1970s and 1980s, the pattern reversed and volunteer support at many institutions became limited.

Another aspect in support of the expansion was a redefinition of what is "historic." During the 1960s, 1970s, and 1980s, the notion of history became more inclusive in terms of class, race, and ethnicity, and Americans came to recognize that the "past" included events more recent than the American Revolution. Much of our history had not been included in studies of the past, and museums, along with other elements of the history community, began to change to become more inclusive. An early example of this change was Sam Houston Park, where the City of Houston, Texas, allowed the Harris County Heritage Society, when it was established in 1954, to begin placing historic structures for preservation. It includes residences from different ethnic groups and classes in the city. The definition of role models also changed, and representative structures from groups outside of the traditional Anglo-American elite became historic house museums. Even in the homes of the elite, interpretation began to expand to include all who lived there, including servants and slaves.

The evolution of the historic house since World War II reflects the many changes taking place in society. It is a complex story of government and private action on all levels and in all parts of the country, as well as the development of new definitions of history and new perceptions of history's scope.

The Present and the Future

Between the late-twentieth and the early-twenty-first centuries, the character of the challenges facing house museums, in particular, evolved in some respects. Some challenges continued, others lessened, and new ones appeared.

1. Changing technology in the areas of interpretation, management, and conservation remains an important issue, although the needs to which the technology is applied and the standards by which it is judged remain the same.

2. The impact of the changing character of the population, with its growing diversity, offers a challenge to many museums as they struggle to serve new audiences with traditional missions and definitions.

3. Funding, whether from government sources, private foundations, or individual donors, remains difficult, and the character of funding priorities changes depending on the particular philosophies shaping public and private funding agencies at the time.

4. Finally, museums that have survived for only one generation face issues associated with passing on the torch of strong leadership and secure funding. The bicentennial celebrations of the 1970s inspired the creation of many new museums. As these institutions mature, they face questions about their continuing value. Whenever the founders of an institution pass from the scene, continued success depends on preparation for this transition. In at least some instances, survival of the museum may be in question.

Technology

Changing technology is a continuing opportunity and challenge to the historic house museum. The computer is a constant in the life of most museums, used for a variety of administrative tasks, as well as collections management. While offering some opportunities to better control data, the computer is not, in itself, a panacea for all administrative problems. As administrations have learned, the cost of entering new data and capturing existing data for use within a system may be expensive. Yet it is also valuable and, once captured, may be passed on to new systems if the organization plans for those upgrades. We are often reminded that, as technology evolves, existing data may be lost if the system that manages it disappears. The history of recorded music—with the Victor system surpassing the Edison system, the cassette forcing out the eight track, and so on—is evidence that information may be lost if the means for accessing it disappears. The same has proven true with computers, which evolve at an especially rapid pace. Careful data management, particularly with records of a museum's collection, is essential. When systems change, all data must be modified to fit the new system. While less paper may be useful, paper still is required to maintain the corresponding documentation.

Similarly, if staffs employ a high technology approach in historic house interpretation, they must be cognizant that systems used for audio and visual programming evolve. Designers and users of museum interpretive technology must seek stable systems that may be repaired over time, and they must be prepared to cope with changing technology. House museums making use of innovative interpretive technology, such as Galveston's Samuel May Williams House and the Moody Mansion, may be frustrated by time. In both institutions, changing technology for audiovisual systems contributed to the failure to continue an exciting interpretive technique. Finding an appropriate way to use new technology is an issue endemic to all museums but, because of a historic house museum's limited budget and the cost of changing built-in systems, professional and volunteer decision makers must be particularly aware of the impact of evolving technology.

The understanding of conservation technologies and research is evolving constantly. Paint analysis is an example. As conservators and researchers have recognized the impact of time, light, and many other factors on paint, the interpretation of paint color, particularly in terms of intensity, has changed radically. Similarly, treatments regarded as the best strategies to use in caring for wood have been replaced when new research has revealed problems caused by previously accepted techniques. All museums must remain current in their knowledge of changing technology for research and preservation. Miss Cunningham's model of careful research remains true to this day. We must not fear using new techniques and technologies, but we must have a clear understanding of their impact.

The purpose of new conservation technologies is to meet the challenge of caring for the structure, which is the single most important artifact in the collection. Often, as we focus on the interior of the structure and the collections exhibited there, we take the continued well-being of the structure itself for granted, slapping on a little paint, changing filters, and just going on without paying much attention to the structure. Yet the environment for our primary artifact is changing. Atmospheric pollution threatens the stability of the surface of the structure and, in some cases, the structure itself. Heavy traffic on nearby streets may also be a problem, generating vibrations that have an impact on the house. The effects of the internal traffic of visitors and staff are equally significant. Most houses were designed to accommodate the needs of a few people, whose activities were spread throughout the house. In a house museum, the number of people passing through on an annual basis is many times greater than anticipated by the builder and, usually, those numbers are confined to a relatively limited path, such as the hallways and small areas of the rooms. This puts a different kind of stress on the house and leads to heavy wear in places not designed to accommodate this traffic. The list of threats to the well-being of the primary artifact is extensive and will become longer as the environment in and around the house changes over time.

Audiences and Interpretation

Just as the technology used in historic houses evolves, so do the audiences who visit. The population changes constantly through age, migration, economics, and other factors. Historic houses once isolated in a rural setting are often now surrounded by suburbs and cities. Our understanding of the past has also changed. While society still values great men and women, it also places value on all those who participated in the past. No longer is it sufficient to speak of the one great figure associated with a structure. While not forgetting the owner, the historic house is challenged by the public and by the museum community to place the house in the context of its time. The family, as well as any servants or slaves, has become an important part of a good interpretive program. When possible, the house must be placed in its neighborhood rather than treated as a structure cut off from the world around it. Without losing respect for the historic leaders associated with the structure, interpretive programming should become more inclusive, reflecting the entire biological family, the remainder of the household, the different generations associated with the structure, and the surrounding community.

At the same time, those responsible for the historic house should consider interpretive strategies other than the classic decorative arts interior. Particularly when collections are typical of a period rather than associated with the structure through use by the owners, there may be other options. A house should be considered a stage for the reenactment of the house's past, and the stage need not be fully furnished. Empty rooms, relying on the evocation of images either by docents or by audio and audiovisual presentations, are an option. Indeed, even rooms that have not been fully restored and allow the visitor to see into the structure of the building are a very successful option. Formal panel or case exhibits that include associated smaller objects are another. The limits on the character of an interpretive program are the budget, available collections, and the creativity of those responsible for interpretation.

Funding

Funding is often at the heart of survival and programming for a historic house. While historic house museums, particularly in smaller communities, benefit from the devotion, knowledge, and enthusiasm of their volunteers and from ties to the community, sites in larger communities face competition for support from a variety of institutions, and individual volunteers find a variety of opportunities competing for their efforts.

Ideally, funding should be generated from within the community. Admission, although a valuable measurement of interest, does not keep the doors open. At this writing, no nonprofit historic house museum operates solely on admission, special event, and gift shop revenues. Financial support from the community, the development of an endowment, and grants from charitable foundations and from government on all levels combine to keep these museums afloat. As valued local institutions, historic house museums receive some of their support simply by being part of the community. At the same time, support for museums may come from other sources, including businesses, foundations, and governments. For these outside agencies, community support is a key factor in determining whether or not they will fund a local museum. At the same time, these outside agencies also demand clear evidence of sound management and an effective, imaginative approach to the use of the structure.

These decisions are also affected by the debate over support from government, on all levels, and from private philanthropy that has taken place in the years since the end of the Cold War. Although more prevalent in the late 1990s, questions about the role of government, particularly in terms of direct support, have long been debated. The evolution by both major political parties of the vision of government as more limited in its programs has a continuing impact on government support for museums. Private sector museums in particular may find government resources on all levels to be more limited. At the same time, there are opportunities in this change. Local and state governments are challenging private groups to assume responsibility for operation of some museums. Although perhaps more limited in scale than governments, these groups are able to give individual projects greater care and attention than can larger public agencies.

At the same time, political leaders debate the character of the tax code. The current income tax code provides opportunities to make donations of many sorts in support of a museum. At times when the nature of the charitable deduction has been limited in some fashion, a substantial decline in contributions to museums has followed. If a different type of tax structure without the charitable deduction replaces the income tax, museums could face severe cuts in contributions.

The world of private philanthropy is increasingly called on to support cultural institutions, including historic houses. But other demands, notably in the social services, create increased competition for philanthropic funds. This competition requires that those responsible for the care of historic houses be prepared to defend the cause with vigor, documenting its importance to the community as an educational institution, as a contributor to the character of the community's environment and lifestyle, as a contributor to an attractive business climate, and as a source of high quality popular entertainment. Public relations, as a tool for demonstrating the museum's significance to the community, is a necessity for a house museum. Only with total involvement of the community will support for house museums continue. And that support depends on a museum's ability to be inclusive in its programs and operations.

Survival

The house museum community faces a fourth challenge—the possible failure of institutions that have existed for only one generation. During the 1970s, the country witnessed a push to create new museums, often historic houses, as a part of the celebration of the bicentennial of the American Revolution. Despite the best intent of the founders, some of these institutions now face a questionable future. Too often, leaders have not trained their successors, have not established endowments to provide for maintenance, operating costs, and capital expenditures, and have not recognized that the character of museums is changing. Standards of performance, acceptable a generation ago, are no longer sufficient. New knowledge of good management, of history, of collections care, and of interpretive techniques continually raises the standard of good performance. If institutions are unable to meet the test of competition and higher standards, they may be faced with the prospect of closing. In this circumstance, the property may be sold to a private individual or corporation while the collections are dispersed to other institutions and to the private sector.

Before a museum is closed and its assets sold, the leadership must make every good faith effort to keep the institution within the public sphere. Historic house museums, in particular, engender strong emotional devotion from those who worked to save, restore, furnish, care for, or interpret the structure. Reaction to a sale is likely to be strong, followed by discussions of lawsuits and government takeover. If the board, as a matter of its fiduciary responsibility, is able to demonstrate that it warned the community of the problem and was unsuccessful in obtaining outside support from individuals or government agencies, closing will cause less controversy.

This very real situation demands that both the museum community and the public, as represented by government agencies, prepare to deal with the loss of such a property. The resources of a failed museum are, in fact, a part of the public trust. As a nonprofit organization, the institution and those contributing to it received benefits in return for their contributions. The public and the museum community must be prepared to protect those assets and require use in accord with the original purpose of the institution.

In assessing the likelihood of the closing of historic properties, smaller communities appear to be in less danger. Support for a museum, such as a historic house, in a small community is driven by a level of commitment from the entire community that may not be present in larger cities. Medium and large communities, where competition for resources exists, are more likely to be settings for a historic house closure. Unless the leadership has developed a continuing cadre of professionals, an endowment, and a demonstrated program of caring for the structure and the collections, a historic house may well be faced with closing.

The fate of the Robert E. Lee Boyhood Home in Alexandria, Virginia, is an example of a result of the failure to pursue new resources.[15] After a number of years of neglect, which led to an accumulation of damages equivalent to two-and-a-half million dollars, the Lee-Jackson Foundation sold the structure to a private individual rather than attempt to keep it in the public sector. The aftermath, for all concerned, proved to be difficult. The purchaser of the house suffered from substantial community criticism, although his willingness to put easements on the property relieved the situation. He also made a good faith offer to the community at large, asking any interested party who wished to preserve the house as a museum to come forward with demonstrated resources. Although community groups sought to develop these resources, the efforts proved unsuccessful.

The sale demonstrates the difficulties of caring for a historic house. By failing to seek substantial outside assistance and by failing to make the difficulties known in a timely manner, the former owners, who held the structure as a public trust, did not serve their own cause. Secret dealings and an unwillingness to make the problems known raised serious questions of propriety. In contrast, the actions by the purchaser demonstrate the appropriate behavior when it is no longer possible to maintain a historic house museum. Those acts did much to end community controversy.

While there will be regrets at the closing of any historic house museum, the circumstances must be carefully considered on a case by case basis. Without appropriate resources from the community at large, whether of public or private origin, the museum and its collections will suffer. At this point, the trustees and the community may well choose to close the museum and dispose of its property, including the structure. If this process is managed in an open and responsible manner, and includes every reasonable opportunity according to good nonprofit management to save the institution, the decision to shut down is an appropriate one. Indeed, in the hands of a private individual prepared to care for the property, such a structure is likely to be in better hands than those of an insufficiently funded nonprofit organization.

Historic house museums and properties face many challenges. To some, they are quaint, fussy places managed without much relevance to the world around them. To some "new historians," whose essays in *Presenting the Past* are a critique of traditional historical analysis and institutions, including house museums, the house museum is isolated from the present, preserving a small bit of history that has little relationship to the world of those who would view it.[16] For these critics, the moral vision of someone like Ann Pamela Cunningham is not sufficient. The museum is then faced with the challenge of better expressing the complexity of life in the past and the relationship of that complexity to the present and the future. For these critics, the element of simply being in a historic structure is not enough.

Often, they are quite right. When considering the slice of history that is presented in many house museums, interpretation focuses only on the domestic life of the family. There is little or no interpretation of issues of work, education, religion, social activity outside the household, and the many nondomestic aspects of life that make the domestic environment possible or needed. It is imperative—even if one does not fully accept the critique of historians who argue that the range of experience portrayed in house museums is too limited—that house museums expand the range of their interpretations.

Moreover, historic house museums must rethink what they are about in terms of the perception of their audience. To those who read museum murder mysteries, the image of the house museum as a fussy, dusty place—as portrayed in Margaret Maron's *Corpus Christmas*—may be a more accurate view of a museum's public image than we would like.[17] Again, there is a sense that the house museum lacks a relationship to the modern world. While some may find this charming, such a response will not be sufficient for an educational institution that wishes to survive in an era of increased economic and community pressure to justify its existence.

The house museum is a complex institution that, like so many others of our culture, has reflected and been affected by the changing values of society. It faces serious challenges: economic support is always an issue; care of collections is a continuing problem; the notion of appropriate interpretation is subject to continual rethinking; and finally, even survival has become a question for some institutions. To serve society, the house museum must develop as an institutional offering more substantial than a vague inspirational message about preserving historical values. While serving the technical needs of the operation, historic house museums must also keep in mind the broader challenge of serving the needs of the culture. It is comforting, and sometimes frightening, to realize that many of the issues facing the modern house museum, while different in degree, are the same ones confronting Mount Vernon in the 1850s. Is the challenge—to maintain the original character of the house—that Ann Pamela Cunningham made in 1874 to the Mount Vernon regents still sufficient? Or, should society reorganize and expand the challenge if the house museum is to continue as a vital institution?

Notes

1. I would like to acknowledge the assistance of five individuals who were kind enough to share their thoughts on the house museum as an institution: the late Dr. William T. Alderson, Mr. Neil Horstman, Dr. William Murtaugh, Dr. William Seale, and Ms. Patricia Williams. The conclusions I have drawn are mine alone.

2. To learn more about the growth of house museums in the years prior to World War II, two books by Charles Hosmer are essential: *The Presence of the Past* (New York: G. P. Putnam's, 1965); and *Preservation Comes of Age*, 2 vols. (New York: G. P. Putnam's, 1981). These two studies provided much of the material used in the narrative of the history of the historic house museum.

3. Hosmer, *The Presence of the Past*, 36.

4. In dollar amounts corresponding to the years 1995–2000, these sums translate as $92,053 and $231,000, respectively.

5. In dollar amounts corresponding to the years 1995–2000, these sums translate as $2,418,000 and $8,060,000, respectively.

6. Edward P. Alexander, *Museum Masters: Their Museums and Their Influence* (Nashville, Tenn.: American Association for State and Local History, 1983), 185.

7. John J. McKusker, *How Much Is That in Real Money?* (Worcester, Mass.: American Antiquarian Society, 1992). This is a handy reference for converting historic currency values to modern currency values and is useful in addressing the idea that it was less expensive in the past.

8. This amount would be roughly equivalent to Mount Vernon's $9.00 admission fee for adults in 2001.

9. Quoted in Alexander, *Museum Masters*, 193–94.

10. At this writing, Mount Vernon has initiated plans to build a new interpretive facility that will address some of these needs.

11. Cited in Sherry Butcher-Younghans, *Historic House Museums: A Practical Handbook for Their Care, Preservation, and Management* (New York: Oxford University Press, 1993), 3.

12. Elizabeth D. Mulloy, *The History of the National Trust for Historic Preservation, 1963–1973* (Washington, D.C.: Preservation Press, 1976), 72.

13. Mulloy, *History of the Trust*, 72.

14. William Seale, *Recreating the Historic House Interior* (Nashville, Tenn.: American Association for State and Local History, 1977).

15. Built in the late-eighteenth century, the home on Oronoco Street served private families, including the Light Horse Harry Lee family, until the 1960s when the Lee-Jackson Foundation acquired the building and made it a museum. In February 2000, the Foundation sold the structure to a private individual.

16. Susan Porter Benson, Stephen Brier, and Roy Rosenzweig, eds., *Presenting the Past: Essays on History and the Public* (Philadelphia: Temple University Press, 1986).

17. Margaret Maron, *Corpus Christmas* (New York: Doubleday, 1989).

CHAPTER TWO

INTERPRETATION PLANNING: WHY AND HOW

Barbara Abramoff Levy

Interpretation planning is not only important, it is essential. For an interpretive experience to be both engaging and effective, it must be built on a solid foundation that takes into consideration the strengths and needs of the site and the audience. A good teacher won't walk into a classroom without defined plans tied to a curriculum; if she did, her chances for success would be random. The same holds true for historic house museums. The likelihood of success of an interpretive program is increased measurably if the staff has made decisions about what they want to teach, why it's important, and how they are going to go about it, all based on careful consideration of the site and the audience.

Not planning is dangerous. Skipping the planning process risks wasting time, wasting money, and losing audience as the site tries to find a way to bring people in the door and keep them coming back. An interpretation plan influences nearly every choice made at the site—choices regarding tour outlines, educational programs, fund-raising, exhibits, furnishings plans, preservation and conservation, collections plans, collaborations, even the merchandise sold in the shop.

An interpretation plan is the educational blueprint for a museum. It articulates the interpretive vision and lays out the content and structure for the visitor's interpretive and educational experiences. In his seminal book *Interpreting Our Heritage*, Freeman Tilden offers a definition of interpretation, which can be summarized as follows: Interpretation is an educational activity meant to reveal meanings and relationships by means of original objects.[1] An interpretation plan is meant to guide a site in determining what meanings and relationships it wants to reveal, as well as how and for whom it should do this.

The job of an interpretive plan is to answer three basic sets of questions.

- First, *what is the site about?*

  Answering this question requires considering why the site is important or unique, identifying the strengths of the collections, and defining and articulating the strongest storylines.

- Second, *who is the interpretation for?*

  A successful plan requires understanding the museum's audiences, figuring out what they need and want from their visit, and being clear about what it is the staff hopes people will come to see, understand, or experience at the site.

- Third, *how will the museum go about communicating what the site is about while meeting the needs of the audiences?*

  Designing an overall interpretive program that meets the needs of the site and the audience requires that the proposed programs be well thought out, pedagogically sound, engaging, and audience specific. It also requires designing effective assessment tools that enable staff to measure the relative success of the programs so that changes can be implemented.

Interpretation plans vary greatly because they must address the idiosyncrasies of particular sites. Like Historic Structures Reports, plans are tailored to meet the needs, the size, and the resources of the site, the issues that need to be addressed, the timing of the planning process, and the reasons for the planning. An interpretation plan can be comprehensive for multiple buildings at a larger museum complex or more narrowly focused for a single historic house. No matter what the size of the site or scope of the plan, however, every interpretation plan must express a clear sense of what the site wants visitors to learn and experience and how they will accomplish and measure this. The interpretation planning process becomes a forum for developing those learning objectives and for creating a framework for putting them into action.

Preparing to Plan

Before beginning the planning process, preparation is essential. Good preparation entails four elements: self-analysis, knowing the history of the site, understanding how people learn in the museum, and organizing and designing the planning protocol.

Self-Analysis

As a museum enters the self-analysis phase, it is important to take a very close look at the institutional mission. If necessary, it should be clarified and updated. This is a critical step, because the interpretation plan should be a tool for accomplishing the mission; a conflict between the interpretive mission and the overall mission is a recipe for failure.

The next step is to conduct a resource inventory, which describes the following:

- *All of the collections.* Include natural features (landscape) as well as cultural collections (objects, buildings, archives, and so on).

- *The site's visitor services and access features.* Include roads, signs, compliance with the Americans with Disabilities Act (ADA), parking, the number of people the site can accommodate, the number of public bathrooms, food services, museums shops, etc.

- *Current interpretation and educational programs and materials.* Include: tours, exhibits, brochures, school programs, adult and general public programs, family programs.

- *Current staffing.* Include the number and type of staff and staff training. Be sure to include volunteers if they provide visitor services.

- *Available background interpretation and supplemental materials.* Include selected relevant materials like room books or object cards, interpreter handbook, tour outline, site history, etc.

- *Current audiences.* Include visitation numbers and program attendance figures if they exist. Also describe the site's current audiences.

Continue by listing any other existing plans and reports that have an impact on interpretation at the site. If a strategic plan or a Historic Structures Report, a social history report, landscape plans, furnishings plans, collections plans, visitor study evaluations, financial plans, or older interpretive plans exist, retrieve them, scan them, and decide what information in those documents is still relevant and which earlier decisions are likely to have an impact on the new interpretation plan.

Then, *evaluate.* What are the strengths and weaknesses of: the collections; the physical plant; visitor amenities and services; staffing and staff training; current interpretive programming and materials; visitation; written materials and available research; current audiences, etc.? Although this is a somewhat subjective exercise, it is extremely valuable to know what staff and others think about the site before planning begins. For this to work, however, it is essential that all participants feel free to be honest without fear of recrimination.

One of the most important activities in the self-analysis process is clarifying the site's interpretive vision. Planners can accomplish this by considering what would be, in the best of all possible worlds, the ideal interpretive experience at the site, and then by developing a *vision statement for interpretation* that articulates the site's "highest and best use." This provides an opportunity for staff and others involved in the planning to reach a consensus about what is most important to them. The vision statement should develop out of an examination of the planners' motivations and goals. Why did the site decide to plan? What do staff members hope to achieve? The vision statement need not be long and detailed, but it should be specific enough to provide a focus for the planning process. It must also define the goals and objectives of the plan.

In the analysis phase, it is also useful to spell out *specific needs* that the interpretation plan must address. These are the larger problems that have become clear during the preplanning stage. Is ADA compliance a problem? Is the history and story told in the site's current interpretation complete and sufficiently inclusive? Is the site trying to attract different audiences? Are there public bathrooms on site? Is a school program needed? Brainstorm these issues and make a list of them. Use the list as a reference throughout the planning process, and add to it as new issues and needs arise.

When the site resource inventory and self-analysis are complete, and all of the relevant questions have been raised, everything should be put in writing. Circulate a draft to the planning team and others for discussion and revision. Planners must first hammer out and come to a consensus on the necessary policy, vision, and mission issues before they can begin to consider what story the site should tell and how it should tell it.

Know the History of the Site

No matter how well organized a site's interpretive content or how successful its presentation, the underlying pedagogical value of an interpretation depends on the quality of the history on which it is based. Good interpretation requires an understanding of the history of the site, familiarity with its contextual history, and in-depth knowledge of the content-related strengths and weaknesses of the site, its stories, and its collections. Before beginning the planning process, read, review, research, and communicate with historians and ask them to help planners focus on what is most important about the site's interpretation. Analyze primary source materials, documents, photographs, maps, illustrations, books, and objects, as well as spaces, monuments, landscapes, and buildings, and understand what they can teach about history. Remember to use both the site's collections and the collections of others to help enhance the study of history. In this way, when the historical "stories" are identified and organized later in the planning process, they will be based on accurate history and reflect intellectual integrity.

The lack of good or complete research or of an ongoing research program need not be an excuse for postponing interpretation planning, however. Research is an important activity for museums, but it is never complete. Even at those sites where research is done regularly, it is virtually impossible for research to keep up with interpretation needs, and impractical to try to adapt an interpretation every time a new bit of information is uncovered. However, the planning process is an ideal opportunity to figure out what is known, determine what research needs to be done, and put a *research plan* in place to help fill the gaps. Once a clear and well-defined research plan is in place, the museum can enter into collaborations with local historians, graduate students, and history professors at local colleges to help do the work. In the meantime, proceed with the interpretation planning, designing the plan to be flexible enough to accommodate changes in information or knowledge as research progresses.

As staff and others examine the research needs, develop a research plan, and put that plan into action, they will inevitably reveal further research needs. Keep an ongoing list of those needs, integrate them into the research plan, and when important research milestones are reached, incorporate the new material into the interpretation where appropriate.

Whatever the state of the site's historical knowledge, it is important to write a *three- to five-page essay articulating the historical significance of the site.* This valuable tool provides an opportunity for the planning team to reach consensus about what (and who) is important in the site's history, provides a jumping off point for the development of themes, and is extremely valuable for creating interpreter training programs, writing brochures, creating interpretive signs, and even writing grants. Be certain that the site's significance as it is articulated is actually illustrated by the site's evidence—the collections, the spaces, and so on. Once consensus is reached on the historical significance essay, create a packet of basic history materials for all planning team members. Include the essay and any other useful materials—site brochures and other publications, background readings, selected primary source materials, bibliographies—so that everyone on the team can read, digest, and be up to speed on the essential history of the site and any relevant contextual history.

Understanding How People Learn

People visit museums for a variety of reasons, but certainly the majority of our audiences come voluntarily, in their precious free time, looking for an experience that is both pleasurable and educational.[2] Because interpretation is meant to be educational or instructive, it is important to understand something about how people learn in museum settings. Visitors will cease to pay attention if they lose interest.

One sure way to lose an audience is to provide interpretive experiences that are crammed with too much information, much of which is poorly organized. As George E. Hein points out in his book *Learning in the Museum*, "[I]t is not sufficient for experiences to be 'lively, vivid, and interesting'; they must also be organized to be educative."[3] Interpretation should consist of well-organized and comprehensible content presented in an entertaining and engaging way.

Barbara Levy, Sandra Lloyd, and Susan Schreiber, in their book *Great Tours! Thematic Tours and Guide Training for Historic Sites*, describe an organizing strategy for effective teaching in museums. "The most effective, *memorable* learning often occurs when we are asked to focus on a few important **big ideas** that are used as an umbrella for smaller ideas. . . . This teaching strategy, when employed creatively and dynamically, is extraordinarily effective because it focuses on a few big ideas, then uses these ideas as umbrellas to group related information and illustrations. It also provides the opportunity to repeat the key ideas several times. When done creatively, this process is easy to follow because it is organized and reinforces the major concepts that are important to remember."[4]

Examples of the efficacy of grouping on memory are all around us. Think about a social security number or a long distance telephone number. Remembering nine or ten numbers strung together is difficult for most of us, but as soon as those numbers are broken down into smaller groups we are able to remember them easily. Grouping ideas in a teaching situation is equally valuable, particularly when learners are relying on their memories and not keeping notes. Grouping like ideas serves as a kind of aide-mémoire by helping visitors find a relevant location for what they hear or see in their mental filing cabinets.

For most people repetition is also a key to retention. The more we hear or see an idea repeated, the greater the likelihood that we will remember what we heard. However, repeating an idea over and over in the same way is boring and invites the familiar glazed look of a visitor who has stopped listening. By using a "big idea" organizing structure (also known as a thematic structure), an interpretation can use many different elements of the site's history and material culture to illustrate and reinforce a limited number of essential concepts. In this way, the constant but varied reinforcement acts as repetition, helping visitors remember what is important, but avoids the inevitable boredom caused by verbatim repetition.

In addition, there are a variety of teaching tools that are effective because they help people learn and remember:

- Relate history to visitors' experiences. People tend to have more interest and remember better when they can relate what they are learning to something they already know or something they have experienced. Teachers often use comparing and contrasting as a means to do this. It is very effective in interpretation also.

- Use a variety of teaching techniques to provide the best chance of reaching people at different developmental stages and with diverse learning styles.

- Use animated, engaging delivery techniques in all interpretive media. Strive to stimulate visitors' curiosity and interest.

- Make creative use of the unexpected. This prevents visitors from always anticipating what will happen next, and it keeps their minds focused on what the interpreter is trying to say.

Organizing and Designing the Planning Protocol

It is unwise to jump into planning without having thought through how the process of planning should take shape. The plan will ultimately rise or fall depending on how well the planning process is organized and managed.

First, establish who will be on the planning team. It is a good rule of thumb to aim for about five to seven people. The team should consist of enough people to share the work and to be creative, but not so many people that the process becomes cumbersome and inefficient. The needs of each site will be different. The team's makeup will depend on the individuals involved at the site, the size of the site, and the nature of the planning attempted.

The planning team should include people who have expertise or are working in the areas of management and administration, collections, education, interpretation, and public programming. It is useful to include an interested board member, and it may also be helpful to include people with knowledge of building or landscape maintenance or preservation, the museum's finances, or visitor services. In addition, consider including someone who represents the site's visitors—someone in the community who is very involved with the site, perhaps a long-time volunteer. This person could bring a helpful perspective.

The planning should be conducted according to a schedule. Establish a deadline, and develop the schedule based on the deadline. Make it realistic—long enough to accommodate busy people, but short enough not to allow the planning to languish. Schedule interim deadlines for specific products so that the team feels it is making progress all along. Undoubtedly, these deadlines will change, but they will help the team stay on task. The planning schedule should also include checkpoints for the other interested parties—the board, staff, community members—so that they all have an opportunity to review and comment on the work while it is in process, not just at the end.

The team needs a chairperson, someone to keep everyone on schedule, run the meetings, produce the written materials, and divide work among the team members. Actual policy making, however, should be done as a team, often through discussion, but also with the assistance of various activities. Consider designing activities that will help team members think creatively.

To be effective, the team must establish and abide by a set of ground rules. These might include requirements to think creatively, respect others, be productive, work toward consensus, and stay within the schedule. With ground rules such as these, as well as a diligent effort to adhere to them, the team will be a model of productive organizational behavior and will cultivate a creative and positive work environment.

As mentioned earlier, it is important to engage the board, staff, and others—visitors, for example—in the planning process on a regular, predetermined schedule. Solicit their input, and take it seriously. The planning process will benefit from their perspective and the implementation is far more likely to be successful when they have a personal investment in it. Soliciting the input of others can actually help the team stay on schedule, especially if it must submit drafts to the board by specific dates.

Finally, the team should keep and circulate good meeting notes to serve as a record of progress of the process and to ensure that the products developed are based upon the team's decisions. Some groups tape their meetings instead of writing notes because it frees up everyone to participate more fully.[5] Meeting notes, however, are more useful. The meeting record is easy to copy and circulate, and reading the notes requires team members to think, one more time, about what transpired. In addition, when team members review the meeting notes for accuracy, they can clarify and edit the transcript so that areas of consensus are indisputable.

The Plan's Content

An interpretation plan should cover five major topics: background and justification, organizing and articulating the primary content, where to interpret the themes, how to interpret the themes, and plans and schedules for developing implementation and follow-up strategies.

Background and Justification

The background and justification section contains many of the materials gathered or prepared in the preplanning stage. It should include the site's mission statement, interpretive vision statement (including goals and objectives), the essay of historical significance, and a description of the site based on the resource inventory. The team should discuss all of these elements, then come to a consensus about them and include the results in the plan.

Organizing the Content

Determining the focus and scope of a site's interpretive content provides a skeleton on which successful interpretive programming can be built. For this structure to be effective, it must clearly convey a limited number of themes. Sam H. Ham, in his book *Environmental Interpretation: A Practical Guide for People with Big Ideas and Small Budgets*, says:

> [W]hen interpretation has a theme it has a **message**. We call this thematic interpretation. When our communication isn't thematic, it seems unorganized, difficult to follow, and less meaningful to our audience. This is simply because they can't easily see where the communication is going, and they don't know how to connect all the information they're receiving. But when the information we present is thematic—that is, when it's all related to some key idea or central message—it becomes easier to follow and more meaningful to people.[6]

Themes are essential to successful interpretation, and therefore critically important to interpretation planning.

Each *interpretive theme* should be of primary importance to the history of the site. It must also express what it is the site wants visitors to know or understand. Consequently, topics—the Civil War, women's work, or the Industrial Revolution, for example—are not themes because they do not establish what is most important for visitors to know about the topic. For themes to do this, they should be specific and stated in full sentences.

How many themes should a historic house museum have? As Levy, Lloyd, and Schreiber note, "Most sites will find that three to five significant ideas or *themes* typically work best. When these themes are woven together, they provide a *storyline* that is a succinct, yet compelling summary of the important ideas, events, and features that make a site special."[7] Often, limiting the interpretation to no more than five themes is difficult, because the more interpreters know about their sites, the more excited they get, and the more things they want to tell visitors. Having the discipline to know what not to say is essential to effective interpretation planning and to interpretation in general. In some ways, the most difficult aspect of interpretation planning is choosing what *not* to interpret. There is a danger in telling visitors too much—more than they can assimilate and, usually, far more than they want to know. This is critical given the brief length of time visitors usually stay at historic house museums. Say less, not more, and say it in a really engaging, disciplined manner.

The three- to five-page site history essay developed during preplanning is a useful tool for the theme development process. After rereading and digesting the essay, begin a discussion about the most important ideas. As the discussion progresses, write the ideas on a board or flip chart where everyone can see them. At first, they need not be expressed in full sentences, but once a reasonably short list has been determined, turn each phrase into a full sentence or two. Post the sentences where everyone can see them, and work toward choosing the three to five themes that are most important.

Sometimes the process of articulating a theme begins slowly. One way to facilitate the expression of themes in sentence form is to ask planning team members to complete the sentence fragment "Visitors will understand that . . ." using one of the phrases that emerged from the discussion. In this way, the team will be forced to decide what it is about the phrase or concept they want visitors to learn. For example, the topic "American Revolution" might generate a theme like: "Visitors will understand that Jonas Smith was a leader in local patriotic activities, organized the local militia, and led the men who defended the town against British regulars," or "Jonas and Sally Smith were staunch patriots who believed adamantly in the cause of the Revolution. Their beliefs and actions created a rift with Sally's family who felt equally strongly that the colonies should remain a part of England." Aim for a complete and specific idea, one that visitors will take away with them and remember about the history of the site.

Once the team drafts the themes, work with them to ensure they are not only specific, but also substantive and meaningful. Answering the following questions can be useful in achieving this. First, is the theme of critical importance? If it is, could it be expressed more clearly or would it make more sense if it were expressed in some other way? Is the theme sufficiently complete, or should it be expanded to include other critical ideas or topics, or narrowed to include fewer? Finally, and by no means least importantly, can the theme be illustrated by the material culture and ideas at the site?

Remember:

- A theme is what the site wants visitors to understand or know about its history.

- Each theme should be a discrete idea that contains a message visitors will receive.

- Limit the number of themes to three to five.

- Well-written themes should be specific enough to have focus but not too narrow. Think of each theme as a "basket" that will hold other, smaller concepts.

- Be sure that the material culture at the site supports the themes; themes should be inherent in or illustrated by the historical "evidence."

- Themes are the single most important element of interpretation. They give it unity and coherence.

Where to Interpret Each Theme

With the story line written and the themes identified, the planning team must next determine the appropriate interpretive venues. Deciding where to interpret each theme at a historic house or site depends on the strengths of the collection in each place. Collections include historic structures, architectural elements, landscapes, monuments in the landscape, and spaces, as well as objects, documents, photographs, maps, art, and other items more commonly thought of as part of the museum's collections. Although some moving of objects can and often will take place as a result of the interpretation planning, the locations of many collection components will not change. For example, historic room use is often fixed. The kitchen will remain the kitchen; therefore, the cook stove will not be moved to the parlor.

This portion of the planning is best accomplished in the actual spaces themselves. Team members should meet in those spaces, using flip charts to record ideas and decisions. In each space to be interpreted, including the landscape, answer four questions. Which theme or themes are most strongly evoked in that space? Which people are most strongly associated with the space? What activities or events took place there? And which stories related to the space are important? Next, analyze the material culture in that space and determine which elements best illustrate the themes, people, activities, and stories. Use this as an opportunity to come to consensus about what the museum will communicate to visitors and how it will use the extant evidence to support those ideas. Proceed from space to space, repeating the procedure. Use a flip chart or other means to record ideas and conclusions, and when finished, put everything in document form to circulate for comments. When reviewing the resulting document, check for balance among the themes and ascertain that the themes are still relevant. Expect to revise and revise and revise.

When deciding what to interpret, planners must also consider historical context. Context is the background visitors need to know in order to be able to understand the message and its relative importance historically. For example, if the daily life of immigrant factory workers in New York were an essential part of the interpretation, then visitors would need to understand something about the context of New York at the time, the nature of factory work, and what crowded tenements were like. Selecting relevant context for an interpretation is like taking a photograph in which the interpretive message is included. The picture cannot be too comprehensive or the message becomes small and insignificant. However, when the picture is too much of a close-up, the message has no frame of reference. Without context, it is difficult for visitors to make sense of the message. Determine what visitors need to know about such contextual elements as the background of the site, the history of the period, the context of the neighborhood, and social experiences to be able to assimilate the themes and perceive them as relevant to their own experiences. Insert the appropriate context in the draft document in the places where the corresponding issues will be communicated.

How to Interpret

Once the team makes decisions about which information will be interpreted and where, the planning team must tackle the issue of how to interpret. Most historic sites use a mix of primary and secondary interpretation tools, supplemented by printed and published materials. Primary interpretation tools are the principle means of interpretation at the site; they are used every day for interpreting to the largest general audiences. A site can function with primary interpretive tools alone. They include methods such as interpreter-led tours (in the first person or third person), self-guided tours (with accompanying brochures, text panels and labels, audio tours, and sometimes stationed guides), and permanent gallery-type exhibits.

Secondary tools enhance and enrich the primary interpretation, but they do not stand alone. Often, they are repeated on a regularly scheduled basis. Secondary tools include introductory videos; specialized tours or special temporary exhibits; historical demonstrations or reenactments; programs (such as school programs, elder hostels, adult public programs, etc.); hands-on areas; and computer-based interpretation stations. In addition, printed and published materials are important to supplement an interpretive program. Site brochures, videos, CD-ROM, exhibit catalogues, and other publications are all useful in the quest to extend the influence of on-site visitation.

Before choosing which types of tools should be used to interpret the various spaces, the planners need to revisit the issue of audience. Think about whom the site is for. First, consider the principal audience. Who are they? What interests them? How long do they generally stay at the site? What kinds of experiences does the site want them to have?

Based on the audience profile and the kinds of experiences the site wants visitors to have, determine what *learning objectives* should be achieved by the interpretation. In a museum setting, learning objectives are not simply content related, in the way that themes are, but encapsulate what sites want visitors to know, understand, feel, or be able to do when they leave the site. Put these in writing.

Interpretation techniques are not created equal. Choose the techniques and tools that accommodate the strengths and make up for the weaknesses of the themes and collections. The more direct the connection between the idea to be communicated and the medium, the less likely it is that the interpretation vehicle will obstruct learning. For example, let's say that a site wants to interpret a paper clip to a person who has never seen or used one. One look at the clip holding papers and the learner immediately understands what the object looks like and how it is used. If an actual paper clip is not available (or a sofa, a teapot, a spinning wheel, or a kitchen tool, for example), a picture and an explanation have to substitute. Without a picture, words alone are barely adequate. The farther interpreters get from the simplest and most direct mode of communication, the harder it is for visitors to experience the idea. If a five-room historic house once contained a bustling household with twelve people living and working in it, a pristine, clean, "perfect" historic house does not communicate the way the house felt when the family lived there. How can the site interpret the social history of that family? Although it is not usually possible to repeople the site, there are ways to enhance the words used to explain things to people. Use objects to convey clutter, use photographs, add ambient sound, use living history techniques. In short, be creative—think about what visitors should *feel* when they visit the site.

In this process, team members should be certain to consider the needs of special audiences. These include audiences with disabilities or special needs as

BARBARA ABRAMOFF LEVY

well as particular groups of people, such as international visitors, minority groups, senior citizens, and children. Another special audience might be a group of people with a distinctive interest, collectors of antique automobiles, for example, or people who have decorative arts interests. Every special audience consists of people who have an important, vested interest in the site. Planners need to analyze the learning objectives they have established for major audiences and determine whether they are also appropriate for various special audiences. If not, create separate learning objectives.

Now comes the time to determine which interpretation tools to use to achieve the learning objectives. Primary interpretation tools should be selected first because they will accommodate the majority of visitors. The choices should reflect the best answers to the question, "What is the most effective way to tell these stories to this audience?" Make a chart with columns that shows the type of interpretation (tour, exhibit, etc.), the location for the interpretation, the themes it will cover, and the audience for which it is primarily designed. This will make it easier to see what is missing so the site can select the most appropriate secondary tools.

Once the team chooses the primary tools, planners should consider which secondary tools will enhance the visitor's experience, address the needs of different kinds of learners, and offer different perspectives on the site's themes. With regard to special audiences, answer the following questions. Will the primary and secondary tools succeed with this group? If not, what tools should be available for them? If, for instance, the site's primary interpretation tool is a tour of a historic house in which the second floor is accessible only by stairs, visitors who cannot climb stairs need another means, perhaps a video, to experience the second-floor tour.

Create a chart for secondary tools showing the same information as the primary tool chart. Review the two charts to see if all audiences have been provided with an opportunity to learn the themes and experience the site in the most effective way.

Budgets, logistical constraints, and staffing will, of course, affect decisions about interpretation tools. A less desirable alternative for the primary interpretation tool may be necessary because of cost. Sometimes in these cases it is possible to use secondary tools to enhance a less desirable alternative. For example, if a self-guided tour is what the museum can afford, but the planning team believes that visitors need interaction with a human to gain a strong sense of the themes, they might arrange for regularly scheduled demonstrations or periodic first-person interpretations, which would supplement and enhance the visitor's experience without committing the museum to financial commitments it cannot sustain.

56

These kinds of choices can also be considered interim—ways to implement new interpretive ideas and test them out while raising money for more expensive possibilities.

Once the team makes the preliminary decisions, write a draft report that describes the interpretive program. Be sure to explain which primary and secondary tools the team selected and why, which themes and learning objectives each of these will cover, when they will be offered, where they will be presented, and which audiences they are meant to address. Also include a description of the likely impact of the choices on the budget, staffing, and physical plant. Be specific and as descriptive as possible. The more explicit the program description is, the easier it will be to write a scope of work, create a contract for consultants, and develop a work plan for staff.

It is also useful to include brief "visitor scenarios" in the report that describe the experiences particular types of visitors (a family group, bus tour, group of seniors, architecture buffs, etc.) will have from the time they arrive until the time they leave. The scenarios help planners and others imagine the visitor experience. They are also useful as a means to examine the viability of the plans for each audience.

Implementation and Follow-Up

All of this preparation, information gathering, and decision making leads to the implementation and follow-up phase. The first step in this process is preparing the *scope of work and budget*. To do this, first describe in detail the work that must be done to create each element of the interpretation. Next, specify who will be responsible for doing and supervising the work. This may include the creation of new staff positions. It also requires deciding which projects contractors or consultants will do. Then, figure out how much each element will cost. Be as specific as possible. Think through the ramifications of every single decision the team has made.

The team can then determine how the plan will be implemented. First, decide what the order of priority is for the interpretation projects, and create an *implementation schedule* for all aspects of each of those projects. If planners discover—as most sites do—that the proposed scope of work is far too big, try breaking the schedule into phases or interim steps. This not only makes the projects more manageable, but also helps the museum avoid costly mistakes by allowing time to evaluate, make changes and adaptations based on those evaluations, and raise money. Provide time in the schedule to test drafts of products like tours and brochures and to make revisions.

It is likely that the work plan will need to be edited, possibly even setting aside some projects. At the same time, however, be sure to include as high priorities some interpretation tools that will not require fund-raising. This will allow staff to begin work immediately and to see some things happen quickly.

Create a draft of the implementation plan at this stage which includes the scope of work, work responsibilities, budget, and implementation schedule. Circulate it, get comments, discuss it, revise it, and work with the interested parties until everyone is on board. Defend the choices. Don't try to move ahead with implementation until the institution and its partners accept the ideas with enthusiasm.

Because implementation of an interpretive plan often requires raising a significant amount of money, it is helpful to develop a specialized and realistic fund-raising plan specific to the interpretation and accompanied by a corresponding schedule. Integrate it into the work plan.

The impact of the implementation on the physical plant and landscape is another important consideration. Often, an interpretive plan will require changes in the physical features of the historic building(s), site, or landscape. Is an increase in the number of parking spaces needed? Does the site need more bathrooms or a ramp for wheelchairs? Will a visitor center be built? Are there safety and security concerns? Describe the alterations or additions needed, how they will impact the site, and determine how much each alteration or addition will cost. Integrate this into the work plan and schedule.

The new interpretation may affect other areas, as well. The furnishings plan might need to be revised, a landscape plan created, a financial plan prepared. Perhaps the museum's collections are inadequate or more historic research about servants or slaves or some other topic is needed. Determine how and when such issues will impact the implementation, and adjust the work plan and schedule accordingly.

It is also important to consider how the site will measure whether the interpretation is accomplishing the articulated learning objectives. As the scope of work is developed, think about how the site will evaluate program success. There are many ways to do this. As Judy Diamond says in *Practical Evaluation Guide: Tools for Museums and Other Informal Educational Settings*,

> You want to study the visitors at your museum, . . . but where do you begin? You may want to know how well your new exhibit or program works. What does it communicate to visitors? How can you make improvements? What do you need to know about your audience? What are your visitors learning?

These questions can be answered by conducting evaluation studies at your institution. There is no single recipe for evaluations; each study should be designed to meet the specific needs of the institution or program being studied. There are, however, many different evaluation research methods to choose from.[8]

Team members should create an interpretive evaluation plan or employ a consultant to design and implement an approach. Sometimes a consultant specializing in audience research and evaluation will train a museum's staff to conduct the evaluation themselves. The plan should also include a schedule for the evaluations that parallels the implementation schedule from the very beginning. This will ensure that visitor input arrives early and that the staff can make necessary adaptations before the interpretation is fixed and permanent.

Finally, the interpretation plan should address how and when the site will make adaptations to the implementation based on evaluations. This includes budgeting for necessary changes. Often budgets for interpretation disappear when everything is installed, except perhaps for some maintenance money. Museums tend not to allow for the inevitability that there will be mistakes, omissions, or other reasons to make adaptations. The budget and the schedule should include provisions for this, reflecting the probability that there will be mistakes and that money and flexibility are necessary to make things work as they should.

Create another draft of the scope of work, budget, and schedule that includes the fund-raising plan, changes to the physical plant, other necessary changes, and the evaluation plan. Circulate it as before, and work to build consensus. As soon as possible, put the plan into action; don't let the ideas get stale or interest wane.

Planning will not solve all of a site's interpretation problems, but it will go a long way toward clarifying what visitors will experience. It will also help a site realize its potential as an educational institution. The planning process may seem like pushing a boulder up a hill, especially when simply keeping the site running from day to day is a challenge. It does, however, offer significant rewards.

Interpretation planning is not easy or short, but it can be invigorating. It is a way to enjoy an experience with peers in an environment entirely different from the workaday world. It enables museum professionals to think about situations at their sites that they may not otherwise have a chance to consider. It provides an opportunity to begin, at least theoretically, with a clean slate and to fix problems and address the issues that really matter. It fosters creativity, new perspectives, and new ways of thinking. All in all, interpretation planning is not an onerous process; it is an exciting, enriching, and fulfilling experience that benefits not just the planners, but everyone who visits the site.

Notes

1. Freeman Tilden, *Interpreting Our Heritage*, 3d ed. (Chapel Hill: University of North Carolina Press, 1977), 8.

2. Alison L. Grinder and E. Sue McCoy, *The Good Guide: A Sourcebook for Interpreters, Docents, and Tour Guides* (Scottsdale, Ariz.: Ironwood Publishing, 1985), 105.

3. George E. Hein, *Learning in the Museum* (London: Routledge, 1998), 2.

4. Barbara Abramoff Levy, Sandra Mackenzie Lloyd, and Susan Porter Schreiber, *Great Tours! Thematic Tours and Guide Training for Historic Sites* (Walnut Creek, Calif.: AltaMira Press, 2001), 4.

5. Tape recordings of meetings tend to go unused. Recordings are only useful if they are transcribed promptly, which is time consuming and costly.

6. Sam H. Ham, *Environmental Interpretation: A Practical Guide for People with Big Ideas and Small Budgets* (Golden, Colo.: Fulcrum, 1992), 33.

7. Levy, Lloyd, and Schreiber, *Great Tours!*, 4.

8. Judy Diamond, *Practical Evaluation Guide: Tools for Museums and Other Informal Educational Settings* (Walnut Creek, Calif.: AltaMira Press, 1999), 15.

CHAPTER THREE

INTERPRETING THE WHOLE HOUSE

Rex M. Ellis

Something is happening. Something is happening in the field of history, especially relating to the study of African-American history and culture. How America learns history, as well as whose history it learns, is undergoing scrutiny, debate, and challenge. Mainstream museums—science, natural history, art, children's, historic site—are addressing minority history in their exhibits and interpretive programs like never before. This movement extends beyond the museum and into the arena of popular culture, as well. Steven Spielberg's production of *Amistad* (1997), complete with a teacher's guide and educational materials, is one example. Others are the public television series *Africans in America: America's Journey through Slavery* (1998); Ethiopian-born filmmaker Haile Gerima's film *Sankofa* (1993); and the 1998 movie based on Toni Morrison's Pulitzer Prize–winning novel *Beloved*. The popular movie *The Patriot* (2000) included scenes relating to the Gullah community of the South Carolina sea islands. Something is indeed happening.

A new cadre of public historians is making significant links between academic research and public accessibility. They have inspired fellow scholars, writers, artists, teachers, and communities to take a second look at what they thought they knew about topics like slavery. At the conference *Transatlantic Slaving and the African Diaspora* held in Williamsburg, Virginia, in 1998, more than 700 people met to discuss the latest research on the African slave trade. Researchers also announced the development of a CD-ROM chronicling the majority of existing records relating to the slave trade in the eighteenth and nineteenth centuries. In 1999, Microsoft released its first version of *Encarta Africana*, a comprehensive multimedia encyclopedia of the history and culture of people of African descent. University of Maryland professor Ira Berlin's prize-winning volume, *Many Thousands Gone: The First Two Centuries of Slavery in North America* (1998), and Phillip Morgan's *Slave Counterpoint* (1998) represent two of more than 2,000 texts on slavery published in the last five years of the twentieth century. In April 2000, the Smithsonian Institution held a conference on slavery titled *American Slavery in History and Memory*. The conference explored the many ways the topic of slavery is introduced, discussed, and presented in print, film, radio, museums, and schools in the United States. For most attendees, the study of slavery in America must be comprehensive and is far from finished. All participants acknowledged a need to continue discussing slavery and its influence on American identity.

New scholarship, innovative technology, and renewed attention to African-American history and culture have fostered new, popular, and sometimes controversial ways to look at and examine the past. As an example, concerned parties have reignited arguments about whether reparations should be paid to African Americans for the indignities they suffered during slavery. Randall Robinson, author of *The Debt: What America Owes to Blacks* (2000), writes, "The United States was complicit in this massive injustice. And the injustice did not end with the lives of the slaves and the slaveholders. The great-great-great-great-grand-children of slaves are owed not just for their forebears' labor, or for the humiliation of performing it, but for every devastating failure since, engendered by their government on the basis of race."[1]

Perhaps the most publicized of these recent glimpses into the past was the controversy over the relationship between Thomas Jefferson and his slave Sally Hemings. Dr. Eugene A. Foster and a team of British and Dutch geneticists at Oxford, Leicester, and Leyden Universities conducted DNA tests on Jefferson's descendants. The results have changed what many Jefferson scholars thought they knew about Mr. Jefferson. That Sally Hemings was the mistress of one of this country's Founding Fathers and the mother of one or more of his children were notions previously inconceivable to the best and brightest scholars. Now Dr. Foster's study "indicates a sexual relationship between Thomas Jefferson and Sally Hemings."[2]

An unprecedented amount of activity is taking place in popular culture for a subject that has traditionally been discussed by a few historians and still fewer historic house museums. Why is it happening? What is causing such a ground-swell of activity? How are Americans reacting? What is the significance of it all? The answers are not yet clear, but the level of interest and the associated activity will continue to change the ways history is taught and the methods used to teach it.

One of the most effective and traditional venues for teaching history is the historic house museum. The twentieth century witnessed a surge in the creation of these museums in America, but for most of that time, their interpretive emphasis was on white, often upper-class, mostly male residents. As competition for audiences and funding increased, and as the field of history in general opened up to diverse perspectives, historic site staffs began to explore ways to make the interpretation of their sites more inclusive. This comprehensive approach included racial and ethnic minorities (not just African Americans), who were part of their past as well as their present. Museums now are forced to deal with a more sophisticated audience. Because public access to research is more immediate and more comprehensive than ever before, the public will begin to hold teachers of history in the twenty-first century to ever-higher standards of accuracy and inclusion. Historic house museums will be judged by these standards, as well, and their survival will depend, in many cases, upon the extent and effectiveness of their efforts to interpret their sites more fully.

Embracing Change and Broadening Perspectives

One of the challenges in the world of historic house museums is embracing change in an atmosphere that reveres the past. As new historical evidence is uncovered and public curiosity increases, change becomes necessary in all institutions of history. Museum professionals must balance what they think they know with what the public desires and needs to hear; they must attune their stories to visitors' willingness to listen and learn if the public is to understand the importance of those stories. Museum curators and educational scholars spend a great deal of time researching and reading (usually about subjects that support their own particular interests). The particular conclusions they reach can cause them to unwittingly hamstring themselves into the arrogant belief that they already know most of what is "important" to know about any given aspect of their site's history. This perception of knowledge provides a safe, comfortable haven. Therein lies the rub. In this sort of intellectual climate, new data can be suspect and unwelcome because too often the first instinct is to deny that the new information has any merit. Forgetting that there is no statute of limitation on conclusions that can be derived from historical analysis, they assume that the new information must be wrong. Such responses in historic house settings may spring, in part, from discomfort about how to present the past in a new way.

Traditionally, the public viewed historic sites as legitimate places for teaching and learning history. It valued the way these museums conducted research, gathered information, utilized artifacts, and communicated. As social and public historians have continued to push the envelope and test the public's readiness to receive new information, they and the general public have come to expect historic sites to update their information and integrate it accurately and creatively into the way they teach about the past. If historic house museums are to remain competitive they must meet and fulfill these expectations. In addition, there is a great need to keep abreast of what is happening in the field so that information can be updated and new methodologies implemented.

Museum educators are also under constant pressure to make it all meaningful to vast numbers of schoolchildren. This pressure has many sources: decreased resources for field trips; demands to do more on the site in less time; the pressure to teach creatively to counterbalance school systems that are less and less successful connecting with their students; questionable preparation by student visitors; and a hesitancy on the part of school administrations to pay teachers for preparation in addition to the regular school day. Add to this questions about what is true, what is false, what is known, and what is not known, and you've got a moving target that frustrates even the most ardent interpreters. But being open to new ideas must be a prerequisite of their work. It is the act of opening our minds to the possibilities inherent in the stories we tell that makes the educational enterprise exciting and engaging.

There are fine examples of historic house museums dealing with changing information. The interpretive staff at Monticello embraced change and chased the truth when the results of the Jefferson-Hemings DNA tests were revealed. For years, few believed that someone like Thomas Jefferson would have an affair with his slave Sally Hemings. He was simply above it intellectually, socially, and morally. They thought they knew. Then, suddenly, under the glare of widespread public attention, Monticello had to adapt to this new understanding of the past, and the controversial nature of this particular past made change difficult indeed. Monticello's administration and staff moved forward with intelligence and grace and promptly updated the story they had been telling on top of Jefferson's mountain.

As historians continue to release the voluminous research they have amassed over the years, the difficulty of the job required of historic sites and house museums does not diminish. No one really knows the extent to which popular films and television shows that deal with slavery and African or African-American history—*Amistad, Africans in America, Sankofa, Beloved,* and *The Patriot,* for instance—have satisfied America's taste for controversy, and what America has learned about history as a result. And one continues to wonder about the truth of what the audiences have learned. There is no doubt that the history most of us revere has now become part of the box office. Unfortunately this also suggests that these sensational storytellers—most of whom seem more interested in box office sales than accuracy—will have a great degree of influence on public perceptions and understanding of history. What these venues present as truth is often their inference that has been stretched to tell a compelling story or wrap up loose ends before the final credits. As a result, the many Americans who get their "history lesson" from film and television are getting some truth mixed with a great deal of fiction for the sake of entertainment.

Consequently, this puts an even greater burden on museums to present history accurately. The stories may not be as glamorous as the versions produced by Hollywood, but they will certainly be more reliable. Effectively presented, they will go a long way in helping debunk myths and shoddy history. Now, therefore, is not a time for mediocrity in presenting the past; and it is not a time for denial, especially if institutions such as historic house museums hope to survive. It is a time to reassess, reembrace, and enliven the search for historical truth. There is no one true window through which we must view the past, so museums must reexamine the belief that the current truth is the only truth and all other perspectives just attempts to be politically correct. If the public is expected to perceive as important the messages historic houses convey in the new millennium, then sites must embrace dynamic history, diverse publics, and technology that is making access to information available to people and communities that never considered visiting their sites before.

The stories museums tell—the essence of their interpretation—will achieve their potential only if they reflect or appeal to a variety of perspectives. To develop an interpretive strategy derived from one point of view is to limit the institution's reach and, therefore, its usefulness. The following is an adaptation of the story of "The Girl with the Large Eyes," which was first included in *Black Folktales*, a collection of stories by Julius Lester. It illustrates my point concerning the new ways museum professionals must begin to see their task of educating the public:

Many, many years ago in Angola there lived a girl with beautiful, large eyes. Whenever she walked through the village, her gaze was more than the young men could bear. On the summer that she was to marry, a drought came upon the region. The crops dried up, the earth dried up and turned to dust, and the people began to starve. And when a man's mind is on food, he cannot think of marriage, even to one so beautiful as the girl with the large eyes.

She had very little time to think of her own misfortune, because it was her duty each day to go to the river bed and to scoop up what clay she could and to squeeze what water she could from the clay. One day, she went to the riverbed. She began to scoop up the clay. She began to squeeze the water, and a fish appeared, and he said to her, "Give me your pitcher." She obeyed, and he filled it with cool, clear water. The next day, the girl returned to the riverbed, and she called to the fish. He appeared and he commanded, "Give me your pitcher." She obeyed. He filled it. Cool, clear water.

Each day the girl returned to the riverbed. Each day, she called to the fish. Each day he filled her pitcher with cool, clear water. And the girl became very fond of the fish. His eyes were clear, like the water he provided each day. His skin was the color of the rainbow. And on the seventh day, she allowed him to embrace her, and she became his wife.

Now, the father of the girl with the large eyes became very curious as to where she was getting this water each day. He was a medicine man. He turned his son, her brother, into a fly. He said, "Follow her. Report back to me." The next morning the brother, the son, the fly accompanied the girl with the large eyes to the riverbed. He watched in amazement as she called to the fish. He watched in amazement as she allowed the fish to embrace her. He flew home to tell his father of this disgraceful occurrence.

The next morning, the father would not allow the girl with the large eyes to go to the riverbed. Instead, he and his son went to the riverbed. And when they arrived, they called to the fish. And when he appeared, they killed him. They picked up the fish; they took him back to the girl with the large eyes, and they threw it at her feet. And they said to her, "We have brought you your husband."

She looked down at the fish—eyes gone cloudy, skin no longer the color of the rainbow—and her eyes began to fill with tears. She picked up the fish and began to walk, wondering what was to become of the child that she was carrying inside her. If they killed her husband, would they not also kill her children? She walked for many, many miles, until she came to a cool, clear stream. Calling her husband's name, she walked into the water until it covered her head. But before she died, she gave birth to many, many children; and they can be seen on the beds of the river today—as water lilies.[3]

The girl saw something her family refused to see. The perspectives of the father and the son were clouded by what they thought they knew about the fish. The girl saw the fish for all that it was—extrinsically, as well as intrinsically. In much the same way, historic sites must strive to see *all* of history and to find ways to teach what they see, read, and understand with responsibility, innovation, and compassion.

Facing the Challenges

Although the task may seem overwhelming, a well-thought-out approach that takes into consideration the following suggestions and ideas can aid museum staffs in developing effective, inclusive site interpretations.

If a subject that relates in some way to a site's mission has the potential to suffuse its interpretation with varied ideas and viewpoints, the staff should not assume that a lack of relevant collections and research precludes their discussing it. Too often historic sites use the excuse that because they have suggestive, but not conclusive, evidence about a topic relating to minority history at their site, they cannot interpret or comment on the minority presence at all. Such a decision is often misguided and causes the site to fall short of what is in the best interests of its educational mission. Artifactual evidence is almost always scant for slaves, servants, indentured servants, Native Americans, and other marginal communities. It is shortsighted and irresponsible, however, to allow that lack of evidence to justify silence about those individuals and their roles in the site's history. Better to use it to teach a lesson that all of history is a series of puzzle pieces. Some aspects are complete but so many are not (and this is not exclusive to the history of minorities).

Guided by its mission and its particular historical footprint, the staff of a historic house should work on expanding the collection, research, archaeology, and documentation to fill these gaps. Resources to aid in that investigation must be found. The alternative is obvious: no visitors and no credibility. A carefully constructed analysis of the scope of a site's collection is helpful in determining what is missing. The goal is not to make the site's story something that it never was, but to integrate all aspects of life and activity into the story to expand its truth and meaning.

When site-specific documentation about a known minority presence is limited, a museum's staff should study evidence available elsewhere in the region to determine what situations, people, and topics might parallel their site's history, or help the public understand interconnections that may exist. As mentioned before, history is a puzzle consisting of a set of pieces that are incomplete because all of the facts are not, and simply cannot be, known. Historical interpretation, therefore, must extrapolate from the known truth. Museum staff might have to speculate, for example, on how a slave or servant's quarters were furnished, because the primary source documentation is not available.

As a caution, however, information that a museum presents must be based on sound reasoning and careful analysis of the information that does exist. It must involve more than an educated guess, though it should not be treated as factual or indisputable. Additionally, audiences should be aware of what is fact and what is inference. Most are able to accept and respect the difference but they must be made aware of the distinction. Taking this step can lead to a more fully developed interpretation that brings history to life and enhances understanding of that which is known as well as that which is conjecture.

Good History and New Perspectives

In addition to strengthening their collections and seeking other repositories of information, historic house museums should ask new questions of the collections they already possess. This can be an effective way to integrate new, inclusive perspectives into interpretation. Determine which artifacts can be used in different ways. Relevant archival materials can supplement this approach with valuable insight and data. Inventories, deeds, wills, parish records, baptismal records, diaries, census data, tax assessments, travelers' accounts, court cases, newspaper ads—although they alone do not tell a complete story, these types of documents provide insight into our diverse patrimony.

Oral histories in particular can shed new light on the intangible qualities of the past, opening the door to understanding through someone else's view of history. Efforts of the Works Progress Administration reward researchers with useful information for sites in many states, especially Virginia, North Carolina, and South Carolina. Too often, pockets of history such as these are not explored as fully as they could be. Analyzed in tandem with such resources, objects, archaeology, documentary evidence, photos, and the rest grow in interpretive value.

Historical interpretation *must* be based on accurate history and responsible research. This is particularly vital for interpreters of minority history about which visitors often have misconceptions, little knowledge, or misunderstandings. With African-American history—as with other marginalized histories—the depth and breadth of information is often limited. Therefore, facts that are available must be correct. If the accuracy of a site's interpretive information comes under scrutiny, it must hold up or the interpretive effort will be wasted and credibility lost.

However, there is no overcoming—via artifacts, documentation, or otherwise—the difficulty of discussing controversial issues like slavery. At the Arlington House, a National Park Service site outside Washington, D.C., which is the pre–Civil War home of the Lee-Custis family, slavery is handled very carefully for this reason. The subjects of slavery and of Robert E. Lee as a slaveholder can be fraught with controversy on a daily basis. Stephanie Batiste-Bentham, an African-American interpreter who worked at Arlington House, remembers that visitors would often pull her to the side and question her about slavery on the site. It was no accident that these visitors were more willing to hear the story of slavery in the slave quarters than they were in the main house. Not only were they more accepting of the slave story in traditional slave spaces, but they also avoided questions that dealt with unpleasant aspects such as master-slave relationships. At the same time, white visitors wanted to hear Lee described as a "good master," while African-American visitors expected to hear the unpleasant parts in all of their gory detail. Most visitors did, however, share a desire to hear about the slave experience from an African-American interpreter.[4]

Another challenge is talking about slavery with interracial groups. One story at the Arlington House is particularly exemplary:

> Batiste-Bentham was conducting a tour of the second floor of the house when from the floor below, ascending the back staircase a black female visitor approached playfully chanting the refrain, "I's in the master's house, I's in the master's house." This visitor was not aware of the tour group and they could not see her, but her improvised refrain created a long, embarrassed silence especially among the white visitors.[5]

Astute interpreters find ways to acknowledge frankly and honestly the awkward nature of these types of situations and the challenges that are inherent. In many of these cases, simply admitting what most visitors already feel can take the conversation to new levels of interaction and thus be rewarding for both the interpreter and the visitor.

When I first worked at Colonial Williamsburg, we developed a tour called "The Other Half," which interpreted the African-American population of the town. The initial reaction to my proposal for the tour was mixed. I was told that a half-day tour (which was changed to a two-hour tour) dealing with the other half of the population was a wonderful idea, but that because no space—out of the thirty-eight reconstructed or restored buildings, out of the 173 acres that constitute Colonial Williamsburg—actually focused on the slave population of Williamsburg, such a tour did not seem practical. My response, however, was that such a tour would complete the story of the town of Williamsburg. Even though someone else might have designed it, certainly somebody black helped build it.

The tour was implemented first in the summer of 1981. It focused on the beginnings of African and African-American presence in the colonies and began at the Governor's Palace, which was one of the first buildings built in what was then called Middle Plantation. Visitors entered, not through the front door, but through the rear of the building. The goal was to challenge visitors—on various levels and planes and by various juxtapositions of ideas and objects—to see the town from the point of view of the Africans and African Americans who lived and worked there. The setting of the tour was not new, but the way visitors saw it created an entirely different perspective and level of understanding. It was a success because it offered a different perspective of the colonial period, one that was valid and compelling. Providing diverse perspectives is still one of the most important qualities of successful interpretation.

Informed Interpreters

Because they do the storytelling, interpreters must always possess the most up-to-date information available. They must also have the knowledge and skills to present it properly. Interpreter training should focus its attention on presenting the information, as well as on understanding its historical context. When talking about subject matter that is controversial by its very nature, presentation method and style can create a successful and entertaining educational experience or doom it to failure. When content is controversial, interpreters should be as comfortable as possible when presenting it. They must be confident of their command of the information and its accuracy, as well as the way they tell it. Too often sites focus on content knowledge and assume that the facts will produce a superior presentation. However, they must give a commensurate amount of time to communication of the content. Organization of information, personal style, body movement, listening, group dynamics, rhythm and pace, diction, time, and focus cannot be left to individual intuition. It must be an integral part of ongoing and comprehensive training.

During my earlier tenure at Colonial Williamsburg, one of the interpreters encountered a problem in which an absence of information prevented him from potentially transforming a bad situation into a teaching opportunity. The interpreter, who was an African American, was outfitted in his eighteenth-century garb, standing at his post, when a visitor approached him and said:

> Let me ask you a question. I know that you people came here under a system of slavery, but you have to admit that it's the best thing that could've happened to you. When you look at Sammy Davis, Jr., Bill Cosby, all the extraordinary sports figures, and all the wonderful things that you people have been able to do since you've been here, you've got to admit it's the most wonderful thing that could've happened. I know it was under a system of slavery, but you were over there in Africa swinging in trees. We bring you here, and we educate you, and put these marvelous opportunities in front of you. You've got to admit, it's the greatest thing that could've happened to you.

During a training session, the interpreter described this encounter to me. When I asked him what his response was, he said, "Well, I turned around and walked away." I said, "Why'd you do that?" He said, "Because, if I had stayed there, I would have hit him." I said, "Good, because if you had hit him, you'd have lost your job; but then what did you do?" He said, "Well, I went about my work." "Then, what did you do?" "I went home." "Then what did you do," I continued. "Told my wife about it." "Then what did you do?" "Came back to work the next day and tried to forget it." "So, then, what did you do?" Frustrated, he finally asked, "Why do you keep asking me what I did?"

I replied by asking him to tell me something about this man that he talked with. "What do you think? Was the man the worst image of a redneck that you can think of?" The interpreter said, "Yeah, yeah! He was! He was! He said when we were in Africa, we were swinging in trees!" I responded:

> That's why I asked you what else you did. You don't know whether that man was insensitive, arrogant, a bigot, or just misinformed. When he said you were in Africa swinging in trees, you bought it, because you didn't know about the once powerful African kingdoms of Ghana, Mali, and Songhai. You didn't know about the great University of Timbuktu. You didn't know about iron smelting, or the civilizations that rivaled the governing structures of European nations. You didn't know about the complex society that was in Africa long before Europe was Europe. You weren't aware that most scientists now agree that life as we know it began in the continent of Africa. You didn't know that. And because you didn't know it, when that man said you had come from Africa where your ancestors were swinging from trees, you bought it. That's why I asked you what you did, because not one time did you tell me you went to the library to see if what he said was true. Not one time did you tell me that you questioned the veracity of his information. You assumed that he knew your history better than you knew it.[6]

If interpreters are going to handle controversial information, they must know as much as they possibly can about the history. And they must know it thoroughly, because often the only thing that stands between them and insensitive or hurtful remarks by misinformed visitors is the amount and quality of information they have at their grasp. Sometimes even this is not enough to prevent an unpleasant situation. A visitor with his or her own agenda might confront an interpreter, who must accept each circumstance and attempt to pursue the opportunity it provides to teach, hoping that some of the information will get through. Unlike a college or university, historic house museums cannot choose who can come to them to learn, so their visitors will have a variety of opinions and perceptions. Some are more open to new information than others, but the interpretive goal of any historic house museum should always be to present information responsibly. This means arming interpreters with the best information and interpreting skills possible.

Programming and Outreach

The lifeblood of historic house museums is programming and outreach (fig. 3.1). Exhibits can be highly effective interpretive channels, but public programming can further enhance inclusiveness and understanding, providing an approach to teaching history that is lively and entertaining as well as instructive. Theater, music, historical reenactment, and other types of living history programs have proven successful at house museums and historic sites, large and small, throughout the country. Such programming can go a long way toward adding life to what seems to be a stagnant, dull situation.

A case in point is the "Getting Word" program begun by Diane Swann-Wright and Lucia Stanton at Monticello. For more than six years and over 22,000 miles, from the Pacific Coast to Massachusetts, Stanton and Swann-Wright have researched and compiled an impressive cache of stories and oral histories relating to the black descendants of Thomas Jefferson. They located African-American family members who were active in the Underground Railroad and others who passed for white and even served as officers in the Union army. Swann-Wright, who is African American, conducted the interviews, and Stanton, who is white, handled the documentary research and created genealogies.

Figure 3.1. **This mock hanging at Colonial Williamsburg shows two convicted criminals being taken to the gallows for execution. It is one of the many programs aimed at providing the audience with interactive experiences. Colonial Williamsburg believes the audience should actively participate in the learning process. Courtesy of Colonial Williamsburg Foundation.**

The program was an important link to the work done by Dr. Foster and his DNA team of scientists.

Another example of effective program development is the work of Dorothy Spruill Redford at Somerset Place Historic Site in rural Crenshaw, North Carolina. Somerset Place is an antebellum plantation that interprets life in coastal North Carolina prior to the Civil War. During its eighty-year existence as an active plantation (1785–1865), it included as many as 100,000 acres and became one of North Carolina's most prosperous rice, corn, and wheat plantations. It was also home to more than three hundred enslaved men, women, and children of African descent, eighty of whom were brought to Somerset directly from West Africa in 1786.

Since 1990, Redford has transformed the site. Once seen as a "whites only" site, a new day has dawned. Today, visitors to the site begin their tours in the slave buildings before they ever set foot in the main house. Twenty-five percent of the visitors are African Americans, and plans are under way to reconstruct all of the outbuildings inhabited by enslaved Africans who lived on the property. Programs and initiatives like Somerset and "Getting Word" represent a rising interest in efforts that have been mounted by the National Park Service, the Pennsylvania Historical Commission, the National Trust for Historic Preservation, Old Salem, Greenfield Village, Mount Vernon, and many other historic houses and sites across the country.

Partnerships and collaborative efforts can add dimension and further the outreach of museum programming. Community organizations, senior citizens' groups, ethnic and neighborhood associations, schools, and any number of other entities can offer resources and alliances that will open the door to new audiences. Internships can also extend a site's reach, as can programs involving young people in the interpretive process itself. Together, the University of Virginia and Monticello provide a good example of a successful partnership between a historic site and a local university. The university's history department offers a semester-long course on the history of the area of Virginia where Jefferson's home is located. At the end of the semester, students have the opportunity to become summer docents at Jefferson's plantation. Many of the students choose to interpret Mulberry Row, site of the quarters that housed enslaved Africans at Monticello and the center of service-related activity for the 5,000-acre plantation and house.

Plan for Controversy

Although changing a long-established interpretive plan to make it more inclusive may generate anxiety, museum personnel should not fear it—they should plan for it. Any challenge to long-held assumptions about the past or, especially if a site is highly revered by its community, almost any type of change at all is going to ruffle feathers at some level—staff, board, targeted audience, local community, or beyond. The staff at Colonial Williamsburg did not anticipate the widespread uproar caused by its 1994 reenactment of a slave auction. The National Museum of American History probably never thought the exhibit *Science in American Life,* which also opened in 1994, would cause a stir, but it did. The exhibit explored the intersections between science and society. No one could have imagined that the American Chemical Society and the American Physics Society, which funded portions of the exhibit, would raise concerns, but they did. The following year, the National Air and Space Museum had its troubles. The Enola Gay exhibit, *The Last Act: The Atomic Bomb and the End of World War Two,* created nationwide controversy in the spring of 1995. More than seven years later, the controversy still reverberates around the institution. To be sure, these types of controversies occur, and they should no longer come as surprises, especially at a point in the development of museums when the public has increased its knowledge of history as well as its expectations of what museums do.

Repeating mistakes is not a luxury most house museums can afford. Therefore, learning from controversial exhibitions is vital. When developing an exhibit on sweatshops, curators at the Smithsonian's National Museum of American History not only focused on the background and presentation of sweatshops in America; they also studied and evaluated previous exhibits. They tried to learn from *The Last Act, Science in American Life,* and others that had been steeped in controversy. The exhibit, *Between a Rock and a Hard Place: A History of American Sweatshops, 1820–Present,* looked at the garment industry, particularly in El Monte, California. Exhibit planners examined concerns from all sides of the issue and informed interested parties of their intentions and progress. The primary intention was to focus on the history of technology from a social historical perspective. The curators, Harry Rubenstein and Peter Liebhold, understood that careful planning, commitment to balance and fairness, and, finally, strong institutional support were essential to the success of the exhibition. They made sure that goals were stated up front in the exhibition and that the public was alerted to the nature of the show before they visited it. They also used other people's words— those of people involved with the sweatshops—to help tell the story. Finally they allowed all of the stakeholders, from the workers to unions and industry leaders, to have their say in the exhibition. Throughout the exhibition, visitors were encouraged to describe their reactions in comment books set on tables in each section of the exhibit.

But the curators also did their homework. The information they gathered influenced how they chose to exhibit the collections and present the data. They also spent considerable time writing responses to visitors' questions once the exhibit was up. As a result, the exhibit was well received and thus able to accomplish its educational goal. The exhibit team made certain that they consulted all pertinent viewpoints; they attempted to understand not only the perspectives that would be presented, but those that would not be; and they arrived at a cogent argument reflecting various perspectives without seriously jeopardizing the points they believed were important.

Finally, there was tremendous support from the administration. In fact, at the beginning of the exhibition, chief curator Lonnie Bunch and museum director Spencer Crew fashioned a statement regarding the museum's position. It is worth quoting:

> History museums are educational institutions that strive to make the American past accessible, useful, and meaningful to the millions who view their exhibitions, read their catalogs, and participate in public programs. Museum exhibitions often celebrate and commemorate the past and, in doing so, create a collective memory that helps provide Americans with a common understanding of the past. Equally important is a museum's obligation to explore all aspects of the American experience.
>
> History museums interpret difficult, unpleasant, or controversial episodes, not out of any desire to embarrass, be unpatriotic, or cause pain, but out of a responsibility to convey a fuller, more inclusive history. By examining incidents ripe with complexities and ambiguities, museums hope to stimulate greater understanding of the historical forces and choices that shaped America.
>
> Museums make the greatest contribution to public education when they provide audiences with tools to both celebrate and critically analyze American history. Ultimately, museums mount these kinds of exhibitions because they have confidence in the American public's tolerance for candor and its appreciation for important historical stories.[7]

These administrators understood the importance of the museum presenting a united front, and the curators understood the importance of aligning their exhibition with the mission and goals of the museum.

Instead of shying away from controversy, then, museums should embrace it for the lessons it can teach. No matter how carefully a historic house, historic site, or museum approaches a topic, someone is going to take issue with the way the story is told (and possibly even the institution's right to tell it), saying, "You have not done it or said it right," or "That's my story; that's not your story." You can be sure that something or someone will be questioned. As information becomes more accessible, the ability of museum audiences to know and understand what a site is doing, to comment, and to raise legitimate questions about it in valid and scholarly ways will grow. Practitioners of history, therefore, must be knowledgeable, prepared, and willing to confront the controversies that will inevitably arise. Remember, for every ten who complain, there are hundreds who appreciate the risks taken and the dedication required to go the extra mile to tell a full and inclusive story.

Consult Others

A wise museum staff will enlist the aid of the community (museum and otherwise) as it prepares to assimilate a new interpretive subject. As more people and views become involved, the opportunities for diversifying messages and audiences increase. The resulting messages presented will also be more accurate and better conveyed.

At Head Smashed In Buffalo Jump—a native-Canadian museum in Alberta near the town of Lethbridge, which is not far from the state of Montana—a member of the Blackfoot tribe, one of the tribes the museum studies and interprets, greets visitors. He walks around the museum and escorts visitors through it, as if the museum belonged to him. Because the museum features the history of his community, he takes great pride in guiding visitors through and showing them around. The visitors hear a voice that heightens the benefit of the educational experience in a way the museum could not otherwise accomplish. By recruiting someone from the community to be, in this case, part of the interpretive effort, the museum is creating an inclusive experience that many others in the historic house field would like to replicate for their visitors.

Although historic sites are realizing that going into the community for counsel is prudent, they often make the mistake of assuming that the only community interested in their exhibition is the community whose artifacts they are exhibiting or to which they are targeting their programming. Certainly, the African-American community should be involved in developing programming relating to that community, but one should not assume that that project would benefit or interest only African Americans. Likewise, to assume that Native Americans are the only people who will be interested in a Native-American exhibition is a missed opportunity. Such assumptions and approaches actually ghettoize minorities and their history in a naïve and dangerous way. No aspect of history is insular, and to treat it and teach it as such is to disregard the multifarious nature of the past.

Universal Topics

By interpreting universal themes, any historic site, no matter what its mission, can address topics to which visitors with diverse backgrounds can relate. An abundance of widely understood issues are inherent in the domestic environment most house museums interpret. Food, for example, is a topic with which all visitors can make associations. Simply comparing and contrasting the foodways and the kinds of food common during the interpretive period with those understood by contemporary cultures enlivens the experience and allows the site to draw the visitor in. Agriculture, the world of work, child rearing, domestic life, relationships between men and women, generational challenges—all are examples of topics that people everywhere can appreciate. Most house museums already address some of these, in one way or another, in their interpretations. The key to using them to broaden audiences is being alert to how they might interest and pertain to the experiences of people today. Interpreters should be trained not only to address such topics, but also to help visitors make the necessary connections.

Making connections is fundamental to good interpretation, and it is also essential to building diverse audiences. In turn, audience diversification can only be sustained if, for every visitor who comes through the door, the museum answers (through its interpretation) the visitor's question, "Why should I listen to you?" The site must offer some way for its visitors to connect with the site's message, and if it does, they will listen and be more inclined to return.

Good Stories

Good stories are essential to effective interpretation. Interpretive stories at historic house museums can be told through labels, brochures, historical dramas, tours, videos, and a variety of other channels. Whatever form it takes, however, a good story attracts people; it does not, by its very nature, exclude. Poor writing, excessive detail, and disrespectful content are not characteristics of a good story. Rather, good stories provoke thought and appeal to a wide range of interests. When writing an exhibit label, some museum curators have a tendency to write what others might consider a "book on the wall." "Wait a minute," a curator might plead. "This is the first time in fifteen years somebody has asked me about my ceramics collection. I'm telling them everything I know, because it's going to be fifteen years before they ask me again!" And so they write on that label everything anyone could possibly ever want to know about chamber pots or colonoware or glazing. Whether for an exhibit label or an interpretive tour, museum professionals must avoid this inclination. A possible exception is when the purpose of the exhibit or tour is intentionally specialized and developed for a narrow audience. In general, though, interpreters should resist the temptation to get bogged down in obscure minutia that is of interest only to a precious few. This information may be legitimate, but usually it is not important enough to risk alienating a large part of the potential audience. All in all, it makes for neither a good story nor inclusive interpretation.

Redefine Success

Finally, as a historic house or site develops and implements programming for underserved or minority audiences, it should redefine its definition of success. One of the steps in the planning process should be to decide what outcome would signify that the effort was worthwhile. In 1989, Colonial Williamsburg opened a slave quarter that visitors passed on the way to the centerpiece of Carter's Grove plantation, the mansion of Robert King Carter (fig. 3.2). Although the house was the primary focus of visitors to the plantation, the new tour plan created a physical presence and introduction to the issue of slavery before the opulent mansion could even be seen. Soon after the slave quarter opened, the director of Carter's Grove received a letter from a disgruntled man who visited the quarter. He wrote that he had been an annual visitor to Colonial Williamsburg for the past twenty years. Each visit had energized him as he prepared to teach his traditional course in early American history. His letter was to inform the administration that he considered the slave quarter exhibit reprehensible and that he would not teach that kind of history to his students. He would, therefore, not be returning to Colonial Williamsburg.

The director's reply went something like this:

Dear Sir,

We are very distressed that you had a terrible time at Colonial Williamsburg, but we want you to know that your letter is evidence to us that we are on the right track. Please find enclosed the price of your ticket. We hope that you will reconsider and that at some point you will come back and visit. We are proud of all of our exhibits and programs and hope you will return to see them again and again.

For me, the boldness of the sentiment expressed in that reply was revolutionary, because the director was acknowledging that success is not measured by the number of smiling faces leaving a site. It is difficult at best to introduce a topic as controversial as slavery and have people view the exhibits, hear the interpretation, and leave the museum with smiles on their faces. If they leave the museum laughing and joking, it is possible that the message has not been delivered or that the museum has been in some way misguided or mistaken in the implementation of its interpretive plan.

Figure 3.2. Slave Quarter at Carter's Grove. In 1981, Colonial Williamsburg staff began reconstructing a late-eighteenth-century slave quarter at Carter's Grove, a plantation owned by the foundation ten miles southwest of Williamsburg. Foundation tradesmen, using eighteenth-century construction techniques and methods, built three dwellings and a corncrib on an excavated foundation of a late-eighteenth-century quarter that housed African-American workers living on the site. The construction of these dwellings represented a significant shift in Colonial Williamsburg's interpretation of rural life in the colonial Chesapeake region. Furthermore, it cemented the foundation's commitment to presenting the lives of enslaved Africans as an integral part of its overall story. Courtesy of Colonial Williamsburg Foundation.

Places Where We Can See Ourselves

Soon after I became employed at the Smithsonian Institution, my mother-in-law visited. As many people do, she thought the Smithsonian was one place, one museum. Mulling over which of the eleven Smithsonian museums (surrounding the mall area) I should take her to, I settled on the National Museum of American History. I thought she might enjoy the exhibit *Field to Factory*, which interprets the complexities and effects of the Great Migration by focusing on the lives of the migrants as they traveled from rural towns and communities in the South to new lives in the North.

As we walked through the exhibit, my mother-in-law saw a push plow and a hame, a sort of collar worn by a draft horse to help control it. She looked at the latter and said excitedly, "Do you know what that is? That's a hames. That's a hames that you put on top of a horse. I can't tell you the number of days that I went out to that field trying to get Jasper." (Jasper was one of the draft horses her family owned when she was growing up.) She continued, "Trying to get Jasper to come out of that field was a real mess. Sometimes I'd bring him oats, sometimes barley. We took the oats and the barley, and we'd go out there and sometimes he'd see me and he'd run away because he knew I was coming to put him to work."

She continued to talk about growing up in rural Suffolk, Virginia, about that horse, about how she could plow as well as any boy her age, and about how her sisters did more work than her two brothers. As she talked, other visitors approached and started listening, because the more excited she was, the louder she became. Idaho, Kansas, Oklahoma—people from all over began talking about the horse or the oxen or the farm implements that they remembered. This conversation between total strangers went on for close to forty minutes. At the end of the day, as I was driving her back home, she looked over at me and said, "It must be nice to work in places like that museum when you can go in there and see yourself."

For me, the experience of my mother-in-law reflects the greatest success a history museum can achieve. Because of the commonality of domestic life, regardless of the differences in conditions that characterize it, historic house museums should be as eager as other types of museums to strike a personal chord with diverse segments of the population. And if they create spaces and messages in which and through which all who visit can in some way see themselves, they will have responded to what is happening in the field of history and will have truly succeeded in interpreting the whole house and, in a sense, the whole world.

Notes

1. Randall Robinson et al., "The Case for Reparations: Why? How Much? When?" *Ebony* 55 (August 2000): 76.

2. Excerpt from the *Statement of Daniel P. Jordan, Ph.D., President, Thomas Jefferson Memorial Foundation* (statement delivered at a DNA Press Conference at the International Center for Jefferson Studies, 1 November 1998), available at www.monticello.org/plantation/hemings_statement.html (visited 16 June 2002).

3. Adapted from Julius Lester, *Black Folktales* (New York: Grove Press, 1991), 33–36. Used with permission of the author.

4. James Oliver Horton, "Presenting Slavery: The Perils of Telling America's Racial Story," *Public Historian* 21 (Fall 1999): 28–29.

5. Horton, 29.

6. Conversation with Neal Black, Colonial Williamsburg Foundation, March 1985.

7. Spencer Crew, director, and Lonnie Bunch, associate director for curatorial affairs, National Museum of American History, Smithsonian Institution, April 1998.

CHAPTER FOUR

MAKING GENDER MATTER: INTERPRETING MALE AND FEMALE ROLES IN HISTORIC HOUSE MUSEUMS

Debra A. Reid

Social history uncovers new information that revolutionizes our understanding of the past because it emphasizes ordinary people and their daily concerns. Living history museums embrace social history, but other types of museums have been less receptive. Ironically, historic houses, the type of museum most associated with intimate details of interest to social historians, respond slowly to new historical information for reasons rooted in their origins.[1]

Disfranchised but politically astute women coordinated many of the early efforts to preserve historic houses. Patricia West documents their use of domesticity and other popular forms of "womanly persuasion . . . to 'make friends' with male politicians" to ensure success. The founding mothers practiced consensus history, exaggerating the power of the domestic sphere to ensure civic virtue and de-emphasizing divisive issues such as slavery, suffrage, and segregation. In contrast, social historians hint that the domestic sphere was a myth, that the influence of women in the home did not necessarily elevate their position relative to men, and that home life could include domestic abuse, violence, and desertion. Is it any wonder that the findings of new social historians are particularly threatening to house museum founders and staff, and that incorporating new social history into house interpretation proves challenging?[2]

Women's History and Accuracy

New approaches provide the foundation for studies of previously unstudied individuals. Social historians rely on a variety of materials, believing that the unspoken is as important as the written record. They pour over public records, quantifying data and analyzing it, and they ask new questions of traditional sources. By doing so they discover the illiterate and marginalized. The court records of Plymouth Colony, Massachusetts, the diaries of individuals such as midwife Martha Ballard of Augusta, Maine, and the oral histories of women on Texas cotton farms take researchers into the privacy of homes. Many women's historians adopt an interdisciplinary approach to their inquiry by incorporating material culture as evidence of complex relationships between women, home, and work. They theorize on topics as diverse as male and female spheres of influence and labor, universal female subordination, and the extent to which women determined their own destiny. These quantitative and qualitative resources help us hear more voices and comprehend a more detailed narrative of the human experience.[3]

Barbara Melosh argues that women's history has become more influential than other social history subfields. She and others believe that it has the potential to restructure historical inquiry beyond the traditional study of great men and great events, but the goal is not as simple as filling in the blanks left empty by traditional narrative. Instead, women's historians want to contextualize past experiences and explain how inequality in law, society, and culture affected women as well as men. The historical status of women as a dependent social group makes this contextualization possible, but women also assumed and exercised authority. As Elizabeth Pleck explains, women had "powerful and intimate ties with their opposites based on kinship, shared residence, and common interests in the rearing of children." This makes for complex relationships defined as much by personal preference as by outside forces such as law and culture.[4]

Women's historians have documented the experiences of many different races, cultures, and socioeconomic groups, but comparable work on women's "opposites" in the home has lagged behind. Less is known about men and their perceptions of kinship, intimacy, and home life. This makes it difficult to balance interpretations of the male and female experiences. The term "gender studies" more accurately reflects the efforts of those who compare and contrast the experiences of the two sexes. People engaged in gender studies consider the ways culture—such as family and peer groups, schools and churches, and employers and laborers—defines appropriate behavior for boys and girls, men and women. Critical analysis helps explain how gender acculturation affected daily interaction, life choices, and perceptions of the world. The home, the space in which males and females regardless of age communicated intimately, provides a place to start the study. House museums can further our understanding of the significance of the exchange.[5]

Homes and Gender Studies

Henry Glassie's 1972 study of rural Virginia, *Folk Housing in Middle Virginia*, concentrated on houses because most Virginians "left no writing but they did leave those houses." By 1982, Glassie's analysis of folk housing reflected the influence of women's history and gender studies. His earlier concept of houses as a male product changed. In *Return to Ballymenone* he recognized the Irish female as homemaker, commanding as influential a position as that of the male house builder. According to Glassie, the kitchen served the individual, the farm economy, the family, and the community. It provided shelter, kinship, support, and opportunities for peer review for both sexes. Additionally, the kitchen provided the means to sustain the family. Women orchestrated the preparation of food-stuffs, a process that consumed their energies before prepackaged foods became available. Those without hired help found only limited time to undertake tasks outside the home as a result, but this did not negate their influence outside or within the home (fig. 4.1).[6]

Recognizing the role women played in constructing and sustaining a home can help researchers move the understanding of gender relations in the past beyond the traditional ideas of women at work in the kitchen and men at work outside the home. The staff at the David Davis Mansion in Bloomington, Illinois, found that Sarah Walker Davis, not her husband, a United States Supreme Court justice, made most of the decisions about building, plumbing, and heating their Italianate house, built between 1870 and 1872. While visitors may assume that men made such decisions, the reality at the Davis Mansion proved more complicated.[7]

Other sites may find less direct evidence of a woman's involvement in home construction, but reinterpreting data can uncover complicated economic relationships that indicate the ways women contributed financially. The Gillard-Duncan House—relocated from its original site to the grounds of a regional branch of the Texas State Library in Liberty, Texas—documents the lives of Dr. Edward Joseph Gillard, his wife Elizabeth DeBlanc, and their Creole extended family. The Gillards concentrated their resources on corn, cattle, cotton, and land, and the women played as important a role in their success as did the men. The Gillards' adopted daughter, Eliza, stabilized the family's position in the community by marrying William B. Duncan, fourteen years her senior, a veteran of the Texas Revolution, and an established stock drover. William's correspondence informed Eliza of physical and financial challenges he faced while on the road with live-stock, challenges that affected their personal as well as their economic future. On October 25, 1853, he wrote, "I am over the Nechez with my beeves about six miles from the ferry at Mrs. Thomas'. . . . lost one . . . two I had to leave on the road, as they broke down . . . beef is very low; but perhaps they only tell me so for the purpose of buying my beeves. I am determined not to sell this side of Lafayette [Louisiana] unless I get a good price." Four days later he wrote, "the night before I crossed Sabine was one of the worst I have seen lately: it rained all

Figure 4.1. Women of all ages helped in food production. Two-year-old Debra A. Reid learns to pluck chickens, with the help of her aunt, Mary Surman Hammel, in the Reid family's kitchen, Rockwood, Illinois, 1962. Courtesy of the author.

night and was cold: we had to set up all night to keep our beeves from breaking the pen—they have never broken a pen since we started—which is great luck."[8]

Why did William provide such detail to Eliza? Because women brought dowries and expertise in farm or plantation management to their marriages, and as a result husbands believed that wives should be kept informed. Texas law considered marriage a species of partnership, with each party contributing financially. The property that women brought to a union included cattle branded with marks registered in the woman's name. In some instances, women recorded brands for their newborn daughters, evidence of the degree to which women used the law to bolster their status within a patriarchal society, if not directly challenging the division of authority. The more property and knowledge a girl could accumulate before marriage, the more enviable a partner she became. Making good marriages mattered because after marriage women lost control. Stock and other items became community property with each partner owning an equal share or interest, but with the husband assuming ultimate authority for its care and management. With the authority came the worry. Husbands believed that well-informed wives would become independent widows capable of managing plantation affairs for the family's well-being. This gave men such as William Duncan another reason to keep their wives informed of plantation operations. The second Mrs. Duncan, Celima DeBlanc, a relative of the Gillards who grew up in the Gillard household along with Eliza, found herself managing the plantation after William died at forty-nine years of age in 1867. Her knowledge of business affairs contributed to the persistence of the plantation.[9]

The Gillard-Duncan House could do more, as could most historic houses, to interpret human interaction and male and female strategies. Period room installations, the preferred static interpretive technique in house museums throughout the nation, celebrate family history and emphasize original furnishings predominately. Brochures can further the effort to broaden interpretation, and the Gillard-Duncan House brochure recognizes the role women played throughout its history. It does not, however, stress the involvement of Gillard or DeBlanc women in family business or in the daily administration of the plantation during and after the Civil War. A simple shift in emphasis could go a long way in furthering visitors' understanding of the interaction between men and women on the Texas frontier and of Southern economic development.[10]

Sensitivity to gender issues helps researchers gain new understanding of the arrangement and meaning of spaces within the home, as well. One of the most durable but least understood historical theories relates to women and the domestic sphere. Elizabeth Blackmar takes a critical look at the ideology that linked women to the home and housework and men to the workplace, public life, and productive labor. She does this by questioning the real influence of prescriptive literature such as Catharine Beecher's and Harriet Beecher Stowe's *The American Woman's Home*. Barbara Clark Smith takes a different approach, claiming that it is not enough to document women's history with material evidence. Historians must also locate "men's history and men's artifacts in their partial and gendered context."[11]

Analyzing domestic artifacts and space arrangements indicates that some things change, and some remain the same. Daphne Spain, in her study of home design, contends that middle- and upper-class Americans gradually abandoned gender segregation. Nineteenth-century home interiors reflected legal and social inequality, with spaces for male owners nearer the front and side entrances and spaces for women and servants nearer the back. By the second decade of the twentieth century, however, homes contained more open spaces, defined not by gender distinction but by the quest for family interaction, thus reflecting a more egalitarian society marked by the passage of the Nineteenth Amendment in 1920 that granted women the right to vote. Despite the relaxation in gender separation, class- and race-based segregation continued. Comparing the arrangement of servants' work and living spaces at several house museums reflects this. During the 1830s at Lindenwald—Martin Van Buren's home in Kinderhook, New York—the cook lived in the cellar while other servants lived on the third floor, removed from the family rooms on the second floor. African-American slaves during the mid-nineteenth century at Hampton Hall in Towson, Maryland, occupied different spaces within the house based on their rank. The chef slept in the storage area so he could protect the most valuable commodities while the highest ranking male servant, the butler, worked out of a pantry that linked the servant and family areas of the house and gave him the opportunity to regulate interaction. Servant spaces remained separate from domestic areas into the twentieth century as evidenced at the McFaddin-Ward House in Beaumont, Texas. Louis Lemon, the McFaddin family's African-American male cook for thirty-seven years (1915–1952), did not even live in the home. He had a sleeping room in the carriage house.[12]

Prescriptive literature and period house designs, despite their popularity as primary sources, tell only part of the story of space definition within historic homes. Beds and bedrooms offer a more representative artifact to assess the ways class, kinship, or personal preference affected the use and meaning of spaces. The prominence of a bed and its coverings denoted status or lack thereof in colonial America. Beds dominated communal spaces in simple houses and reflected the wealth of more prosperous individuals. During the late-nineteenth and early-twentieth centuries, reformers encouraged the growing middle class to abandon the communal house plan for a design that provided more privacy. In progressive homes, beds never appeared in public spaces, and parlors became the locus for socializing and conspicuous consumption. Regardless, most Americans still owned small homes with few bedrooms. In these, several children of both sexes slept in one room, or even in one bed, and many slept in areas considered "public" by middle- and upper-class residents. Thus, bedrooms and parlors took on multiple meanings depending on the age, status, and relationships of residents. For the lower classes, getting an individual bed or bedroom marked a major life transition, one dictated by gender mores. Kinship likewise affected bedroom allotments and locations. With family members, servants, and guests sharing a residence and jockeying for position and influence, spaces within the home became contested.[13]

Additionally, houses provide a bridge to move gender out of the private recesses of women's history and into the local and national story. Instead of the community containing numerous houses, Glassie conceptualized the community as "the space linking hearths." Events in the home move out into the community as community and world issues move into the house. "Like a spiraling swastika, space spins, its four directions extend, then curve, spiraling down and up, merging to embrace half the world, returning, and turning through the house to center precisely on the hearth." The domicile—a haven for family, a status symbol, the setting for rites of passage, a product of culture—provides the perfect site to interpret gender and its influence on local, national, and even international events.[14]

Preservationists link houses and communities in ways that museum staffs must understand to comprehend the selected pasts they collect and interpret. Visitors who receive information on preservationists' goals are more likely to comprehend the multiple meanings of a house museum. For example, Historic Deerfield, Inc. includes fourteen historic houses scattered along a mile-long street in rural western Massachusetts. Visitors escape their hectic present and marvel at the exquisite landscape, buildings, and decorative arts that exude an eighteenth-century aura. White middle- and upper-class women active in Deerfield between the 1870s and the 1920s made this possible by aggressively preserving artifacts and challenging modernity with their own version of the arts and crafts revival. They marketed the identity they created to tourists using "community parlors" located in preserved houses along the street and furnished with crafts for sale. Their success created a rich heritage that Henry and Helen Flynt began buying in the 1930s and institutionalized in 1952 when they created Historic Deerfield. By understanding the perspective of the late-nineteenth- and early-twentieth-century female preservationists, visitors can recognize that the eighteenth-century streetscape they see reflects a myth that Deerfield women created and nurtured.[15]

House Museums and Gender

Status, rites, culture—these intangible concepts become concrete when reflected in things. Museums provide an important service as they preserve and interpret this material evidence. Asking questions that focus on the materials, production methods, ornamentation, uses, consumption patterns, and cross-cultural comparisons helps visitors understand *things*. Such traditional material culture analysis, however, fails to expand awareness of gender relations. In 1987 Christie Farnham argued that as long as this analysis remains "framed in terms of traditional masculine and feminine characteristics that are stereotypical of the Euro-American experience, feminist theory building will be imprisoned in a . . . frame of limited possibilities." To effectively incorporate gender, interpreters of material culture must recognize the feminine as well as the masculine perspective when conducting fieldwork and documenting artifacts. With this double perspective, the collections exhibited within house museums can help visitors learn about the ways that women, as well as men, constructed material culture but were also constructed by it.[16]

Exhibit and program reviews assess whether or not museums have used their resources effectively. One of the earliest of these reviews, cowritten by Barbara Melosh and Christina Simmons, describes the ways women's history exhibits have evolved from 1964 to 1984 from "unselfconscious" depictions of women in traditional family and social roles to analytical interpretive exhibits that incorporate social-historical questions and scholarship. Museums draw on academic scholarship to enliven exhibits but augment this with new sources including material culture, film, and audio recordings. Visitors may find the museum exhibits more compelling because of the evidence and delivery used, but flaws still exist. Melosh and Simmons caution that the story often features uncritical biography of heroines rather than analyses of "the roots and context of the women's public accomplishment—social class, sexual and marital life, women's oppression, and internal struggles and conflicts." Founders, sponsors, and visitors encourage museum staffs to avoid such controversial topics as they devise storylines. Melosh believes this timidity must be overcome for museums to contribute most effectively to historical inquiry.[17]

Historic houses, a museum's largest artifact, contain the material culture to further our understanding of gender. With such rich resources, house museums have an obligation to add to knowledge by documenting the range of activities that occurred within and outside their walls and to share the findings with the general public. A *self-study* can help staff members identify the strengths and weaknesses of the site, its history, and its collections, and formulate themes of local, regional, and national significance. This process starts with an analysis of topics currently addressed and continues with a listing of relevant topics requiring further study. The collection informs the self-study.

The M'Clintock House in Waterloo, New York—one of several sites preserved in the Women's Rights National Historical Park in Seneca Falls, New York—offers a good example of how a staff built on collections to introduce related themes in a property devoted to women's rights interpretation. Attendees to the first women's rights convention, held in Seneca Falls in 1848, drafted the Declaration of Sentiments in the M'Clintock home. Staff members could have glorified the women's rights cause, but they avoided it by researching the family's Quaker beliefs, involvement in the abolition movement, and business pursuits to get a more complete impression of the family that lived in the home between 1836 and 1856. This helped the National Park Service staff expand the interpretation beyond women's rights to incorporate the whole family and the ways that each member furthered social reform by challenging race and gender inequality. Relationships of spaces within the home help tell the story, as well. A small room behind the pantry on the first floor supported a discussion of nonfamily residents and frequent visitors to the M'Clintocks, including two free African Americans who lived there during 1850. A rear door that offered direct access to the M'Clintock drugstore made it possible to discuss the shared responsibility of the family business. Elizabeth gained firsthand experience in shop management, operating it along with her father. This sensitized her to the importance of equal access to work and pay, aspects of the women's rights cause that she championed.[18]

Next, sites should conduct a *"gender sensitivity" study* that begins with a basic inventory of the role women played. The National Park Service (NPS) completed an eye-opening assessment during the 1980s and 1990s. Previously, many staff and visitors believed that women had no place in NPS properties such as battlefields, prisons, forts, and natural parks, or even at "presidential and Great Men sites." By the mid-1990s the NPS identified three categories of sites, ranked by the involvement of women: (1) sites that focus on women's history, (2) sites that include women's history, and (3) sites that surprise us with women's history. The process made it possible for several properties that previously focused on accomplished males to incorporate the female perspective.[19]

Fort Ticonderoga, a reconstructed military site near Ticonderoga, New York, that documents the French and Indian War and the American Revolution, is operated by a private nonprofit organization. Though Anglo and Native-American women populated the site in the eighteenth century, visitors received little information about their experience or about the nineteenth- and twentieth-century history of the site. The staff devised a character that helped them incorporate the female perspective and tourism—a well-heeled female traveler visiting the site during the 1830s. Most visitors did not recognize the anachronous clothing styles and usually mistook the woman either for an officer's wife or a camp follower, an indication of closed attitudes about the role women played in the military during the colonial era. Once visitors learned about their inaccurate assumption, they had to grapple with the fact that they were talking with a tourist removed from them by nearly 170 years, but a woman with the same purpose—visiting Fort Ticonderoga. Visitors would not have responded the same way to a male interpreter, and he could not have gotten visitors to think about gender as effectively as did the female character. This approach helped fort staff explain the importance of the site as a cultural icon, not just as a military site.[20]

The gender sensitivity study is only one-half complete, however, unless the museum staff conducts a comparable inventory of the male role. This will prove more challenging because little secondary research exists on the man in the house, and few museums have assessed the domestic presence of the male. House museums, founded by women who celebrated the domestic sphere and documenting the birthplace or residence of men who made their reputations outside the home, rarely pay attention to evidence that attests to the male presence in the house, unless that male is a servant. Interpreters generally impart biographical and business details about the man of the house in the foyer, hallway, library, or billiard room. Rarely do they refer to men in the rest of the house, even in bedrooms where the male residents spent approximately one-third of their day, or the dining room where they entertained and conducted business.

What role did men play in a home on a daily basis, on weekends, on holidays? Idealized views of family members interacting in a domestic setting, often around an open hearth in the parlor, appeared frequently in period literature, and many featured men and boys (fig. 4.2). These images often served as propaganda, created by the middle class to reinforce their ideals and influence those with other values. Yet, historic house museum interpretation could benefit from a closer reading of the evidence. Occupation affected the degree of male interaction in domestic scenes. Farmers and tradesmen who worked at home might have had a more visible presence in the household on a daily basis, and the family had more direct access to and responsibility for the business. In contrast, men who worked away from home had less direct involvement in the daily working of the household, and the family had less direct contact with the business. Age and race played a role as well. Life cycles affected a man's willingness to help women. Courting provided incentive to younger men to assist with knitting (fig. 4.3), while new fathers as well as grandfathers might act as baby-sitters. Evidence exists but many house museums have not moved in the direction of integrating men of various ages and occupations into the home interior. Staff members at the David Davis Mansion are working on this as they plan ways to interpret David Davis's presence, a husband absent from his Bloomington, Illinois, home during his tenure as a U.S. Supreme Court justice, by expressing his perspective through his letters and other documents generated by his family, friends, and enemies.[21]

Figure 4.2. This idealized family scene depicts African Americans in an extended family setting surrounded by middle-class material culture. It was marketed toward recently freed slaves to encourage them to pursue Anglo-American ideals. Plain Counsel for the Freedman, 1866. Courtesy of the Library of Congress.

Visitors want to know about the family and what the home meant to all family members including the elusive male. The Newark Museum's Ballantine House, located in Newark, New Jersey, responded to this visitor expectation by creating storybook panels that present nine mini-dramas. Visitors encounter John Ballantine's three-quarter length professional portrait on the main landing, and they read his reflection on what the house meant to him in a monologue story-

Figure 4.3. A young man holds yarn for his sweetheart to use in her knitting. *Harper's Bazaar,* 1868.

book on the second floor (fig. 4.4). Also, visitors gain impressions of him through the eyes of his daughter and various servants who discuss his taste as exhibited in the billiard room, his need to close himself off in the library when he worked at home, and his interaction with a wealthy Jewish store owner over an evening meal. These scenarios populate the historic house with men and women with strong opinions and the ability to express them. It makes the house a home.[22]

Living History and Gender Interpretation

After the self-study identifies themes and the influences of gender, the museum staff must decide the most effective interpretive venue to convey the information.

Figure 4.4. Storybook illustration depicting John Ballantine primping in front of a mirror in his bedroom. Male grooming rituals receive little discussion in most historic house museums, but the interpretation of the chambers at the Ballantine House discusses Mr. Ballantine's personal grooming ritual. Courtesy of the Ballantine House, Newark Museum, Newark, New Jersey.

Interpretation takes many forms in house museums, including static exhibits, guided tours, interactive displays, and costumed interpreters performing chores and discussing the past with the public from a firsthand perspective. Staff must analyze their resources to determine the best approach. Each supports gender interpretation, but living history offers one of the most promising venues. Living history allows interpreters to respond to visitor interests, helping them plumb the depths of home life in intimate detail. The delivery, more flexible than text on a wall, can influence visitor perceptions by forcing them to engage in discussion with an interpreter, ponder and process information, and articulate ideas, all evidence of higher learning that static exhibits may not prompt. Furthermore, living history generally occurs within complex environments populated with visual, tactile, audible, gustatory, and olfactory clues. Engaging all senses makes the experience more memorable, particularly when the interpretation links to the sensory evidence.[23]

Living History Defined and Assessed

Jay Anderson, author of the most authoritative history of the living history movement to date, describes the technique as "a simulation of life in another time for the purpose of research, interpretation and/or play." Living historians do things (cook, clean, plow, spin, sew, haul wood); they wear historic attire (replicated clothing based on original garments and accoutrements); and they present the mind-set of an era, either by experiencing it as a real or composite personality (first-person), or by describing it (third-person). This method, however, has its limitations. It can be expensive to outfit and train staff, and the delivery depends on skills difficult to find and retain for the low wages that history museums tend to pay. Effective living history takes a commitment of time and energy that exceeds the resources of many house museums. Once trained, interpreters may compete with the historical processes for the visitor's attention. Cooking, spinning, or weeding can become a crutch for discussing just that activity and little beyond it. Despite the best planning and training, a visitor may still leave thinking only about women cooking and sewing in the house and men laboring in the fields. Living history offers opportunities for visitors to glimpse a woman's life beyond "women's work," but this may be possible only if sites de-emphasize popular living history programs, such as cooking and spinning, and encourage interpreters to undertake other historically accurate but less visually engaging undertakings. Female interpreters might cover Grange songbooks, recruit members for a reform society, or discuss their concern over a widow's tenuous legal position in relation to her late husband's estate, thus providing information on a woman's concerns beyond the home.[24]

Reviews of programs at two living history museums, Conner Prairie Pioneer Settlement and Plimoth Plantation, offer evidence of the ways living history can inform visitors about gender issues despite the challenges. Melosh and Simmons found that Conner Prairie, near Noblesville, Indiana, used the chores female interpreters undertook within the museum's historic houses to show how family and social responsibilities consumed women's energies but contributed to a viable household economy at the same time. Women raised the labor force, they generated income that could sustain a farm through a cash-crop failure, and they recognized the tedium of their lives and hoped daughters might fare better. Interpreters discuss and engage in daily routines in Prairietown in 1836, but as they do, their interactions and conversations with visitors stress the inequality of life and the separate and sometimes antagonistic spheres in which men and women functioned in the past. Nancy Grey Osterud observed similar male-female interaction at Plimoth Plantation, near Plymouth, Massachusetts, in 1992 and praised the delivery: "Servants as well as masters, women as well as men, presumed and, when challenged, articulated relations of inequality." Age, sex, wealth, social status—all affected community standing and interpersonal relations in 1627 Plymouth Colony. Osterud contends that "the humanity of the interpreters" made communication of such complex issues possible. Furthermore, she declares that living history forced interpreters and visitors to "pay attention to 'world view' and to the subjective dimension of the past," that is, the personal beliefs and inconsistencies of humans. Because living history worked, visitors "alternated between apprehending some facet of seventeenth-century culture and discovering its irreducible difference from the present."[25]

Critics, on the other hand, claim that locating women's history within the historic house museum and the medium of living history limits the interpretation to domestic issues and to "nostalgic associations of home" with a conflict-free family revolving around a warm spice-scented kitchen. Visitors may learn more about preparing an oven to bake bread than about the women and men involved in its production. The historic house limits interpretation of women and men only when thoughts do not move beyond the "separate spheres" approach. Part of this relates to mind-set. Visitors, and staff, must be escorted into a new world-view, a perspective that replaces our modern-day sensibilities and stereotypes with an appreciation for and understanding of past culture.[26]

Osterud observed the way that gardening, the mainstay of much living history, could impede interpretation by emphasizing similarities of attitudes toward gardening and techniques of gardening then and now or reinforce differences by providing a concrete example of a different worldview. A visitor to Plimoth Plantation visibly relaxed when greeted with familiar ground in the form of an interpreter working in her garden. The role-player conversed about soil and sun but did not stop with such generalities. Instead, she refocused the conversation back to the issues, back to the fundamental differences of 1627 Plimoth where residents balanced the humors in their bodies with "cold" and "hot" vegetables. A less adept or experienced living history interpreter might never have steered the conversation away from garden layout, cultivation techniques, and plant varieties. The visitor would have learned something regardless and would have felt comfortable in the process, but the issues of differences in worldview would not have surfaced so powerfully.[27]

Butter making provides another example of a process that can result in simplified interpretation. Sherry Butcher-Younghans, in her handbook on house museums, summarizes the potential of butter making to enliven interpretation, but she stops short of explaining how it can also limit learning. A visitor may walk away understanding how butter was made, that it was traditionally women's work, and that it was one of the products of a self-sufficient farm. Visitors may think they know more, but the information they acquired may be outdated from the perspective of a historian such as Joan Jensen whose study of women in the mid-Atlantic region showed the ways dairying linked women to the market. Furthermore, visitors have not been provoked to think about gendered work. How does gender relate to gardening and the butter-making process? To answer the question, staff members have to ask: Who selects the vegetables to grow, who plants them, cultivates them, harvests them, prepares them, and preserves them for future planting? What does the responsibility for the garden mean to males and females or to the family? In the case of butter making, why did women make butter? What role did children play in the process? What role did butter play in farm and regional economics? What did this mean to men and women on the farm or in towns? The answers will vary from site to site, reflecting personal preference, culture, race, and class.[28]

An important final example relates to fire. How many times does a visitor to a historic house express amazement at the historic reliance on fireplaces for heat and the hearth or stoves for cooking? In *More Work for Mother*, Ruth Schwartz Cowan explains the significance of the transition from using hearths to using cast-iron stoves for cooking. Fundamentally, the change in fuels freed those responsible for cutting, hauling, and ranking wood (often the men and boys of the household), but did not decrease work for the cooks (servants or family members, often women and girls), who still had to secure fuel and tend fires. More broadly, she argues that "labor-saving" devices really increased expectations and thus workloads for women. Process-focused interpretation often fails to explain gender inequality or the social, economic, and cultural factors that caused the inequality. Interpreters who understand processes, who rely on collections and primary sources as evidence, and who read the latest interpretations of the era and event have the resources necessary to present the complexity to visitors.[29]

Yet, even employees who base interpretation on research and believe they explain gender hierarchy may find their programs challenged by an informed public that disagrees. Staff at Oliver H. Kelley Farm, a state historic site near Elk River, Minnesota, experienced this during the late 1980s when Amy Sheldon, an associate professor of linguistics at the University of Minnesota, challenged the presentation of men's and women's work as stereotypical and inaccurate given the role the Kelley women played in the farm and in public life. While the quality of the arguments and their protracted nature make the discussion unique, comparable debates should be expected because women's historians disagree over the extent that gender determined divisions of labor or involvement in public life. Different opinions can help visitors and staff reimagine gender relations and perceptions then and now.[30]

Incorporating Gender-Sensitive Living History into House Museums

What must historic house museums do to present effective living history interpretation? Policies at most museums prohibit fires of any sort in historic houses, but working fireplaces, cookstoves, and candleholders greatly affected historical human interaction and patterns of work. Introducing the foodstuffs necessary for living history programs likewise poses threats to collections because pests may enter the home. And gardening, a popular outdoor activity and one necessary to discuss the creation of foodstuffs, relates to gender but not to the home interior directly. Secondary studies can help interpreters discuss these activities generally, but site-specific evidence provides the most important resource to create interpretation that deals with substantive issues presentable using living history techniques without reliance on the activity. For example, researchers at Conner Prairie accumulated evidence from central Indiana to support the representative characters they constructed to populate the homes of Prairietown. Timothy Crumrin, the museum's historian and archivist, studied the history of women and their legal status in Indiana to fully understand the ramifications of marriage as it related to property ownership, divorce, and abortion in the 1830s. This helped interpreters construct more meaningful public presentations that start with a process but lead to bigger issues.[31]

For example, the butter-making equipment owned by Robert Cole in colonial Maryland takes on new meaning when interpreted as evidence of the strategy English colonists used to accumulate capital. Butter came from cows; cows needed feed; feed forced farmers to diversify. Farmers in the Chesapeake accumulated capital more rapidly as a result, and this gave them a more stable lifestyle and helped the English culture take root more rapidly than in other regions of the Chesapeake tobacco belt. Historians and anthropologists made these connections based on extensive research in public documents and personal papers related to Robert Cole's heirs. Court documents, years of record keeping by overseers of Cole's estate, and material evidence provide detailed documentation of household tasks, foodstuffs consumed, and personal routines. The data informs interpretation at Historic St. Mary's City, near Saint Mary's City, Maryland. Staffs at house museums without such treasure troves should not despair. It takes time to accumulate evidence from a region, compare attitudes, and compile a composite or representative database, but it is possible. Only then can staff formulate a furnishings plan, a crucial step in developing a more balanced approach to interpreting the domestic interior and gender relations. Alarmingly, administrators often do not support the research function. This makes it difficult for many sites to progress from a generic interpretation of influential personalities toward an analysis of society, culture, and values, let alone gender.[32]

What can house museum staff members do who want to make interpretation more meaningful and inclusive of gender, but who feel uncomfortable with adopting living history as described by Anderson? A broader definition of living history could better serve their needs. Stacy Roth, in *Past into Present*, a study of first-person interpretation, defines living history as "anything that evokes a link with the past: cultivating heirloom plants, singing a song learned from grandmother, . . . preparing an old recipe, hiking an old trail, attending a religious service. . . . If it touches a connective chord with the past, be it mystical or deliberate, it is history expressing itself in vital form." This moves the application of living history beyond open-air museums and historic sites to traditional house museums and exhibit galleries. It becomes a means of engaging the visitors by involving them intellectually, helping them forge connections and reflect on the significance of the things they encounter—not as information to reinforce preconceptions, but as evidence to help them reconsider and reconceptualize information. Staff members at the Smithsonian Institution's National Museum of American History based their reinterpretation of the Ipswich House on this investigative approach. Through the exhibition *Within These Walls . . .* , documents inform the public about the roles and responsibilities of women, men, and children who lived and worked in the house between the 1760s and World War II. The interpretation focuses on five phases of house occupancy, each representing transition periods in the nation's past. The histories of occupants such as Lucy Caldwell, abolitionist, or Katherine and Mary Lynch, laundress and mill worker, or Mary Scott, who was active on the home front during World War II, turn the house into a dynamic space. With the broader definition of living history, historic house museums can guide visitor perceptions of gender in many ways, not exclusively through the medium of a costumed interpreter.[33]

The Ballantine House interpretation shows how living history, broadly defined, can enliven period rooms without the addition of costumed interpreters. During the planning process, staff members decided they would reinterpret the decorative arts collection to stress the meaning of objects in the home, not an object's rarity. They knew visitors came to find out about the people in the home, so they refocused their inquiry from *what* was in the collection to *why* it was in the collection. And they gave voice to several Ballantine House residents who expressed their ideas about an object or a space within the home. Members of the reinterpretation planning team believed this would make the meaning of objects clearer; visitors would better understand why the Ballantines chose particular objects to fill their rooms because the things tangibly indicated "who they were and what they believed in." Furthermore, servants' perspectives made it easier for many visitors to relate to a late-nineteenth-century millionaire's mansion. This relativism helped engage visitors to get them to think about what the museum said and to formulate their own opinions, not just accept the museum's rhetoric as given.[34]

Visitors to house museums can become their own interpreters, an effective way to expand their perceptions about gender. The method can rely on living history either strictly (as in Anderson) or loosely defined (as in Roth). An example from the Washburn-Norlands Living History Center in Livermore, Maine, attests to the power of this approach. The Washburns, a family of politicians, built an Italianate mansion on a hill and used it as a summer home. Their story is secondary to that of the year-round residents, including a hired family and neighbors to the north and south. The interest in neighbors as well as the builders made it possible to develop interpretive themes that related to community formation and growth, rural life during the industrial era, and gendered responsibilities on the farm. Participatory programs and inquiry learning provided the foundation for all programs, including a four-day "live-in," developed in the mid-1970s to help teachers earn recertification credit. During the program, participants adopt the identities of neighboring family members: they live on the property and they research their character using primary sources. The program immerses participants in life as it was in Maine in the 1870s, an experience made most memorable by two days of "gender shifting." One group of participants, men and women included, assumes female roles one day and male roles the second day. At program's end, participants compare the types of work and express frustration about the repetitive and monotonous nature of many domestic tasks, particularly cooking, that consumed their energy from before dawn to bedtime each day. The saying "men work from sun to sun, but women's work is never done" takes on new meaning for the participants.[35]

Does the Washburn-Norlands program reinforce stereotypes about the woman's sphere? Not for the open-minded participant. The primary sources indicate the ways the women and men participated in community life, interacted with each other in business and pleasure, and still managed to maintain homes and raise children. The chores drive home the nature of farm life as one of mutual dependency and constant work. The evidence about individuals and personalities indicates the ways that some women and men rebelled from the expectations, leaving the farm for the city or the West, or staying single while others rapidly remarried to preserve extended families and maintain farms and lifestyles. Living history strictly defined can create memorable interpretive moments.

For instance, circumstances sometimes changed the daily routine. Women visited neighbors and extended family frequently and stayed for long periods of time. If the wife left her home for a visit and did not arrange alternatives, the husband found himself cooking. Bachelors fended for themselves, sometimes with but often without the assistance of hired help, as did men whose wives suffered an illness that kept them in bed. Older couples may have had children to assume the household chores, but families without daughters or without the resources to hire help relied on younger sons to assist with household chores. Older men also found themselves enlisted for duties other than childcare. Site-specific documentation of a man in the kitchen may not exist, but a critical analysis of representative evidence can result in interesting scenarios. Male interpreters can cook and perform other domestic chores such as sewing or knitting with impunity (fig. 4.5).

Putting the Pieces Together

Developments at the George Ranch Historical Park near Richmond, Texas, provide a case study of how staff can use living history techniques to present gender-sensitive house interpretation. Ranch owners built the house in Richmond to gain access to town-based resources and business and trade networks after Reconstruction. The Ryon-Davis House served as ranch headquarters between the 1880s and the first decade of the 1900s. Research indicates that entrepreneurs such as the rancher J. H. P. Davis challenged planters for local control throughout the South at this time. Museums that concentrate on male boosters, as do most sites such as the Ryon-Davis House, neglect an important component of

100

Figure 4.5. Todd R. Williams, an interpreter at the Jourdan-Bachman Pioneer Farm, Austin, Texas, cooks the noon meal in the homestead cabin and explains that he has to fend for himself while his wife tends to sick relatives. Photograph by Debra A. Reid, 1994. Courtesy of the author.

the story, the role that the ranch women played in the political struggle of the white middle class to secure supremacy in the New South.[36]

J. H. P. Davis gained his position because of his involvement with the Ryon women. He married into a prominent local ranching family through which the property descended matrilineally. His mother-in-law, Polly Ryon, appointed him manager of the Ryon Farm and Pasture Company that she created in 1886. He managed the property but did so under her watchful eye as she cared for her grandchildren following the death of her daughter, Lizzie Ryon Davis. Polly lived with the family temporarily after her house burned in 1888, and then permanently as her health failed. A portion of the company passed to her granddaughter, Mamie, in 1896 following Polly's death (fig. 4.6).[37]

These two generations of Ryon-Davis women—Mary Moore "Polly" Ryon and Belle Ryon Davis—offer an opportunity to consider a transition period not

Figure 4.6. Interpreters depict Polly Ryon, the ranch owner, and her son-in-law, J. H. P. Davis, manager of the Ryon Farm and Pasture Company, conducting business in the parlor of the Ryon-Davis House, relocated to the George Ranch Historical Park. Courtesy of the George Ranch Historical Park, Richmond, Texas.

just in Southern history but in women's history, as well. Analyses of Progressive era activities tend to concentrate on urban, middle-class women, their relationships with peers, and their involvement in clubs and programs of social reform, including suffrage. Research on ranch women—especially those in transition between rural and town life—and their relationships with wards, domestic servants, and the families of tenants and sharecroppers receive less attention. Evidence shows that Polly Ryon managed the ranch for more than fifty years—beginning when she inherited nearly nine thousand acres and a cattle herd as a teenager, to her divestiture of responsibility for twenty thousand acres and eight thousand head of cattle upon her death in 1896. Letters to her granddaughter document Polly's continued interest in the daily aspects of the ranching operation until her death.[38]

Belle, a Ryon relative from Kentucky, arrived as Davis's second wife and stepmother to his children in December 1888. She quickly assumed public responsibilities that followed a middle-class southern pattern. She participated on the local school commission and in women's clubs in Richmond, Texas; played a role in securing a public monument memorializing the "war" that ousted Reconstruction government in the county; assumed leadership positions in the Baptist church; and eventually advocated suffrage.[39]

Servants made it possible for Belle Davis and other women in Richmond to channel the energy not expended on domestic chores toward volunteer work and social pursuits. Male and female African Americans worked in the Ryon-Davis House, but the activities of female domestics are better documented than are the male. Jacquelyn Dowd Hall and Anne Firor Scott summarize the importance of the female domestic as deriving from "her multiple identities—as nurturer, economic provider, and community builder among her own people as well as interracial mediator and participant in the intimate dynamics of white family life." The evidence from the Ryon-Davis House supports the ways black women continued as nurse, maid, and cook for white rural Southerners after slavery ended. This system restricted African-American women to low-wage positions and undermined their obligations as wife, mother, and homemaker. In contrast, domestic labor offered African-American women alternatives to working as farm laborers, and allowed them to draw support "from a dense network of secular and religious working-class organizations." Projects that document the activities of black women and compare their experiences to those of other middle-class African Americans such as the wives of ministers, undertakers, and other businessmen and farm owners provide valuable information to studies of gender as well as race.[40]

Living history techniques provide a viable approach to presenting the perspectives of the male and female residents of both races at the Ryon-Davis House. Vignettes could include ranch association meetings, women's club meetings, or discussions between Belle and her husband about their Progressive agenda and their reliance on domestic laborers such as the cooks Francis or Rachel. Interpretation in either the "cook's house" or the kitchen could include discussion of blacks leaving their farming families to seek more money, better conditions, or a change of environment away from Richmond. The discussion could arise between white interpreters regarding the difficulty in keeping domestic laborers, or between black interpreters concerned about the young leaving home, fear of unknown places, or excitement about new prospects. Storyboards can augment the interpretation and ensure that all perspectives find expression.[41]

In conclusion, interpreting gender at house museums may prove difficult given the influence of founders with contrary ideas about women's, men's, and children's roles and responsibilities, but the effort brings increased understanding to staff and visitors alike. Incorporating gender begins with a self-study of the site and its history, collections, and resources. The assessment should document the perspectives and labor of women as well as men and children. Significant themes must be selected, and gender must be incorporated into the explanation of each. Once the assessment is completed and themes identified, the staff should determine the best interpretive technique to impart the information. Living history offers an alternative and its application can range from the most detailed re-created event to inquiry-based interpretation that provokes visitors to process information rather than just accept it. House museum staff can select characters from among the historic residents or construct representative characters that can impart the significant issues. The voices of the past can speak through real people in costume performing accurate chores, through dialogue presented on a storyboard panel, or through documents available for visitor analysis. Regardless of method, they should present multiple perspectives of space, collections, and the relationships of the artifacts and sites to larger concepts of regional, national, even international significance. This approach can sensitize staff and visitors to multiple perspectives and multiple constructs and can create more detailed, complex, and accurate depictions of the past.[42]

Notes

1. Social history, an interdisciplinary approach based on the study of ordinary people, came into vogue in the early twentieth century and experienced a rebirth (the "new" social history) in the 1960s. For an overview of various approaches see James B. Gardner and

George Rollie Adams, eds., *Ordinary People and Everyday Life: Perspectives on the New Social History* (Nashville, Tenn.: American Association for State and Local History, 1983).

2. Patricia West, *Domesticating History: The Political Origins of America's House Museums* (Washington, D.C.: Smithsonian Institution Press, 1999), 159, 161.

3. Elizabeth H. Pleck, "Women's History: Gender as a Category of Historical Analysis," in *Ordinary People and Everyday Life*, 51–65; John Demos, *A Little Commonwealth: Family Life in Plymouth Colony* (New York: Oxford University Press, 1970); Laurel Thatcher Ulrich, *A Midwife's Tale: The Life of Martha Ballard, Based on Her Diary, 1785–1812* (New York: Knopf, 1990); Rebecca Sharpless, *Fertile Ground, Narrow Choices: Women on Texas Cotton Farms, 1900–1940* (Chapel Hill: University of North Carolina Press, 1999); Dolores Hayden, *The Grand Domestic Revolution: A History of Feminist Designs for American Homes, Neighborhoods, and Cities* (Cambridge, Mass.: Harvard University Press, 1981); Elizabeth Blackmar, *Manhattan for Rent, 1785–1850* (Ithaca, N.Y.: Cornell University Press, 1989).

4. Barbara Melosh, "Speaking of Women: Museums' Representations of Women's History," in *History Museums in the United States*, ed. Roy Rosenzweig and Warren Leon (Urbana: University of Illinois Press, 1989), 186–87; Pleck, "Women's History," 54–55; Linda Kerber, *No Constitutional Right to Be Ladies: Women and the Obligations of Citizenship* (New York: Hill and Wang, 1998); Mary Beth Norton, *Founding Mothers and Fathers: Gendered Power and the Forming of American Society* (New York: Alfred A. Knopf, 1996).

5. For social and cultural history analyses of masculinity see Michael Kimmel, *Manhood in America: A Cultural History* (New York: The Free Press, 1996) and Mark C. Carnes, *Secret Ritual and Manhood in Victorian America* (New Haven, Conn.: Yale University Press, 1989).

6. Henry Glassie, *Folk Housing in Middle Virginia: A Structural Analysis of Historic Artifacts* (Knoxville: University of Tennessee Press, 1975), 178, quoted in James Deetz, *In Small Things Forgotten: The Archaeology of Early American Life* (Garden City, N.Y.: Anchor Books, 1977), 8; Henry Glassie, *Passing the Time in Ballymenone: Culture and History of an Ulster Community* (Philadelphia: University of Pennsylvania Press, 1982; Bloomington: Indiana University Press, 1995), 327–424; Henry Glassie, *Material Culture* (Bloomington: University of Indiana Press, 1999), 78.

7. *Clover Lawn: The David Davis Mansion State Historic Site* (Bloomington, Ill.: The David Davis Mansion Foundation, 1994), 7.

8. Julia Duncan Welder, a Gillard descendant and local historian, spearheaded the preservation effort. "Gillard-Duncan Home," brochure, Sam Houston Regional Library and Research Center, n.d.; Chessie Duncan Quesenbury, "Liberty's Creole Colony," *National Genealogical Inquirer* (Winter 1979): 229–30; Miriam Partlow, *Liberty, Liberty County, and the Atascosito District* (Austin, Tex.: The Pemberton Press Jenkins Publishing Co., 1974), 124–25; and Terry G. Jordan, *Trails to Texas: Southern Roots of Western Cattle Ranching* (Lincoln: University of Nebraska Press, 1981), 80. William Duncan, Jefferson County [Texas], to Eliza Gillard Duncan, Liberty [Texas], 25 October 1853 and William Duncan, Calcusieu [sic] [Calcasieu Parish, Louisiana], to Eliza Gillard Duncan, Liberty,

29 October 1853, in the Julia Duncan Welder Collection, Sam Houston Regional Library and Research Center, Liberty, Texas (hereafter SHRL). David G. Surdam, "The Antebellum Texas Cattle Trade across the Gulf of Mexico," *Southwestern Historical Quarterly* 100, no. 4 (April 1997): 477–92.

9. Ocie Speer, *A Treatise on the Law of Married Women in Texas Including Marriage: Divorce, Homestead, and Administration* (Rochester, N.Y.: The Lawyer's Co-Operative Publishing Company, 1901), chapter 13, section 168, "Spanish Civil Law," 176. Record of Brands [Jefferson County], 1838–1849, SHRL. Examples include Roselle [Rosalie] Ashworth who registered brands for her newborn daughter Sydney Jane on 29 July 1845, and for her second daughter, Lydia Anne, soon after her birth on 2 August 1847. Speer discussed brands and law in chapter 13, section 181, "Deed Taken in Wife's Name," 187. Kathleen Elizabeth Lazarou, "Concealed under Petticoats: Married Women's Property and the Law in Texas, 1840–1913," Ph.D. diss., Rice University, Houston, Texas, 1980; James W. Paulsen, "Community Property and the Early American Women's Rights Movement: The Texas Connection," *Idaho Law Review* 32, no. 4 (1986): 641–90; Marylynn Salmon, *Women and the Law of Property in Early America* (Chapel Hill: University of North Carolina Press, 1986).

10. "Gillard-Duncan Home."

11. Dell Upton, *Architecture in the United States* (New York: Oxford University Press, 1998), 40–43; 300–1; Blackmar, *Manhattan for Rent*; Barbara Clark Smith, "Applied Feminist Theories," in *Gender Perspectives: Essays on Women in Museums*, ed. Jane R. Glaser and Artemis A. Zenetou (Washington, D.C.: Smithsonian Institution Press, 1994), 145.

12. Daphne Spain, *Gendered Spaces* (Chapel Hill: University of North Carolina Press, 1992), 111–40; Jim McKay and Gregg Berninger, "Interpreting Servants at the Martin Van Buren NHS," *CRM (Cultural Resource Management)* 20, no. 3 (1997): 48; John H. Ferry, "Food for Thought: A View Toward a Richer Interpretation of the House Museum Kitchen," *CRM* 24, no. 4 (2001): 9–11; Judith W. Linsley, "Main House, Carriage House: African-American Domestic Employees at the McFaddin-Ward House in Beaumont, Texas, 1900–1950," *Southwestern Historical Quarterly* 103, no. 1 (July 1999): 28, 47. Even though the servants influenced the McFaddins, and vice versa, servants and family members occupied different zones of the house. Inequity governed the relationships and perceptions of space. Louis Lemon's quarters, small but well kept by a meticulous man, existed outside the house proper, a Southern tradition that removed black laborers from the white domicile.

13. Elizabeth Collins Cromley, "A History of American Beds and Bedrooms," in *Perspectives in Vernacular Architecture, IV*, ed. Thomas Carter and Bernard L. Herman, (Columbia: University of Missouri Press, 1991), 177–86, 235–36; Sallie McMurry, *Families and Farmhouses in Nineteenth-Century America: Vernacular Design and Social Change* (New York: Oxford University Press, 1988).

14. Glassie, *Passing the Time in Ballymenone*, first quote 342; second quote 327.

15. Marla R. Miller and Anne Digan Lanning, "'Common Parlors': Women and the

Recreation of Community Identity in Deerfield, MA, 1870–1920," *Gender and History* 6, no. 3 (November 1994): 435–55.

16. Christie Farnham, *The Impact of Feminist Research in the Academy* (Bloomington: Indiana University Press, 1987), 5, quoted in Joyce Ice, "Feminist Readings of Folk Material Culture Studies," in *The Material Culture of Gender, the Gender of Material Culture*, ed. Katharine Martinez and Kenneth L. Ames (Winterthur, Del.: Henry Francis du Pont Winterthur Museum, 1997), 223, 233.

17. Barbara Melosh and Christina Simmons, "Exhibiting Women's History," in *Presenting the Past*, ed. Susan Porter Benson, Stephen Brier, and Roy Rosenzweig (Philadelphia: Temple University Press, 1986), first quote, 203; second quote, 220–21; Melosh, "Speaking of Women," 187; 208–9, note 1.

18. Vivien Rose, "Preserving Women's Rights History," *CRM* 20, no. 3 (1997): 27–28.

19. Patricia West, "Interpreting Women's History at Male-Focused House Museums," *CRM* 20, no. 3 (1997): 8–9; Heather Huyck, "Placing Women in the Past," *CRM* 20, no. 3 (1997): 5.

20. Frances Davey and Thomas A. Chambers, "'A Woman? At the Fort?': A Shock Tactic for Gender Intergration in Historical Interpretation," *Gender and History* 6, no. 3 (November 1994): 468–73.

21. Debra A. Reid, "It Takes Two: Interpreting Women and Men in Open-Air Museums in the Midwest," *Midwest Open Air Museums Magazine* 22, no. 3 (2001): 10.

22. Ulysses Grant Dietz, Lucy Brotman, and Timothy Wintemberg, "Making a New Home for the Decorative Arts in Newark: The Ballantine House," in *Old Collections, New Audiences: Decorative Arts and Visitor Experience for the Twenty-first Century*, ed. Donna R. Braden and Gretchen W. Overhiser (Dearborn, Mich.: Henry Ford Museum & Greenfield Village, 2000), 83, 89–92.

23. Melosh and Simmons, "Exhibiting Women's History," 209–11, 220; Melosh, "Speaking of Women," acknowledges the contribution living history museums and historic houses can make to women's history "because of their focus on community and domestic life" (p. 185), but she mentions them briefly. She criticizes Tryon Palace and Gardens (p. 188), located in New Bern, North Carolina, finds strengths and weakness at the sites associated with woman's suffrage such as the Sewall-Belmont House in Washington, D.C., and the Women's Rights National Historic Site in Seneca Falls, New York (pp. 194–97), and criticizes historic house museum tours for perpetuating traditional ideas of women and domesticity (pp. 201–2). Melosh, however, praises those that offer new insight into little discussed themes such as sexuality and servant attitudes (p. 202). Neither article considers the ways that living history as a technique presented in a historical environment can inform visitors about complicated past events.

24. Jay Anderson, *Time Machines: The World of Living History* (Nashville, Tenn.: American Association for State and Local History, 1984), 3; Debra A. Reid, "A Story to Pass On: Interpreting Women in Historic Sites and Open-Air Museums," *History News* (March/April 1995): 12–15.

25. Melosh and Simmons, "Exhibiting Women's History," 210–11, 220; Nancy Grey

Osterud, "Living Living History: First Person Interpretation at Plimoth Plantation, Plymouth, Massachusetts," *Journal of Museum Education* 17, no. 1 (Winter 1992): 18–20.

26. Kerridwen Harvey, "Looking for Women in the Museums: Has Women's Studies Really 'Come a Long Way'?" *Muse* 11, no. 4 (Winter 1994): 24; Melosh, "Speaking of Women," 202.

27. Osterud, "Living Living History," 19; Reid, "A Story to Pass On," 19.

28. Sherry Butcher-Younghans, *Historic House Museums: A Practical Handbook for Their Care, Preservation, and Management* (New York: Oxford University Press, 1993), 182, 184; Joan M. Jensen, *Loosening the Bonds: Mid-Atlantic Farm Women, 1750–1850* (New Haven, Conn.: Yale University, 1986).

29. Ruth Schwartz Cowan, *More Work for Mother: The Ironies of Household Technology from the Open Hearth to the Microwave* (New York: Basic Books, 1983).

30. A symposium on the topic of women's roles and their interpretation at Oliver Kelley Farm appeared in *Oral History Review* 17, no. 2 (Fall 1989). It included three articles, one by a concerned visitor, one by the site manager, and one by a women's historian, respectively. See Amy Sheldon, "Gender, Language, and Historical Interpretation," 92–96; Thomas A. Woods, "The Challenge of Public History," 97–102; and Joan M. Jensen, "Comment on Gender Issues and Historic Interpretation at the Kelley Farm," 102–5. Thomas A. Woods continued his defense of Kelley Farm interpretation from feminist critics in "Varying Versions of the Real: Toward a Socially Responsible Public History," *Minnesota History* 51, no. 5 (Spring 1989): 178–85. Participants in the 2000 Rural Women's Studies Association conference visited Oliver H. Kelley Farm in June and conducted a plenary session, "Public Interpretations of Private Places: Presenting Women's Roles in Living History Farms and Historic Plantations." Participants included Debra Reid (chair), Joan Jensen, Jim Mattson (current Kelley Farm site manager), and Joanne McNeal (director of a developing site in Virginia). The disagreement continued with a majority of the audience believing the interpretation balanced historical perspectives, and the rest believing that the division of labor that interpreters presented failed to educate the public about the negative aspects of patriarchy.

31. Timothy Crumrin, "These Things Not My Own: The Legal Status of Women in Early Nineteenth-Century Indiana," *Midwest Open Air Museums Magazine* 20, no. 2 (1999): 5–9.

32. Lois Green Carr, Russell R. Menard, and Lorena S. Walsh, *Robert Cole's World: Agriculture and Society in Early Maryland* (Chapel Hill: University of North Carolina, 1991); John D. Krugler, "Behind the Public Presentations: Research and Scholarship at Living History Museums of Early America," *William and Mary Quarterly* 48, no. 3 (July 1991): 347–86.

33. Stacy Roth, *Past into Present: Effective Techniques for First-Person Historical Interpretation* (Chapel Hill: University of North Carolina Press, 1998), 9; Lonn Taylor, "The House from Ipswich: Reconstruction and Reinterpretation in a Museum Setting," and Shelley Nickles, "Within These Walls . . . Reinterpreting the Ipswich House" (presented at the joint meeting of the Organization of American Historians/National Council of Public History, Washington, D.C., 12 April 2002).

34. Dietz, Brotman, and Wintemberg, "Making a New Home for the Decorative Arts in Newark," 86; quote, 84.

35. Billie Gammon created the live-in program during the early 1970s, and I participated in and managed them between January 1983 and December 1984.

36. "Out of Slavery's Shadow: Interpretative Planning for a Post-Reconstruction Texas Ranch" (Planning grant application, National Endowment for the Humanities, 1997); Debra A. Reid, "Ranch Women in the New South: The Home, the Community, and the Ryon-Davis Family—Richmond, Texas, 1880–1900" (report completed in partial fulfillment of consultant requirements for "Out of Slavery's Shadow," NEH Planning Grant, 26 February 1998 and 17 March 1998); C. Vann Woodward, *The Origins of the New South, 1877–1913* (Baton Rouge: Louisiana State University Press, 1951, 1971); Edward L. Ayers, *The Promise of the New South: Life after Reconstruction* (New York: Oxford University Press, 1992).

37. Mrs. Mary Booth Myers, during an oral interview conducted 3 February 1991, noted that Polly moved to town to the Ryon-Davis house as she grew older (pp. 20–22). This likely occurred after the "Old Prairie Home" burned in 1888. "Family Biographical Sketches and Notes: Mary Moore (Polly) Ryon," 2, in 1997–1998 Davis House Complex NEH Planning Grant, Research and Site Planning Documents (hereafter Davis House NEH Planning Documents).

38. "Family Biographical Sketches and Notes: Mary Moore ('Polly') Ryon," 2, 3, 5. Davis House NEH Planning Documents; Petition of J. F. Dyer et al., from Fort Bend County, 14 Feb. 1881, RG 100–399 Petitions, Texas State Archives, Austin, cited in "[JHP Davis] Civic Associations: Memberships in Cattlemen's Associations," 1, Davis House NEH Planning Documents; *The Richmond* [Texas] *Opinion*, 28 January 1887, p. 2.

39. Reid, "Ranch Women in the New South," NEH report. J. H. P. Davis Papers, box 1, folder 4, George Foundation Archives (hereafter GFA); A. J. Sowell, *History of Fort Bend County* (Houston, Tex.: W. H. Coyle & Co., 1904), 331, cited in "[J. H. P Davis] Political Involvement," 7, Davis House NEH Planning Documents. J. H. P. Davis Papers box 1, folder 8, GFA, cited in "[J. H. P. Davis] Civic Associations," 7, Davis House NEH Planning Documents. "[J. H. P. Davis] Civic Involvement," 9, Davis House NEH Planning Documents. *Richmond* [Texas] *Register*, 12 July 1890, p. 1. Polly described Belle's religious devotion in a letter, M. M. Ryon to Mamie Davis, 23 Feb. 1896, Mamie Davis George Papers, box 1, folder 2, GFA, cited in "Family Biographical Sketches and Notes: Mary Moore (Polly) Ryon," p. 4, Davis House NEH Planning Documents. Megan Seaholm, "Earnest Women: The White Women's Club Movement in Progressive Era Texas, 1880–1920" (Ph.D. diss., Rice University, Houston, Texas, 1988). For Belle's support of suffrage see *Rosenberg* [Texas] *Herald*, 16 May 1919. In 1918, ninety-eight local suffrage societies existed including one in Rosenberg. A. Elizabeth Taylor, "The Woman Suffrage Movement in Texas," *Journal of Southern History* 17 (May 1951): 194–215, reprinted in *Citizens at Last: The Women's Suffrage Movement in Texas*, consulting eds. Ruthe Winegarten and Judith N. McArthur (Austin, Tex.: Ellen C. Temple, 1987), 30; Judith N. McArthur, *Creating the New Woman: The Rise of Southern Women's Progressive Culture in Texas, 1893–1918* (Urbana: University of Illinois Press, 1998).

40. Debra A. Reid, "African-American Domestic Servants in the New South Addendum, Ranch Women in the New South: The Home, the Community, and the Ryon-Davis Family, Richmond, Texas, 1880–1900" (prepared in partial fulfillment of consultant requirements for "Out of Slavery's Shadow," NEH Planning Grant, 21 April 1998); Jacquelyn Dowd Hall and Anne Firor Scott, "Women in the South," in *Interpreting Southern History: Historiographical Essays in Honor of Stanford W. Higginbotham*, ed. John B. Boles and Evelyn Thomas Nolen (Baton Rouge: Louisiana State University Press, 1987), 486. Jacqueline Jones discusses the ways domestic service hurt African-American women in *Labor of Love, Labor of Sorrow: Black Women, Work, and the Family from Slavery to the Present* (New York: Basic, 1985), 127–34. Tera Hunter's study of the political activities of Atlanta's black domestics and washerwomen documents activism. See *To 'Joy My Freedom: Southern Black Women's Lives and Labors after the Civil War* (Cambridge, Mass.: Harvard University Press, 1997).

41. "Servants/Workers of Davis House Complex," Davis House NEH Planning Documents; M. M. Ryon to Mamie Davis, 31 March 1896, Mamie Davis George Papers, box 1, folder 2, GFA, cited in "Family Biographical Sketches and Notes: Mary Moore (Polly) Ryon," p. 5, Davis House NEH Planning Documents.

42. For an exercise in interpretive planning that builds gender sensitivity, see Debra A. Reid, "Fleshing out Jane Doe: Creating Scenarios to Interpret Female and Male Perspectives," appendix to "It Takes Two," 15.

CHAPTER FIVE

GROUNDS FOR INTERPRETATION:
THE LANDSCAPE CONTEXT OF
HISTORIC HOUSE MUSEUMS

Catherine Howett

During the period of my life in which I was developing a strong interest in landscape and horticultural history, the restoration projects under way at Thomas Jefferson's Monticello—projects that were able to draw on exceptionally rich resources of archival and archaeological evidence—served as a cynosure for my reading and thinking about the theory and practice of landscape design in this country. In the throes of that enthusiasm, I planned a family trip one summer to visit Charlottesville, Virginia. I wanted my children to see that an American president whom they knew chiefly as the author of the Declaration of Independence had also devoted his energies to the design of a very unusual and beautiful farm and home, intended to support and to nurture his private and domestic life and that of his family.

What proved most memorable about that trip, however, was not my daughters' learning experience, but my husband's. He is an art historian, and had studied Monticello—or thought he had—as part of a course in American architecture taken while pursuing doctoral studies. He remembered that he had learned a good deal about Jefferson's stylistic sources, the gradual evolution of the building's design, its relationship to other projects here and abroad, and its influence on American architectural tradition. His professor had covered all of this material in great detail, but without any consideration of the house within the context of Jefferson's ambitious program for the entire site. The class was shown not just contemporary views and diagrams of the building, but various plans, sections, and elevations in Jefferson's own hand. Yet not a single illustration had been chosen from among the many drawings that reveal his continual preoccupation with working through relationships between the house and the hill—the lawns, fields, orchards, vineyards, woodlands, gardens, architectural embellishments, and the "roundabouts," his walks and roads. All of these features were part of Jefferson's complex visual and kinesthetic plan for this landscape, a plan inspired by the concept of a *ferme ornée* or "ornamental farm" associated with the development of the English landscape gardening movement. The house was certainly a critically important part of that conception, but no one familiar with the historic record can fail to appreciate that in Jefferson's mind it never took priority over his larger vision of the place that he intended to create at Monticello.

Landscape as an Essential Primary Source

The expansion of historic preservation advocacy over the course of the last several decades of the twentieth century probably helped to increase public awareness of the ways that cities and towns, streets and neighborhoods, and all of the buildings, gardens, grounds, and simple spaces green or gray that constitute our familiar world—all of these *landscapes*, in other words—are physical expressions of a dynamic network of forces that came into play to make them what they once were or what they are today. There are social and cultural forces at work, of which historic traditions and current fashion are obvious examples, as well as individual creative and imaginative forces, such as Jefferson's love for the Blue Ridge Mountains or his passion for classical architecture. There is also the inexorable force of pragmatic limiting factors, such as empty pockets, or expansive ones that may make exciting things happen—perhaps a wealthy spouse, a corporate donor, or an enlightened municipal government.

Developing a curiosity about how places have come to be what they are is the beginning of a proper sense of history, connecting us with what has happened in the past. Historical awareness and understanding, in turn, make it possible for us to make informed judgments of quality and significance related to places that concern us. Whatever judgments we do make about a landscape—this park provides recreational benefits to the whole community; this historic property is worth a preservation campaign; this strip mall is going to increase the risk of flooding in the neighborhood and is an eyesore to boot—all such judgments ought to be based on critical thinking informed by history and a respect for the built world as a carrier of meaning and value across generations.

One hopeful sign of a dawning enlightenment with respect to such issues has been the dramatic growth in publications that address landscape subjects, not just for an academic audience but for readers within the surprisingly large segment of our population that has rediscovered the garden—and often, by extension, garden history; or joined community groups promoting the cause of public parks, street trees, or greenways; or become concerned about the degradation—

ecological, but also aesthetic and spiritual—of many environments that impact their lives. The number of related organizations that have come into being—the Alliance for Historic Landscape Preservation in 1978, the Southern Garden History Society in 1982, the New England Garden History Society in 1990, the National Association of Olmsted Parks in 1990, to name just a few—similarly attest to a growing landscape sensibility that holds promise, finally, of investing the discipline of what is now commonly called *landscape studies* with a proper importance within educational programs at every level, from elementary school to university. Although it still is not possible to major in landscape studies at most universities in this country, the number of courses and related degree programs is expanding at such a rate that there is reason to hope that before long many more Americans will be introduced to this important domain of humanistic learning and research as part of their general education.

In the meantime, however, those working with historic properties face a daunting challenge in helping visitors to see and understand, in more intellectually and affectively stimulating ways, the places that museum professionals present and interpret through tours and other kinds of educational programming. I use the word "places" rather than "houses" or "properties" deliberately, because it is not uncommon for historic house museum administrators or staff to have absorbed the same bias that blinded my husband's professor to the essential nature and function of Mr. Jefferson's beloved house on its still *more* beloved hill. It has often seemed to me that the familiar hard work of rescuing or repairing or otherwise renewing a historic house must so engage the minds and hearts and design energies of all concerned that it is easy to lose touch with the ordinary, everyday understanding of the priorities that always operate in the building or buying of homes.

Recall the old saw that realtors cite: "The three most important things to consider in purchasing or selling property are location, location, and location." The word itself derives from the Latin *locus*, meaning *place*. Thus even a seemingly landscape-less condominium on the thirty-fifth floor of a downtown high-rise may take its primary value not from the building but from the place it occupies; a lot of scruffy housing is made genteel and highly desirable real estate by occupying the right block in the right neighborhood. And in a real sense, it is the site as a whole, not the house, that is the true *locus* of any historic residential property. After all, among the values that may move a prospective home owner to choose a particular location, it is most often the character and appeal of the site itself—prompting the imagination to anticipate the very look and feel of the desired home place—that operate as powerful determinants of the actual design and construction process. This priority in causation and importance was even more true in our country's past than it is today, since a postindustrial and urbanized twenty-first-century culture has tended to erode historic societal traditions that once attached greater value to place, landscape, and to land itself, even at the scale of small residential properties or modest communities of homes along pleasant streets. Nevertheless, the appeal of certain landscape values persists to a remarkable degree even today, and at least partially accounts for the suburban world that recent generations of Americans—voting, in a sense, with their cars— have brought into being.

Landscape Design Decisions Reveal Cultural Values

Here we have, then, values that attach to physical places but which obviously are generated from within that vast force field of individual and personal, societal and cultural preferences that I have described. Thus, although we may seem to be talking about just physical place—the site itself and the landscape that embraces the house as a central component—in fact we are talking about ideas and desires, neither of which may have been acknowledged or even consciously identified by those whose goals, choices, and actions they determined. When we look back at the stages in a residential property's evolution at which specific decisions were made about how the site would be developed, we can be certain that the same strong impress of landscape design models that had captivated the imagination of the decision makers—an owner or owners acting independently or in collaboration with one or more designers—helped to generate the specific ideas and design intentions that eventually added up to built outcomes, the place that was finally (or perhaps only partially) achieved.

Although the house has not survived, drawings of alternative schemes for treatment of the landscape surrounding the 1799 Elias Hasket Derby House in Salem, Massachusetts, document just such a decision-making process (figs. 5.1, 5.2a, 5.2b). The distinguished American architect Charles Bulfinch had been initially involved in designing the mansion, but the commission was subsequently awarded to Salem's brilliant local builder and craftsman Samuel McIntyre. McIntyre would help Elias Derby realize his dream of a jewel-like neoclassical house set within gardens and grounds of surpassing elegance, exceptional even in that city of fine homes. One visitor observed that the handsome townhouse on the corner of Essex and Washington Streets seemed "more like a palace than the dwelling of an American merchant."[1] The three landscape plans proposed by McIntyre each represents a very different approach to the question of which style would be most appropriate, ranging from the most conservative solution, the classical quadripartite garden (fig. 5.1); to a blend of the old orthogonal geometries with curvilinear elements and informally disposed flower beds (fig. 5.2a); to the most radical plan (fig. 5.2b), which substituted a meandering roundabout within a "naturalistic" woodland grove for any formal garden features at all.

The Derby family belonged to an elite living in one of the wealthiest mercantile and shipping towns on the Eastern seaboard during the years near the close of the eighteenth century when the new nation was still defining its culture, as well as its government and constitution. From the perspective of landscape history and the evolution of landscape tastes and fashions, each of the design options suggested to his client by Samuel McIntyre reverberates with meaning. Shall Americans retain the discipline and order of a style impressed with suggestions of the old world's socially hierarchic and politically monarchic societies? Or shall we affirm our sophistication and the more liberal social and political attitudes of the new nation by laying out the garden in the manner of the English landscape designer and author Humphry Repton (1752–1818)? Repton's books already were familiar to a class of wealthy and well-traveled Americans sympathetic with the revolution in landscape taste that had, over the course of the century, completely transformed the character of the estates of the English aristocracy and rural gentry.[2] Repton had introduced a hybrid style, combining formal and informal elements in what its creator argued was a sensible, practical accommodation to living requirements; the large scale of the kitchen garden in McIntyre's plan (fig. 5.2a) does suggest, however, a distinctly American heightening of these functional values. (Thomas Jefferson had elected to imitate Mr. Repton's style in the design of the important west lawn at Monticello, with its irregular beds of flowers framing the path that curved gently about the lawn; and he, too, provided for a large kitchen garden close to the house.) Or might Elias Derby choose to express, through the design of the grounds of his house, a bolder and more daring commitment to the romantic and picturesque values—nature freed at last from any suggestion of human control—that the more radical exponents of the English school had espoused?

As it turned out, Elias Derby, like most of his peers in this country, still preferred the older way of doing things and opted to express his probity and respect for tradition by choosing the very simple four-square garden (fig. 5.1). His contemporary, William Paca, however, building a splendid townhouse farther south in Annapolis between about 1863 and 1865, apparently preferred to be more innovative in matters of landscape taste. We see him posed, in a portrait by Charles Willson Peale (fig. 5.3), within a softly naturalesque landscape that clearly articulates, through its neoclassical pavilion and chinoiserie bridge, its owner's awareness of English picturesque principles. Evidence establishing the major features of Governor Paca's garden, including the location of the pavilion and bridge seen in the painting, were uncovered under a hotel parking lot during

Figure 5.1. (this page) and Figures 5.a.–b. (opposite page)   Three alternative design proposals by Samuel McIntyre for laying out the grounds of the Elias Hasket Derby House, Salem, Massachusetts. Courtesy of Peabody Essex Museum.

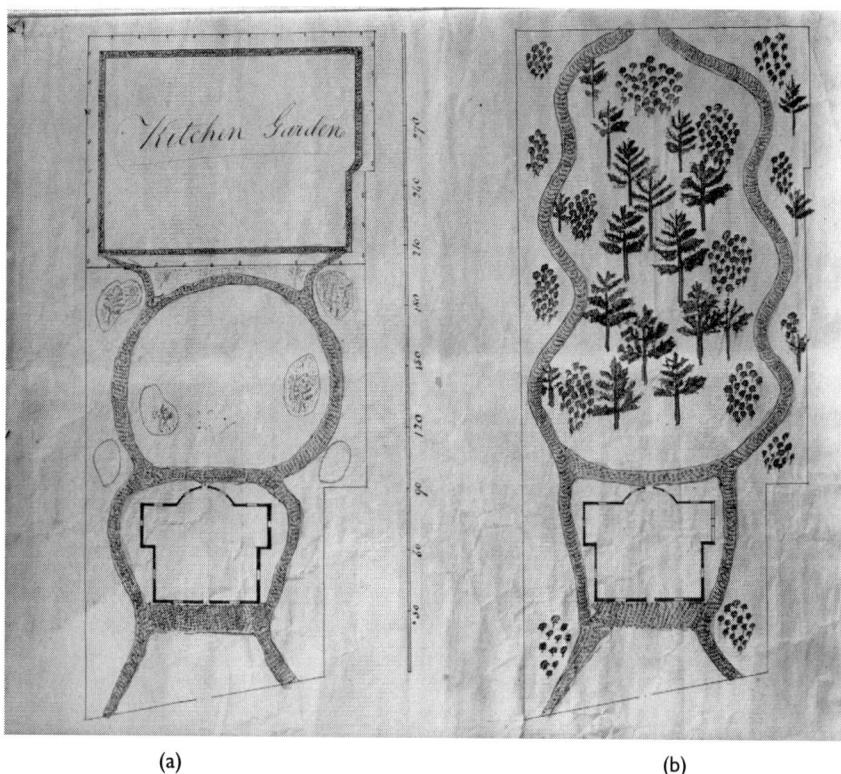

(a)   (b)

the course of archaeological investigations carried out in connection with the recovery and restoration of the Paca house, beginning late in the 1960s. The plan of the gardens subsequently installed on the site (fig. 5.4) indicates that the very stylish "wilderness" section of the garden represented in the Peale portrait was actually the terminal feature of a more conventionally regular and geometric garden layout. Within less than fifty years of completion of both the Derby and Paca gardens, the prolific American garden writer and tastemaker Andrew Jackson Downing (1815–1852) would chide those of his countrymen who persisted in relying on what he termed this "antike" style of garden design in lieu of more fashionable interpretations of the "Beautiful" or the "Picturesque" derived from the English landscape gardening school and anticipated by Paca's "wilderness."[3]

The example of these contrasting design options and decisions illustrates very well the clusters of meaning and contesting ideas and desires that inhere in such choices, which are themselves compounded of conscious and unconscious, pragmatic and symbolic motivations. The point must be made, of course, that this grounding of *any* design in a particular configuration of ideas and attitudes about what constitutes an appropriate and desirable landscape is not limited to choices about high-style landscapes and gardens.

Challenges in Interpreting a Large Vernacular Landscape

The original eight-hundred-acre DeKalb County, Georgia, farm that surrounded the house and its fenced lot seen in a late-nineteenth-century photograph (fig. 5.5) gave expression to precisely the same sort of shifting conflation of ideas, habits of mind, and habits of practice—in this case conventions of agricultural, horticultural, and garden design practice—that we have seen operating in decisions about the laying out of grounds around two eighteenth-century urban mansions. Robert Smith, the original owner of this property, is known to have been a successful and prosperous agriculturist. Even more importantly, in the way he farmed, favoring a mixed agricultural economy rather than staple-crop monoculture, Smith was more typical of farmers in the Georgia piedmont—indeed more typical of much of the South—than the planter class mythically represented in *Gone With the Wind*. Smith and his wife undoubtedly laid out their farm and in every sense "designed" their domestic landscape working out of their own understanding of what was appropriate, using familiar vernacular traditions of practice and also, perhaps, ideas garnered from their reading of the popular agricultural journals addressed to Southern farm families of the time. Late in the 1960s, the Atlanta Historical Society seized an opportunity to purchase and move the threatened circa 1840s farmhouse—now called the Tullie Smith House after the last of Robert Smith's descendants to live in it—to the grounds of what is now the Atlanta History Center, where the house became the centerpiece of a "living history" project aimed at interpreting mid-nineteenth-century farm life typical of the region.

The Tullie Smith Restoration, as the project and site were originally described, provides a useful example of the difficult issues that may arise when, with the best will in the world, the administrators of a historic house recognize the imperative to interpret its landscape context. The Atlanta Historical Society set about a program of collecting nineteenth-century farm buildings and structures—a kitchen, dairy or "sarce" house, smokehouse, barn, corncrib, and a cabin—from various locations, placed them in relationship to the house as appropriately as the severe limitations of space (barely three acres) allowed, and tried to give visitors a sense of the look, feel, and function of these historic building types. After research to establish the most common vernacular treatment of the

Figure 5.3. Portrait of William Paca by Charles Willson Peale (MSA SC #1545–1056). Courtesy of the Maryland State Archives, special collections (Maryland Commission on Artistic Property).

Figure 5.4. Design for the garden of the William Paca House by Laurance S. Brigham, ca. 1976. Courtesy of Historic Annapolis Foundation.

space within the house lot on such farms, a "swept yard" effect was replicated and garden beds laid out, using only horticultural species introduced by the 1840s. In a larger garden space beyond the house lot, a kitchen garden was established, and also a few rows each of representative Georgia field crops—cotton, tobacco, sorghum, and so forth—so that urban schoolchildren and others might see how such plants actually looked.

By comparison with architectural preservation, the theory and philosophy of historic landscape preservation has been subject to substantial rethinking and revision over the quarter century since the Tullie Smith project was undertaken. Certainly the current administration of the Atlanta History Center is sensitive to the issues of historicity and authenticity that inevitably emerge in their interpretation of this farmstead complex. The house has, after all, been enframed within a landscape setting that can never re-create in a realistic way the visual character of a typical nineteenth-century piedmont farm, much less the actual landscape of Robert Smith's farm in the 1840s. The same problems of scale and spatial relationships among buildings, gardens, fields, and woods that make the present setting so different from the original one also compromise the possibility of showing visitors how such a farm *really* worked—the way, for example, that acres

Figure 5.5. Photograph, ca. 1880, of the Smith family homestead, DeKalb County, Georgia. Courtesy of the Atlanta History Center.

of uncleared woodland provided mast for hogs and perhaps grazing for cattle, while the hundred or so acres kept in cultivation produced fruits and vegetables, grains, fodder, and cash crops that sustained the large household physically and economically. Moreover, within the larger visual and functional scheme of fields, woodland, pastures, gardens, orchards, house lot and outbuildings, key elements not related to farming are also missing—slave quarters for one thing, the precinct within which Robert Smith's eleven slaves would have formed a community distinct from the Smith household. The urgency of interpreting this vitally important aspect of antebellum life is not questioned, but neither are there easy answers to the difficult question of how it may be done with honesty and candor, but also with sensitivity to the ethical and social dimensions of its presentation.

Recognizing the Limits to Recovery of the Past

The difficulties inherent in trying to interpret a resource such as the Tullie Smith House—a farmhouse removed from the eight-hundred-acre agricultural landscape that represented its most essential source of meaning—only dramatize a reality implicit in every historic landscape. For even in situations where the original boundaries of the property are intact and the appearance and function of the contemporary landscape replicate the historic past with a high degree of fidelity, in a real sense the original landscape is *not* there, is never truly present to our experience. Houses and furnishings may survive over long ages relatively intact. Landscapes that involve living materials, on the other hand, are human artifacts in which dynamic processes of growth, decay, and death produce continual and essential change over time. The Greek philosopher Heraclitus observed that one never enters the same stream twice; the same wisdom holds true for gardens and designed landscapes. Monticello may be the best documented eighteenth-century landscape in this country, but the Monticello that we visit today still must be mostly invented for us by its curators, using scholarly insight into the remarkable records documenting Jefferson's activities, but using as well a good deal of creative intelligence and imagination.

Even if it were possible to have fastidiously detailed and comprehensive records of a particular historic landscape within a precise period of its existence, the issue of how to deal with other periods, or with the changes that have occurred naturally, such as maturing vegetation, are similarly more complicated and thorny with respect to landscapes than is true for buildings and interiors. Administrators may be willing to remove an offending porch addition, or interpret different periods of occupancy in the furnishings of different rooms, but consider the problems that the National Trust faced in a recent master planning project for Shadows-on-the-Teche in New Iberia, Louisiana. Certain features of the landscape of this circa 1830 townhouse on Bayou Teche, principal residence of a family owning four plantations, are documented in an 1861 painting of the street facade of the house (fig. 5.6).

In the twentieth century, major alterations to the design of the nineteenth-century landscape were undertaken by Weeks Hall, a fourth-generation descendant of the original owners who inherited the house on its now remnant site in the 1920s and eventually made it his home. Hall was a painter and extraordinary plantsman, and the landscape of Shadows (a name he chose for the property) became over time his most significant work of art. While he thought of his manipulation of the forms and materials of this landscape as a work of "preservation"—the same young live oaks whose tops barely were visible over the fence in the painting are seen in great age in a photograph taken in the 1930s (fig. 5.7)—he actually was orchestrating profound changes in the character of the landscape and consequently in the experience it offered those invited to enjoy it. For example, Hall's substitution of high bamboo hedges for the crisp definition of the white picket fence that had previously enclosed the front yard, and oblique

Figure 5.6. Painting of the Weeks family home, New Iberia, Louisiana, ca. 1861, by Adrien Persac. Collection of Shadows-on-the-Teche, New Iberia, Louisiana, a National Trust Historic Site.

paths from the corners of the lot for the original axial walk right up the center, seem symbolic of his transformation of a historic style meant to convey a sense of sunlit rational order and human control into one meant to immerse visitors in an atmosphere of mystery, sensuosity, and shadow, haunted by invocations of some romantic and beautiful, but sadly vanished past.

When the Trust took over the property in 1958, the white picket fencing was restored and other changes were made to the house and landscape. Acts of God also play their own kind of havoc, and in this case a hurricane had inflicted major damage to the live-oak canopy whose shade was essential to what was left of Weeks Hall's garden. Some voices insisted that the Trust should not hesitate to obliterate every vestige of Hall's twentieth-century design and install a "period" garden based on nineteenth-century parterre forms in the front yard, thus synchronizing the landscape with the period interpreted in the interior of the house. Fortunately the Trust appreciated the potential significance of the work that Weeks Hall had done, and challenged the master planning team to develop design strategies that would allow visitors to understand the sequence of landscapes that together constituted the history of the site. Among other changes, the team of landscape architects responsible for the 1992 master plan proposed the restoration of Weeks Hall's bamboo perimeter *inside* the white picket fence that

Figure 5.7. Shadows-on-the-Teche, New Iberia, Louisiana, ca. 1930s. Photograph by I. A. Martin from the Archives of the Shadows-on-the-Teche. Courtesy of Iberia Parish Library, New Iberia, Louisiana.

the Trust had rebuilt to replace the one documented in the painting. The real challenge, while exploring the possibility that multiple-period interpretation can be made comprehensible and appealing as well as historically sound, is to guard against implementation of any one historic period's design in a way that significantly compromises the quality of an important earlier or later landscape feature of the site.

Toward More Appropriate Standards for Interpretation

Consideration of values such as these bring us to the issue of "pure" design strategies in the treatment of historic landscapes. During the past fifteen or twenty years, historic landscape preservation has tended to model itself as a discipline on the philosophical and theoretical foundations of architectural practice. The secretary of the interior's standards for recognizing and adding significant landscape sites to the National Register of Historic Places and the 1996 National Park Service guidelines for the treatment of historic landscapes[4] are relatively recent initiatives by comparison with the analogous processes for buildings. Quite naturally, academics and professionals working to improve the quality of landscape preservation in this country insisted that greater scholarly rigor in research was needed, and higher standards brought to bear on what constituted acceptable landscape preservation practice. At its most extreme, this new enthusiasm contributed to a syndrome that might be described as "Williamsburg paranoia." We so feared the charge of "false history" with which critics excoriated not only Williamsburg but the whole historic preservation movement in this country,[5] that many within the movement began to reach for a defensive weapon. They found it in the implied claim that historic landscape preservation was a quasi-scientific enterprise, working from accumulated documentary and physical evidence for what existed in the historic past to a landscape treatment option that is absolutely verifiable. According to this new rubric, one ought not to restore or replicate a historic landscape unless it is possible to prove that it existed in exactly that form and with those materials—in other words, in many cases, unless you have in hand a plan and a plant list.

The problem with the tone of these new strictures is the presumption that there is, in fact, some hard truth about the past that it is possible to know objectively, based on one's reading of the historic record. The geographer David Lowenthal, who writes frequently about the means by which particular cultural groups celebrate favored readings of the past in memorials and historic sites, has challenged historians and preservationists to accept the fact that there is really no possibility of absolute certainty about the "truth" of any part of our knowledge of the past:

> No historical account corresponds precisely with any actual past. Three things limit what can be known: the immensity of the past itself, the distinction between past events and the accounts of those events, and the inevitability of bias. . . .
>
> The past we know or experience is always contingent on our own views, our own perspective, above all our own present. Just as we are products of the past, so is the known past an artifact of ours.[6]

This is not to say that any one version of history is as good as another, or that the deliberate fabrication, distortion, or suppression of historical accounts and materials in an effort to "rewrite history" is morally neutral. Anecdotal embellishment of historical information as a way of adding drama to an interpretive program and other common deceptions are never less than mischievous and in some instances may be profoundly evil. This is so precisely because human memory, both personal and communal, is by its very nature so precious, fragmented, subjective, and vulnerable. Memory—and its inscription in our narratives, archives, artifacts, institutions, and landscapes—allows us to know ourselves as individuals and as members of society, over generations and even ages of time, and thus to learn from the past. Not just historians but each one of us who shares responsibility for researching or managing historic resources should therefore see that work as a public trust demanding intelligence, high standards of integrity, and a spirit of open-minded and diligent inquiry.

In that spirit, moreover, we can come to see the intrinsic limitations to our knowledge of the past—that it is inevitably partial and never perfectly objective, that history is not like science—less as a constraint than as a liberating opportunity, a challenge to manage and interpret historic resources wisely and well. The roots of history are identical, after all, with the beginnings of human art in oral traditions of storytelling. In a fundamental way, the selection and conservation or restoration of historic sites is similarly a form of storytelling, a way of introducing a new generation to historic events, values, and places that some or all of us believe are important for our society to remember. For this reason, the story that is to be told—the interpretive program—ought to precede and guide decisions made every step of the way during the development of a historic site, bearing in mind that there is never just one possible storyline, one way of interpreting a particular place. Most historic properties are so rich in interpretive possibilities, in fact, having many stories to tell—many voices from the past asking to be heard—that programming can and should be continually renewed, frequently offering visitors new and different stories drawn from the same complex historical text that a house within its landscape represents.

Yet in spite of its centrality and importance to a proper understanding of any historic place, especially a house museum, the landscape story is the one most often left untold—or worse, told badly. The production of interpretive programming for historic houses and landscapes demands not just knowledgeable museum professionals, but creative historians, educators, and artists who approach the landscape itself and the narratives and images through which it is introduced to visitors as consummately a work of *design*, one intended to educate and delight at many levels. The audience visiting a historic house museum might even be compared to a theater audience—a crowd of strangers, metaphorically "sitting in the dark," bringing very different kinds of life experience and education to a "play" that they are invited to engage. At a house museum, that engagement is active and physical as well as intellectual, visual, and emotional.

Like any art, interpretive programming involves transformation—in this case the transformation of raw data, physical structures, and landscapes, the "facts" of history, into a compelling narrative rich in meaning for the lives of men and women, young and old, living at the dawn of the twenty-first century. When the interpretive program succeeds, visitors come to see the house and its landscape— curious relics of another world and another time—as vital, living presences whose stories are in themselves transformative, leaving minds and hearts and memories changed in lasting ways.

Notes

1. Quoted in Marshall B. Davidson, *The American Heritage History of Notable American Houses* (New York: American Heritage, 1971), 140–41.

2. Repton was the author of four illustrated books on landscape gardening, including *Sketches and Hints on Landscape Gardening* (1795) and *Observations on the Theory and Practice of Landscape Gardening* (1803).

3. Downing influenced American taste in landscape design through his popular magazine *The Horticulturist* and through a series of books, beginning with his *Treatise on the Theory and Practice of Landscape Gardening, Adapted to North America* of 1841, which went through four editions in twelve years and sold almost 9,000 copies.

4. Charles Birnbaum with Christene Capella Peters, eds., *The Secretary of the Interior's Standards for the Treatment of Historic Properties with Guidelines for the Treatment of Cultural Landscapes* (Washington, D.C.: National Park Service, Cultural Resource Stewardship & Partnerships, Heritage Preservation Services, Historic Landscape Initiative, 1996).

5. See, for example, Ada Louise Huxtable, "Inventing American Reality," *New York Review of Books* 39 (3 December 1992): 24–29.

6. David Lowenthal, *The Past Is a Foreign Country* (New York: Cambridge University Press, 1985), 214, 216.

CHAPTER SIX

THE HISTORIC HOUSE FURNISHINGS PLAN: PROCESS AND PRODUCT

Bradley C. Brooks

The historic house museum presents a familiar material context for interpreting history, a context that incorporates a diversity of elements, including objects, interiors, architecture, and landscape. None of these stands alone; the relationships between the elements—whether spatial, historical, or aesthetic—are of the utmost importance to the site's achievement of its interpretive goal. Indeed, it is largely in the integrity of these relationships that the site's interpretive potential lies. One of the furnishings plan's chief functions is to articulate what these relationships will be within the furnished historic interior. At its simplest, the historic house furnishings plan is a document that enumerates the objects within the museum's historic furnished interiors, describes their placement, and highlights their relationship to the museum's interpretation.

To maximize the effectiveness of its furnishings plan, a museum should approach it as both a process and a product. Central to the conceptualization and implementation of any historic house, the process of creating a plan—perhaps more accurately described as furnishings planning—helps structure research and guide decisions. As a product, the furnishings plan represents the distillation of its precursor, the interpretive plan, into physical settings, providing an important summary of historical documentation and staff decisions.

Thorough research must be the basis for decisions that shape the furnishings plan, but ultimately it must incorporate much more. A historic house's effort to re-create accurately a complex material culture vignette coexists with concerns about interpretation, conservation, visitor access, security, and board relations, to name but a few. These and almost every other aspect of museum operations will come to be acknowledged, explicitly or tacitly, in the selection and placement of objects.

Historic houses differ greatly in age, location, institutional size and structure, budget, staffing, interpretive strategies, and types of collections. Given the variety under the historic house umbrella, it is not surprising that a single, one-size-fits-all approach to the furnishings plan has not emerged. Plans are as variable as the sites for which they are written. While this flexibility serves well the diversity of historic house museums, it can lead to confusion about the content of the furnishings plan and its role in the museum. Despite the lack of a prescription to fit every situation, some general guidelines are useful in demonstrating the plan's potential not only to shape the appearance and interpretation of historic spaces, but also to allow them to better accommodate museum operations and the conflicting dynamics inherent in the historic house museum.

The Furnishings Plan and the Institutional Environment

Institutional size and degree of centralization are factors that play significant roles in determining the methods and procedures used to create a furnishings plan. A large organization's staff may have members whose responsibilities include researching and developing plans for historic structures, bringing both experience and specialized expertise to the task. Uniform structure and a comprehensive approach to research and documentation are often the hallmarks of plans developed by the National Park Service and other similarly large and far-flung organizations; the size, administrative structure, and geographic extent of such institutions demand standardized written furnishings plan procedures.

Furnishings plans for museums operated by smaller nonprofit institutions often face an entirely different set of circumstances. Frequently founded to undertake the development of a single structure or site, the smaller museum may lack the staff resources of larger organizations, or appropriate staff members may be unable to dedicate the large blocks of time necessary to develop a furnishings plan. In these cases, plan development can proceed in the midst of other tasks, or while partial implementation of the plan is under way.

Some institutions call on consultants to prepare some or all of the material their furnishings plans require. Although consultants provide the skills necessary for such projects, the results of their work may not be rendered in the format that will best serve the client's needs unless the museum has given sufficient thought to determining and specifying exactly what it wishes the consultant to produce.

The process of creating a request for proposals from potential consultants will help refine thinking about furnishings plans requirements, whether or not the museum intends to review multiple bids. The request should spell out in detail the scope of work expected of the consultant, including (at a minimum) essential background on the property, the goals of the furnishings project, the research materials to be reviewed, the components of the final report, its format, and a time schedule for production.

The least desirable—but not uncommon—scenario is that in which a museum has no written furnishings plan. When a new historic house museum is under development, the pressure of deadlines on staff can be intense. Working feverishly toward implementation, they may postpone a final compilation of the furnishings plan with the result that it is left undone as new priorities take its place. Without the touchstone of the plan, incremental changes can creep in more easily, leaving no documentation to assist those who come later in their efforts to sift through the exhibit's history. Years may pass while institutional memory slips away and a succession of staff members, still unable to commit time to completing the furnishings plan, remains confused and frustrated without the documentation necessary to answer fundamental questions about the exhibits they must manage. Years ahead, however, when the time comes to revise the furnishings plan, the effort required to compile it will pay off many times over.

Institutional size and resources affect a museum's approach to its furnishings plan, but political factors have their effect as well. As staff members advance the process of developing and implementing a furnishings plan, their work sometimes encounters a descendant or close associate of the site's builder or owner who holds a position of influence, often on the museum's board. Such an individual may be highly sensitive to implications of furnishing choices that are often overlooked or dismissed as insignificant by museum staff members charged with creating the furnishings plan. Staff members may feel that they bring to the project scholarly, detached—and hence, more historically accurate—analysis of materials and information that can have the most intimate personal meanings to individuals closely associated with the site, creating a situation in which conflict can be sharp and bitter. It is a naive staff member who proceeds with such a task assuming that professional training and experience make him or her the sole constructor of history. A wiser, and perhaps more accurate, view is for the creator of the plan to consider the descendant or associate one of the audiences for whom the plan is created, admittedly an audience with more direct power over the process, but one uniquely able to provide valuable input and support. In such cases, the timely opening of dialogue and establishment of common ground and goals for the site's furnishing and interpretation will better serve both parties.

Revising an established furnishings plan brings its own set of political and logistical complexities. Although the required research and resulting interpretive and furnishings plans may be complete, implementation may move slowly because of the availability of funding. As reinstallations move forward from their initial planning stages, a variety of well-established constituencies will come into play, each with its own needs and priorities. Board members, volunteers, interpreters, potential donors, various staff departments, and the public all may have stakes in the installation as it was and in the changes that will occur. Some should be a part of the dialogue during planning, while others should at least receive ongoing updates on the project's progress.[1]

Institutional size and governance affect the creation of furnishings plans through the broad, organizational cultures they foster; politics and institutional life cycles also leave their marks. Furnishings plans also vary according to the type of historic house for which they are written. In *The Interpretation of Historic Sites,* William Alderson and Shirley Paine Low divide historic houses and sites into three categories according to their primary interpretive goals: documentary sites, representative sites, and aesthetic sites.[2] Perhaps most common of the three historic house types, the documentary house focuses its interpretation on the specific history of a property, often on a particular individual or event. Historic houses that explore the lives of farmers, mill workers, or soldiers, for example, more often take the representative approach, interpreting historical periods or lifestyles rather than individual biographies or achievements. The aesthetic site, which interprets conceptions of beauty or the history of art, sometimes does so with limited emphasis on broader historical context.

Each category of historic house relates to its furnishings plan in a characteristic way; each is predisposed to emphasize certain criteria in object selection. Documentary historic houses are often expressive of contemporary architectural and decorative styles. Such a site frequently contains a high proportion of objects with provenances traceable to the property, or is furnished with objects that research has demonstrated are similar to those used there in the past. For example, the Spencer-Peirce-Little Farm, a property of the Society for the Preservation of New England Antiquities in Newbury, Massachusetts, was remarkable from the time of its building (about 1690) for its masonry construction in an area where frame houses were typical. The museum interprets a sequence of owners and inhabitants and the changes they made to their surroundings from the late seventeenth century to the early twentieth.[3]

The representative site, by its nature, is far less concerned with objects known to have been used at the property, or with their rarity or aesthetic qualities, concentrating instead on objects generally correct for the time, place, and socioeconomic level of the interpretation. Living history museums often use the representative approach. The De Vore Farm at the Old Cowtown Museum in Wichita, Kansas, interprets life on a Sedgwick County farmstead of the 1880s using a wide variety of domestic and agricultural artifacts. Representative interpretations are also popular for more traditional house museums such as the Old Place at The Heritage Society in Houston, Texas, which depicts life in an Anglo settler's cabin in 1824 in Harris County.

Criteria for object selection and placement in an aesthetic site can vary even more widely, depending upon the museum's developmental history and interpretive goals. As Alderson and Low point out, exact interpretive categorization of the aesthetic site can be rather elusive, as it often combines a house and objects of various periods with the aesthetic vision of yet another. Some often-cited examples such as Winterthur (the Henry Francis du Pont estate outside Wilmington, Delaware) and Beauport (Henry Sleeper's house at Gloucester, Massachusetts) expressed their creators' contemporary aesthetic statements using early American decorative arts. While the distinction between the meanings of the objects and their arrangements in interiors may sometimes be difficult to convey, the more clearly the museum articulates its interpretive goals, the more cogent the final product will be.

Furnishings Planning and Interpretation

Whether a site is documentary, representative, or aesthetic, or whether it is a developing museum or an established museum contemplating a major change in its interpretation, an interpretive plan and a furnishings plan are central to every one. At the heart of these plans is research, as William Seale emphasizes in *Recreating the Historic House Interior*, a publication indispensable to anyone involved in such an undertaking. Seale's book describes the many kinds of information the researcher should seek—from historical photographs to wallpaper fragments—and gives advice on its organization and use. *Recreating the Historic House Interior* stresses the importance of information contained in the structures themselves, and describes methods for documenting and analyzing this information. Other chapters discuss architectural and interior restoration, as well as the selection of furniture and furnishings[4] (fig. 6.1).

Of all the material in *Recreating the Historic House Interior*, perhaps the most significant is the chapter titled "The Report." The historic house report, says Seale, "is a synthesis of the research" and corresponds to an interpretive plan.[5] Not simply a compilation of research, it is a carefully crafted narrative that moves from historical background through proposed treatments for interiors, describing the property's interpretive purpose and the mechanisms by which that purpose will be conveyed. "Only when its historical *raison d'etre* is clearly articulated, and its means of expression carefully planned, can [the historic house] perform effectively."[6] Such an articulation is the purpose of the interpretive plan.

Figure 6.1. **View of the great hall of Oldfields, the J. K. Lilly Jr. residence, Indianapolis, Indiana, ca. 1934. Research using visual and verbal documents of all kinds is at the heart of the furnishings plan. Courtesy of Indianapolis Museum of Art.**

Alderson and Low agree, advocating the setting of primary objectives before beginning restoration work on any historic house-to-be, including determining the site's overall interpretive goal.[7] Ideally, the interpretive plan should precede the furnishings plan to allow for the adequate development of all pertinent research and its subsequent analysis and refinement. In reality, of course, a compressed schedule often dictates that the two plans be created simultaneously, demanding vigilance against the increased possibility for errors, omissions, and costly changes to completed work. Every furnishings plan is predicated on an interpretive plan, whether fully articulated and in written form or not. If furnishings planning must proceed without an interpretive plan, the museum should at least establish its core interpretive theme and develop supporting subthemes. These will frame and help support the work of the furnishings plan.

Interpretive goals and furnishings plans cannot be considered independent of one another, either in the context of a developing historic house museum or in the revision of an existing one. When a museum contemplates its interpretive goals, whether determining interpretive period, deciding its approach to treating controversial subject matter, or changing from one major interpretive category to another, it must anticipate the impact on its furnishings plan. Those creating the furnishings plan must remember that it exists so that the interpretive plan may be realized. A furnishings plan cannot be successful without the direction that interpretive planning provides, just as an interpretive plan relies heavily on the furnishings plan for the execution of its vision.

A case in point is Cliveden, near Philadelphia, the summer house of Benjamin Chew, chief justice of colonial Pennsylvania. In 1989 Cliveden received funding to support an extensive project to enrich and expand its interpretation.[8] Cliveden's experience demonstrates the importance of research to both interpretive planning and furnishings planning, and the degree to which the two are interrelated.[9] Although the Cliveden project was one of revising interpretive and furnishings plans, the importance of the relationships among objects, their meanings, and their placement applies equally to new furnishings plans.

The role that objects and their placement would play in a reinterpreted Cliveden was crucial from the beginning. In fact, the collection itself presented a significant given for the staff, a reminder of the ever-present political implications of interpretive and furnishings planning. However unlimited the interpretive reevaluation might be conceptually, staff members recognized that any interpretation that required the removal of the most notable objects from exhibit or that failed to celebrate the site's Revolutionary history would be unacceptable. Both were too much a part of Cliveden's institutional identity. Board members were justifiably proud of them and audiences expected to see them (fig. 6.2).

As the project progressed, curatorial work on the collections focused on research to expand the museum's knowledge about objects that had received less attention during the museum's development in the years preceding the 1976 bicentennial. The result of this initiative was a surprisingly large group of objects whose significance had more to do with Cliveden in the late nineteenth century than in the late eighteenth. When approached from a material culture standpoint without disproportionate emphasis on the objects of greater art historical significance, the collection became a richer interpretive resource, a more meaningful complement to the documentary record. Significant effort invested in basic curatorial research allowed a much broader range of objects to have a voice in the Cliveden story.

After analyzing the museum's rich historical resources, the staff determined that interpretation should focus on Cliveden's late-nineteenth-century occupants and their self-conscious effort to preserve the family's prominent place in Penn-

Figure 6.2. View of the parlor at Cliveden, ca. 1972. The inaugural furnishings plan at Cliveden emphasized the property's decorative arts collection. Photograph by Cortlandt V. D. Hubbard. Courtesy of Cliveden, a National Trust Historic Site, Philadelphia, Pennsylvania.

sylvania's early history, using objects and images that commemorated their ancestors and the notable events that took place at Cliveden.

The new interpretation required a furnishings plan to support it. Objects new to the exhibit, and new juxtapositions of objects previously on display, played important roles in the new interpretation. The museum staff changed room exhibits originally designed to highlight the decorative arts collections, creating installations that reflect late-nineteenth-century furnishing conventions and that re-create documented groupings assembled by the Chews. The new furnishings plan restored to prominent places objects critical to the Chews' presentation of family history, such as portraits and relics of the Germantown battlefield (fig. 6.3).

Cliveden's new interpretation added layers of complexity to the site's story by discussing it as an example of the malleability of history in the hands of rever-

Figure 6.3. View of the parlor at Cliveden, ca. 1915. Cliveden's reinterpretation and revised furnishings plan required a deeper understanding of the way the Chew family used objects for both utilitarian and symbolic purposes. Photograph by Chappell Studios. Courtesy of Cliveden, a National Trust Historic Site, Philadelphia, Pennsylvania.

ent family members, and by investigating the motives and methods of those who construct history. In so doing, the museum created an interpretation much more challenging than that which had concentrated on architectural and decorative arts history, one that effectively uses an expanded selection of objects to give Cliveden's story a more fertile and provocative context.

Contents of the Furnishings Plan

The example of Cliveden demonstrates the interrelationship of interpretive and furnishings planning and the importance of research to both. Research results should figure prominently in any written furnishings plan, but consideration of interpretive and operational issues along with the research will make the final document more useful and the museum more functional.

At the beginning of the process, some time spent planning for the plan will give direction and structure to research strategies that will in turn affect interpretive and operational decisions. Building lists of research sources (beginning with the most promising), oral history informants, and professional contacts will begin to demonstrate the scope of the work and hint at the time required. Even sketching an outline of key operational functions such as visitor reception, orientation, and tour routes will suggest how much space these will require and whether they will impinge on space that might otherwise be part of the historical interpretation. A projected budget will delineate the boundaries of possibility in many areas.

The Curatorial Component

The information that the furnishings plans should include can be broken into three broad categories: curatorial, interpretive, and operational. The primary purpose of the curatorial component is to describe the furnished historic interiors, list their contents, and present their historical and cultural context. In the course of completing this section the museum will answer questions such as these: What objects are necessary and appropriate to the interiors? How should they be placed? Can historic decorative textiles be used, or must the museum purchase new goods for window treatments and upholstery?

This part of the plan should include a brief treatment of the property's historical and architectural background with emphasis on the museum's interpretive period. Individuals associated with the property also require introductory information. Architects and builders, owners and occupants, as well as their families, tenants, slaves, and servants all played roles in making the property what it was. Much of what the museum has to say will be communicated through the lives of these individuals using the objects with which they surrounded themselves.

Of course, information about objects and interiors will have a prominent place in the furnishings plan. Each of the historic furnished interiors should be described and analyzed in a narrative making use of information on architectural and social history, decorative treatments (e.g., wallpapers or decorative painting), furniture and furnishings, typical usage, and, where possible, related documentary quotations or anecdotes from the interpretive period. For each interior, the plan should include a checklist of objects and their locations, along with a photograph and brief catalogue description of each item to be placed in the room. To make the plan as useful as possible for future users, it should include a brief note on the justification for each item's inclusion, whether it be a documentary reference or the curator's informed guess. Scale floor plans, elevations, and details of areas dense with objects, such as sideboards or parlor cabinets, are critical to provide a representation of the room's actual appearance with the objects in place. If specific documents, such as photographs, sketches, or letters, had great influence on the interior's configuration, the plan may include copies of them as well.

Expanding further on curatorial information, photographs and illustrations can reveal a building's structural details, provide evidence of a room's earlier appearance, or show contemporary design sources for furnishings. Notes on sources for object acquisitions and on areas requiring further research acknowledge that work on any historic house or site is not complete when the furnishings plan itself is done. Appendices and a bibliography make the plan more useful as a record and a research tool.

Curatorial concerns about protecting objects from the potential dangers presented by exhibit conditions in the historic furnished interiors must play a role in the process of furnishings planning, as well. These are discussed below as part of the plan's operational aspects.

The Interpretive Component

Interpretive issues, although central to the historic house's effectiveness, often receive secondary treatment in the written furnishings plan. This is unfortunate, as the furnishings plan is created largely to make possible a cogent and well-focused interpretation. The interpretive component of the furnishings plan should make clear the relationship between objects and interiors and the museum's interpretive message, demonstrating the ways that the former support the latter. The configuration of historic interiors and the selection and placement of objects are at once the physical expression of a historic house's interpretive plan and a substantial proportion of its interpretive potential. The better the furnishings plan supports interpretive intent, the more effective it will be.

While the curatorial section of the plan emphasizes objects, the interpretive section emphasizes the story—the historical narrative—that the museum wishes to present. Who were the people who lived here? What were their personalities and interests, their activities? What hardships did they struggle with? What were their accomplishments? In what ways were they representative of their time; in what ways were they innovators? Why are they significant?

Demonstrating the museum's answer to questions like these, the furnishings plan should reiterate the museum's interpretive goals and include for each interior a brief description of the interpretive themes to which it is linked, with discussion of the objects or arrangement of objects that make the link most clearly. The most effective answers will have explicit support from objects. This information, along with curatorial data and much of the research contained in the interpretive plan, will be necessary for training site interpreters and can be adapted easily for that purpose.

The interpretive techniques chosen for the museum will also affect the furnishings plan and museum operations. The decision to have fully guided, partially guided, or self-guided tours will have great influence on: the need for supplementary interpretive media, such as audio/visuals, graphics, labels, and pamphlets; lighting levels by which these may be read; and the need for barriers. Larger tour groups, small rooms, self-guided tours, or installations containing numerous vulnerable objects suggest the need for barriers and other protective measures, while small, guided groups can often enjoy interior settings without those intrusions. First-person interpreters may need to have a different kind of interaction with furnishings and visitors (perhaps supported by specially designated objects or reproductions) than will third-person interpreters.

Interpretive content and furnishings cannot be considered apart from one another; each guides the other. As interpretive content evolves, the furnishings plan must respond. The more detailed and specific the museum's historical narrative, the more the furnishings plan must move from a configuration generally appropriate to the interpretive period toward one with intricately devised material passages that relate to the story.[10] When Winterthur decided to re-create the chaos of an eighteenth-century drinking party depicted in Hogarth's *A Midnight Modern Conversation* in its 1986 Yuletide exhibit, the room setting had to include spilled punch, scattered wine bottles, and overturned chairs to convey the sense of riotous disorder altogether lacking in a generic room installation (fig. 6.4).

The Operational Component

The third category of information—operational concerns—comprises a wide variety of considerations not directly related to either curatorial decisions about the historical appropriateness of object selection or to issues of interpretation. The operational component of the plan reconciles tensions that may exist between museum operations and the historic furnished interiors. What will be the size of tour groups? Must the museum protect historic floor coverings with carpet pathways? Do dark interiors require supplemental lighting? Which locations expose objects to high risk of theft? Will barriers be necessary? While it may not be necessary for the final document to list or explain all of these items, the furnishings plan must accommodate the museum's solutions to these and similar concerns.

Figure 6.4. Furnishings plans rich in specific details may be needed to support the interpretation of human activities in progress. This room setting from the Winterthur Museum's 1986 Yuletide exhibit is based on the drinking scene depicted in Hogarth's *A Midnight Modern Conversation*. Courtesy of Winterthur Museum.

Daily museum operations such as tour logistics and security are critical to the success of a historic house and must receive consideration in the process of devising the furnishings plan. Not infrequently, such practical matters come into conflict with curatorial desires for object selection and placement, for interior lighting levels, and similar issues. This is almost inevitable, given that the historic structure is being made to serve as a museum, a function for which it was not designed. Balancing curatorial wishes and interpretive goals with operational requirements is a delicate but important task. It is better begun while the furnishings plan is in the process stages rather than as an afterthought to the product.

Perhaps the operational question that will have the greatest effect on the furnishings plan is the route that visitors will take while touring the property. Although closely related to interpretive matters, the tour route will have to respond to the location of visitor services such as ticketing and orientation, the size of rooms, doorway locations, and furniture placement. A tour route through a nineteenth-century parlor, for example, may conflict with the location of a center table. The museum must decide whether to move the table or adjust the tour route.

Accessibility concerns may affect the tour route as well. An alternate entry point or route around an obstacle such as uneven floors may be required to accommodate those with mobility concerns; the museum may need to adjust object placement to allow for effective viewing. Whatever choices the museum makes about directing visitors through the property and presenting its interpretation, the desired size and movement of visitor groups will have to mesh with object selection and placement.

Security is another operational concern that affects the furnishings plan. The museum must assess the risks that the historic structure and its furnishings plan present to visitors, staff members, and collection objects. Most importantly, the museum must protect human safety, taking steps to ameliorate hazards presented by constricted stairways, uneven floors, low light levels, low ceilings, and similar obstacles. The security of collection objects is also of concern. The furnishings plan must take into account collections security, keeping objects safe from theft and damage, out of easy reach, and safe from vibration and falls.

The furnishings plan should anticipate the environmental conditions in which objects will be exhibited. Adjustments to window treatments and object placement can lessen threats posed by the high light level common in historic structures. In the case of very fragile, light-sensitive materials, reproductions or replications may be an appropriate solution. Although it is often difficult to regulate relative humidity at absolutely stable levels in historic structures, effective improvement that meets the preservation needs of both collections and structures is sometimes possible, even without a climate control system.[11]

The Final Product

The physical characteristics of the furnishings plan—the product—deserve some comment. While still under development, the plan often changes frequently as new information comes to light, interpretive emphasis shifts, more appropriate objects become available, or as operational plans change. To keep it current, the plan's format must be easy to change, as well. A series of books in loose-leaf format with one book for each interior, each subdivided according to a uniform set of categories such as those suggested above, is a low-tech approach that will accommodate new discoveries or other changes. Electronic formats are similarly versatile, and technologies for integrating images with text are powerful tools for the furnishings planning process but may be impractical for some museums.

It may be necessary to produce a bound version of the furnishings plan for board or governing agency approvals, and hard copies of the plan as implemented will be necessary for reference. While it can be tempting to put the final bound version on the shelf with a sigh of relief and satisfaction, the furnishings plan itself should remain a living document, open to periodic review and revision as the institution matures. Once again, a loose-leaf or electronic format will serve better as the working copy of the plan because these formats can respond to future changes, whether unexpected or carefully planned.

When it combines curatorial, interpretive, and operational information with forethought and analysis, the furnishings plan is a tool whose potential uses extend far beyond the need to document object selection and placement in historic houses and sites. If created through a thoughtful process of carefully assembling and analyzing research and evaluating the many aspects of a site's curatorial, interpretive, and operational requirements, the furnishings plan will become a product with broad and lasting utility for the museum.

Notes

An earlier version of this essay appeared in *Proceedings of the 1996 ALHFAM Conference and Annual Meeting*, vol. 19 (1997), 167–73, a publication of the Association for Living History Farms and Agricultural Museums.

1. See John Lovell, "Re-interpreting the Historic Site Interior: A Few Observations on the Process and Politics of Re-installation," *Courier* (April 1997): 6–8.

2. William Alderson and Shirley Paine Low, *The Interpretation of Historic Sites* (Nashville, Tenn.: American Association for State and Local History, 1985), 12–19.

3. For more information on the Spencer-Peirce-Little house and its interpretation, see Nancy Carlisle, "SPNEA Takes a New Approach to an Old Building," in *Old Collections, New Audiences: Decorative Arts and Visitor Experience for the Twenty-first Century*, ed. Donna Braden and Gretchen W. Overhiser (Dearborn, Mich.: Henry Ford Museum & Greenfield Village, 2000), 74–79.

4. William Seale, *Recreating the Historic House Interior* (Nashville, Tenn.: American Association for State and Local History, 1979).

5. Seale, *Recreating the Historic House Interior*, 12.

6. Seale, *Recreating the Historic House Interior*, 14.

7. Alderson and Low, *The Interpretation of Historic Sites*, 8–12.

8. For a more detailed description of Cliveden and its reinterpretation, see Sandra Mackenzie Lloyd, "Creating Memorable Visits: How to Develop and Implement Theme-Based Tours" (chapter 10 in this volume).

9. I am indebted to Elizabeth Laurent, former curator of collections at Cliveden, for her assistance in providing information about Cliveden and the process of developing new interpretive and furnishings plans for the museum. For an in-depth treatment of the results of the self-study, see "Interpretive Development Plan, Cliveden of the National Trust, September 11, 1991" (photocopy, Cliveden files).

10. For more on this subject, see Nancy E. Villa Bryk, "'I Wish You Could Take a Peek at Us at the Present Moment': Infusing the Historic House with Characters and Activity" (chapter 7 in this volume).

11. Sandra Barghini, "Should We All Be Climate Controlled?" (paper delivered at the annual meeting of the American Association of Museums, Fort Worth, 1993). Barghini's presentation, part of a session considering alternatives to HVAC systems, discussed the use of fans, heaters, and humidifiers to control climate in the Hearst Castle at San Simeon, California. Recognizing the problems of maintaining constant levels of relative humidity in historic structures, conservators have investigated ranges of relative humidity acceptable for various materials. See Richard Kerschner's "A Practical Approach to Environmental Requirements for Collections in Historic Buildings," *Journal of the American Institute for Conservation* 31 (1992): 65–76. The American Institute for the Conservation of Historic Artistic Works and the Association for Preservation Technology International have developed and adopted the "New Orleans Charter for the Joint Preservation of Historic Structures and Artifacts" in response to the tensions that can exist between the needs of the two.

CHAPTER SEVEN

"I WISH YOU COULD TAKE A PEEK AT US AT THE PRESENT MOMENT": INFUSING THE HISTORIC HOUSE WITH CHARACTERS AND ACTIVITY

Nancy E. Villa Bryk

Historic buildings in Greenfield Village—a large outdoor museum close to Detroit that includes the homes of famous and not-so-famous Americans—have been reinterpreted and refurnished to present a specific moment in the lives of the inhabitants. The museum staff has moved away from furnishing houses in which *things* are the focus to homes in which *people* take center stage. Now these buildings are furnished to represent an evocative "moment in time," infused with things that can help interpret the variety of characters who lived within, their important relationships, and their activities. Full of details of everyday life, the buildings help bring the historical characters alive for more than half a million visitors each year.

The family of mid-nineteenth-century lexicographer Noah Webster of New Haven, Connecticut, understood the importance of describing everyday life and activities in their correspondence. Noah particularly treasured learning about the minute details of domestic life that he missed while traveling on business. His wife, Rebecca, reported the sweet scenes in long letters. She begins one particular letter to her husband with the phrase, "I wish you could take a peek at us at the present moment" and proceeds to describe her children's and grandchildren's activities, including "Mary sitting on the carpet by my side studying her Sabbath lessons" and daughter Harriet "drilling at her music."[1]

Other family letters sent to correspondents throughout New England also include descriptions of intimate scenes within the Webster house including granddaughter Mary "in the corner [of the parlor] . . . at her favorite amusement, sewing, because it keeps her quiet . . . and [grandson] William . . . driving around with his stick"[2]; elderly Rebecca Webster "enfeebled" but dutifully "engaged in quilting bed quilts [with only] two or three to finish"[3]; and Lucy Griffin, free black servant, taken ill as family members "sit with her"[4] until she can walk downstairs.

The letters are poignant reminders that while one story within the house certainly revolved around Noah's dedication to creating his monumental *American Dictionary*, the other story to tell is that of the complexity of the Webster household. The rich cache of Webster family letters, published and unpublished, points to intimate scenes of family life that were re-created for visitors, helping paint a particular picture of domestic life in middle-class New England. Visitors deserved to learn about the Websters as the staff had come to know them— frugal, charitable, energetic, sociable, opinionated, occasionally cranky, and openly affectionate. This was hardly the family depicted in a reinterpretation of the house in the 1960s in which the family was presented as austere, dignified, humorless, fashionable, and wealthy—hardly the Websters that are evident in the family letters.

The re-creation of vignettes within houses in Greenfield Village offers the chance for visitors to get an intimate glimpse of the inhabitants, enlivens historical characters within the historic homes by generating emotion and empathy in some visitors, and piques interest in the period and its activities in others. In Greenfield Village's historic homes, visitors may experience a variety of inhabitants and period activities and may discern important relationships implied in re-created vignettes. We try to determine how the house looked within a specific moment in the past, thus filling the house with period furnishings and accoutrements and characters' personal goods. Important activities are implied, as are key relationships within the household. Gone are the days of decorators' exquisite period furnishings and pristine environments. We no longer show the historic house as a period setting but instead emphasize life as it was lived within the historic context.

Re-created vignettes exist within a moment in time. Artifacts and reproductions together create scenes of a precise instant in which it appears as if the characters have stopped activities for just a moment and stepped out of the room. Visitors enter the room as it is set up in the midst of activity and feel as if they have stumbled across a drama unfolding.

What Is a Moment-in-Time Installation?

Theatrical and carefully arranged, moment-in-time vignettes generate messages about the characters, their relationships, and their activities. Thus, several rooms in a house may be furnished with scenes that could conceivably and logically occur at the same time. Houses that include these vignettes are full of objects, details, and ephemera and are visually complex. They generally include a combination of artifacts and reproductions. The latter are often examples of ephemera (newspapers, calendars, pamphlets, letters, advertisements, receipts and bills, broadsides) and clothing for which originals no longer exist but which were essential items in most homes. Sometimes activities are partially finished—a dress may be draped on the sewing machine, or a piecrust may await the rest of the sliced apples that sit in a bowl nearby, as in the Henry Ford Birthplace. There are usually few or no labels in the rooms because labels intrude on the reality of the environment. Instead, vignettes offer clear visual clues as to what is happening (the slices are clearly apples; the crust is realistic; a cookbook sits nearby). Of course, the interpreter within the house interacts with visitors and shares messages, too.

Carefully constructed vignettes in rooms can reflect the stories that convey messages about the characters who lived in the house. These vignettes are stories set within the larger story about the residence's main characters. These small scenes may reveal a trait of an inhabitant that helps us get the bigger messages across to our visitors. For example, in the Smiths Creek Depot in Greenfield Village, we address Michigan women's contributions to their local boys' comfort during the Civil War by re-creating a small ladies' aid meeting in the kitchen that features crates being readied for a shipment of knitted stockings, bandages, and shirts. Letters from local boys are in the kitchen, as are photos; shirts await assemblage; and the crates are in the midst of being packed. The story revolves around the ladies' aid meeting, but the message is that in rural Michigan, as in all parts of the country, Americans were affected by and involved in the war effort.

Why Re-create a Specific Moment in Time?

Moment-in-time installations help convey messages to visitors fairly effectively for a number of reasons. First, historic houses are naturally evocative and may be among the most effective settings for learning within a museum. The houses are fully "immersive"—visitors are drawn into realistic, richly detailed environments that may include period music or dialogue, have wonderful smells emanating from kitchen or hearth, and be interpreted by a costumed staff member. The moment-in-time installation takes this environment one step further, adding another detailed layer of household goods and ephemera that bring people's activities into the third dimension—clothing to show someone getting dressed, toys strewn about, rugs under repair (figs. 7.1 and 7.2). Traditional historic house interiors seldom reveal such activities. Some visitors spend a fair amount of time trying to take in the details of these visually dense interiors—from reading the 1930s reproduction newspapers pasted to the walls in the rural Georgia Mattox Farmhouse (fig. 7.3) to trying to determine who's winning the chess game set up in the boarders' sitting room in the Sarah Jordan Boardinghouse. Those who cannot immediately discern the activity in process tend to spend time studying it, asking questions, interacting with the interpreter. Visitors tend to linger, look, and discuss, discovering things about the people using the cues—generally not subtle—offered. The longer visitors spend looking and discussing, visitor studies show, the more likely they will take at least part of the interpretive message away with them.

Second, the scenes set up within the houses visually represent the stories we want to tell about their notable characters or events. Presentation in the buildings is essential, of course; however, we want to layer our messages using as many

Figure 7.1. This scene in the Noah Webster House implies that the Webster grandchildren had just torn through the parlor. Toys and a tea set (with raisins in the saucers, said to be a favorite of the grandchildren) are strewn under the sideboard. Courtesy of Henry Ford Museum & Greenfield Village.

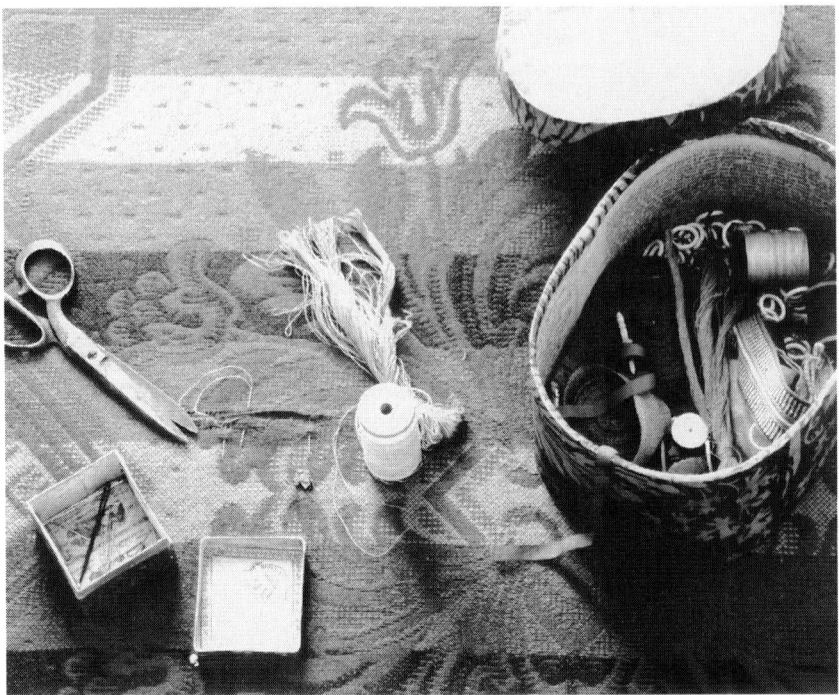

Figure 7.2. Detail of the carpet repair activity in the Webster House hallway. Courtesy of Henry Ford Museum & Greenfield Village.

methods of communication as possible. It is preferable to reflect the stories in what visitors *see* as well as what they *hear*, seeing activities depicted in real objects rather than only hearing them described. It is more likely visitors will remember what they hear if the scene in front of them helps them visualize the message the staff is sharing with them. For some, in fact, these scenes speak the loudest and are the images of domesticity, family, and character they take away with them. The more we can layer our messages using different methods of communication, the more likely those messages will be implanted within the memory of visitors.

Visual learners are particularly comfortable with the historic house environment because it tends to require less mediation to uncover meaning. Labels are not necessary to indicate that children lived within the Webster House because visitors see toys on the parlor floor. Most visitors understand that the Edison Menlo Park Library was a busy office when they see papers being processed, account books open, notes and receipts on bill hooks, and trash in the wastebaskets—the intent being to lead visitors to ask about or instinctively understand the

Figure 7.3. The parents' bedroom in the ca. 1930 Mattox Farmhouse from Bryan County, Georgia, represents preparations for Sunday churchgoing. Courtesy of Henry Ford Museum & Greenfield Village.

import of the inventor's business office. Visual learners who find it difficult to learn from labels in conventional museum exhibits may find the detailed historic interior invigorating—they are more likely to discern activity and learn something about characters from the created vignettes.

Furthermore, the house infused with character and activity moves the historic house from a memorial to one in which the characters or their household may seem more complex, believable, and even likable. Visitors want a glimpse of the lives of the characters within these buildings. At Greenfield Village, characters are depicted as real people with modest backgrounds, personal foibles and quirks, small bedrooms, messy desks, and endless chores. Visitors are fascinated hearing of and viewing small scenes in which young Henry Ford is tinkering with watches and old machinery parts. Some remark on the humble education of Orville and Wilbur Wright as reflected in the family's bookcase in their sitting room—it was the closest they got to college. Others are bemused by the rough-

and-tumble lifestyles of Edison's bachelor employees who loved pretty women and practical jokes, and who carried weapons. These traits make the characters less intimidating and more like you and me, and they help visitors be more sympathetic to hearing the stories of these great people who otherwise seem remote, even superhuman.

Placing additional characters within the house reminds visitors that great accomplishments often include the sacrifices and influence of others within the household. These are, after all, domestic environments, and neither Noah Webster, Henry Ford, nor the Wright Brothers were the only ones who lived in their homes. The Wright Brothers themselves surely would have acknowledged the encouragement of parents and their college-educated sister Katherine, whose unwavering confidence in her brothers' work on the airplane was truly inspirational to them. It is important to mention the contributions of those who ran the houses while the more famous inhabitants were elsewhere—Webster's wife, Rebecca, for example, and servant Kate Williams, who cleaned up after Edison's brilliant but messy bachelor employees in Sarah Jordan's Boardinghouse, where they stayed. These detailed domestic environments can address the relationships, situations, accomplishments, and sacrifices of the children, the servants, the enslaved, seldom-discussed women or mothers, and other significant members of the extended family.

Finally, this type of installation easily accommodates the addition of hands-on household activities, thus engaging the kinesthetic learner. Hands-on activities that reflect the experiences of those who lived within the house add a layer of sound and often smell to the rich environment. The moment-in-time installation also functions well as the backdrop to theatrical presentations, which move emphases from the furnishings and period objects to activities and characters.

The result is an installation that features real people in a believable setting during a second in the past. This installation method is evocative and nostalgic at times, affecting the heart as well as the head. Visitors enter the boyhood home of Harvey Firestone in Greenfield Village, smell the coal stove working, watch food preparation, walk into the sitting room (furnished so that our guests can roam and touch everything), stand before the dining room set for supper, peer into the formal parlor, and truly feel as if they are transported to another time and place. The evening we opened our 1930 farmer's home from Georgia to the public, an elderly gentleman felt so much a part of the re-creation of the Mattox family's parlor-sitting room, set for a checker game and boiled peanut munching, that he hopped the barrier, grabbed the hymnal off the mantel, and began to sing, much to the surprise, then awe, of those around him. The room transported that guest, and all those around him, to another place and time.

When Not to Re-create a Specific Moment in Time

Even if research indicates that the house in question may be full of interesting characters and lots of activity, there are situations when it might be unwise to set up these kinds of vignettes. Museum staff members designing the visitor experience should consider three things before adopting this method: the message they want to convey and whether re-creating a single moment can effectively communicate it, how they want visitors to feel about the inhabitants, and whether the emphasis for interpretation is on things or on people.

It may be unwise to implement a moment-in-time installation if the interpretation plan focuses on change over a long period of time. In this case, it would be very difficult to choose one moment in the house's history of habitation that can adequately illuminate the complexities of change. Instead, an institution may choose to minimally install such houses (as in Giddings House in Greenfield Village, for example). The houses are largely emptied of household furnishings that reflect specific periods because the visuals may sway visitors to set themselves within a period that detracts from the interpretive message. Then, the virtually empty house may be used as a flexible program space in which interpretation comes not so much from material culture as from the words and activities generated by the program presenters. Educators may utilize material culture from a variety of periods by bringing it out for a program and juxtaposing it in a way that helps visitors understand the message, then removing it when the program is over and readying it for another use. Characters' belongings, too, may be brought out as necessary to reflect the different inhabitants of the home at different times, but these too are put away when the program is over. Consequently, a house with a rich and deep story that encompasses many periods and characters, and whose message must reflect that change over time, may not be well suited to the relatively confining nature of the interpretation of a single era that a moment-in-time installation reflects.

Furthermore, the curator may believe that important information about the notable inhabitant is not communicated appropriately in a "lived-in" environment. Slightly unkempt environments, as well as those in which other characters take the stage with the notable inhabitants, are thought by some to take away from the dignity and importance of the notable inhabitants. The curator should, instead, furnish the house in a straightforward manner, neatly and without the implication of activity of others within the household. The famous character is thus positioned as larger than life—even extraordinary, dignified, and very much in control. Interpretation focuses on accomplishments and admirable qualities of the inhabitants rather than on their complex (and sometimes imperfect) characters or on activities that reflect life as lived. Similarly, any discussion of other characters pulls the focus away from that notable main character, raising questions about the roles of other inhabitants and diverting discussion into avenues not considered essential. These houses of great Americans, without other characters or period activities, commemorate and memorialize the historical figure at hand.

Additionally, historic house interpretations that focus on furnishings' styles, period decoration, or the building itself are not compatible with the moment-in-time installation. A sparse installation of furnishings is more likely to emphasize the structure that is the main topic of discussion. If period decoration and furnishing styles are to be the interpretive focus, deep layers of goods such as ephemera, food, or clothing placed on key furnishings may distract attention from the visual examination of the furnishings themselves as visitors focus on the scenes unfolding around them. Within the moment-in-time installation, where characters and their activities take center stage, household goods serve as a backdrop.

Connecting the Domestic Environment to Its Characters

Once the museum staff decides that a moment-in-time installation holds promise for communicating some of the institution's interpretive messages, it still may be difficult to see how the domestic environment can visually communicate significant messages about the house's notable inhabitant. In fact, the first step in devising a furnishings plan that re-creates a specific moment is determining how (or if) the domestic environment in question *can* illuminate the important accomplishments, activities, and defining relationships of the famous, or featured, inhabitant.

Planners should concentrate at first on determining the roles of the domestic environment and other household members in the lives of the notable inhabitant. Some of the following questions may help the curator make visual connections between things (house and environment) and people (the characters and their activities). Answering them will help the staff determine what objects can illuminate the personalities of the inhabitants, imply important relationships, and re-create activities.

Cultural Expectations

How does room use suggest that the family followed prescriptive literature regarding the home? Oral reminiscences indicate that widow Sarah Jordan carefully segregated her parlor from the boarders' parlor, probably an attempt to shield her young daughter from the coarse bachelors—propriety was important to her. They suggest that her parlor was likely set up conventionally to nurture her young daughter.

If the family did not follow the tenets of prescriptive literature regarding room decoration and room use, what does this suggest about this family? The Websters, elderly when they moved into the home now in Greenfield Village, eschewed formalities regarding room use, choosing instead to mix uses and rearrange furnishings to keep from climbing stairs or heating largely unused rooms. These particular mixed-use rooms are good spaces in which to interpret aging and sickness in early America.

Was the family self-conscious about presentation of self? The prominent Firestone family of Columbiana, Ohio, remodeled and enlarged their parlor and built their first true dining room (purchasing all new furnishings for the rooms in the 1880s). They appear to have been concerned about projecting just the right image of middle-class respectability and gentility.

Did the family use furnishings long after the items faded from popularity, and why? The Mattox family used thirty-year-old furnishings. This African-American family bought the pieces shortly after their house was built and handed them down to the succeeding generation. Economics prevented them from buying "new."

Nurture and Family

Were children permitted to explore and experiment within the home? Henry Ford's mother permitted him to repair watches in her dining room where the light was good, so Greenfield Village staff members re-created the repair bench in this seemingly odd place.

Were parents encouraging of intellectual discourse? The Wright family loved good arguments and so the museum staff occasionally re-creates these debates on the porch or in the parlor. Their remarkable family bookcase, now in the sitting room, includes the Wrights' schoolbooks. Books for pleasure reading include *The Origin of Species*, despite the family's conservative religious views. The Reverend Milton Wright thought it important to expose his children to diverse points of view.

Can you re-create scenes that reflect this intellectual interest, such as with a school lesson in progress? The Susquehanna House from St. Mary's County, Maryland, shows the sitting room center table arranged for a school lesson with the plantation tutor, circa 1860.

Adventure and Travel

Was the family provincial or cosmopolitan? What role did travel out of the region or country, or to expositions, play? Can an adventurous nature be reflected within the home? Castle Tucker in Wiscasset, Maine, includes a remarkable collection of souvenirs from the family's domestic and foreign travel and represents the Tucker family's keen interest in the world beyond New England.

How did this travel and adventure affect the inhabitants? The Henry Ford Birthplace contains souvenirs from William Ford's trip to the Centennial Exposition, where William saw the Corliss Engine and other wonders. His descriptions of the exposition further confirmed for young Henry Ford that there were exciting opportunities outside life on a Michigan farm.

Relationships

What relationships were important in forging the characters of the subjects? Did experiences—either loving and supporting or challenging and adversarial—with servants, grandparents, or siblings affect the notable inhabitants? The Noah Webster House depicts mentally disabled Louisa Webster's loving ministrations to servant Lucy Griffin in the room the two shared.

Would it be accurate to manifest the presence of these "other" characters in the house, thus implying their importance or impact on the character in question? Historic houses often feature servants' quarters. Colonial Williamsburg offers "The Other Half" tour that discusses the experiences of the enslaved in the grand white-owned homes.

Were bedrooms set up for use by extended family members, thus revealing something about relationships that are important in your interpretation? The Ford family welcomed grandparents' visits and the first-floor bedrooms were set aside for their use, reaffirming the warm relationships with his grandparents that Henry Ford expressed in his recollections.

Activities

What domestic activities can be re-created to convey an essential message? The Bliss parlor from Longmeadow, Massachusetts, re-created in the National Museum of American History's *After the Revolution* exhibit shows a house in disarray from inventory activities necessitated by the death of the male householder.

What activities and objects help reveal the uniqueness of the characters? The ingenuity of Thomas Jefferson is emphasized at every turn in his home, Monticello.

Are there scenes that visually communicate important activities associated with important characters in this building? The Motown Recording Studio of the early 1960s, re-created in situ on West Grand Boulevard in Detroit, was Berry Gordy's studio and his private home. Today, the dining room table is "set" with a scene showing studio workers readying dozens of 45 rpm records for shipment to stores.

Events or Traumas

Were there events—local, national, or both—that occurred during the occupation of this house that were pivotal in the maturation or careers of the inhabitants? The depression affected the already impoverished Mattox family of rural Georgia, and a moment-in-time installation highlights their resourcefulness during the 1930s by re-creating Carrie Mattox's quilting, sewing, and canning that she shared with neighbors.

Could depicting the events in progress or the aftermath of these events be helpful in conveying an interpretive message? Potential scenes include preparations for antislavery rallies, readying for political campaigns, or collecting funds for fire victims.

Researching People and Their Activities

The only way the museum staff can properly answer the questions asked above is through extensive research into all aspects of the inhabitants' lives. A good furnishings plan begins with a meticulous research plan. Most of us are not going to be able to find books already filled with details on the domestic lives of the inhabitants of our historic houses, and we must turn to primary sources for the bulk of our information. Archival research should begin with research on the building and its owners, including research in wills, census records, city directories, tax records, obituaries, newspapers, insurance maps, estate/inventory records, and other similar records.

Personalities, penchants, and proclivities are more difficult to ferret out but may be revealed in biographies, personal letters, diaries, and recollections of friends or the community. Family descendants may provide access to Bibles with inscriptions, private records and letters, diaries, oral reminiscences, and even recipes handed down that offer insights into ethnic food traditions. Other revealing primary source research may include scanning music books for favorite songs sung at special occasions and analyzing checkbooks and family receipts to learn about spending habits, food preferences, gift giving, book and toy buying, and far more.

Curators and interpretive planners should delve into the lives of all the characters associated with the house, including casual friends. (The owner of Tinker Swiss Cottage in Rockford, Illinois, dined with Oscar Wilde, for example, when the famous author was visiting Rockford during a lecture tour in 1882.) Unusual stories and relationships may unfold that were not obvious from the start. Letters and census records revealed that a fascinating group of inhabitants lived within the Webster household in about 1835, including the two elderly Websters; granddaughter Mary, whom they legally adopted as their daughter (Mary's mother died and the Websters were horrified by the promiscuous lifestyle of their son-in-law, removed granddaughter Mary from the home, and legally adopted her); their daughter Louisa, who was mentally disabled and may have had Down's syndrome; and a number of servants, including Lucy Griffin, a free black servant who lived with the family for many years. Visits from rowdy grandchildren were frequent and their antics were noted with regularity.

Understanding the context of the community is also vital. Community research encompasses everything from knowing specific information about the property and its history of ownership, to learning about the neighbors and the history of the community. Publications such as town newspapers, printed maps with descriptions of neighborhoods and houses, county histories, atlases, town histories, and histories of local churches that illuminate community connections are particularly useful. Especially significant is identifying important events that had local and national resonance, including fires, flood, famine, war, and economic depression. Researchers need to find out how these events affected the course of life of the house's inhabitants and the community.

Analysis of the family's surviving possessions, even if they are not in the collections of the institution, may also be helpful. Evaluate what newly purchased goods reflected about the family's taste, style, and economic situation. Analyze why some objects were used over a long period of time, were remade or patched, were poorly made, or were handed down within the family. Try to determine which goods were purchased locally and which were ordered by mail. What did the family send away for that was not available locally? More important, what objects did they order from larger cities a distance away when the same kinds of objects were available locally? Look carefully at the surviving objects to learn about the inhabitants' chores, hobbies, and leisure time activities (craft supplies, sports equipment, specialty clothing, or music books). Compare the family's prescriptive literature with what you believe to be the look and feel of the household.

Furthermore, what does the building, its physical arrangement, and its decoration reveal about how the family presented itself to others? Determine if the house was significantly remodeled, sketching changes in the physical floor plan.

Analyze why the family altered the house—more privacy, more room for children, more spaces for material goods (closets and pantries). Compare this house type to others in the region with owners of the same class, race, and ethnicity. Is it similar? If not, can the differences be explained? What do the differences suggest about this family?

Finally, once research has allowed museum staff members to develop a thorough understanding of the family and its social and cultural context, it is helpful to learn about other similar families in the region. Gathering more generic information on similar families may reveal much about acceptable or appropriate cultural and social expectations, typical room furnishings, and spatial arrangement of rooms as defined by culture, domestic activities, and fashions. Archival searches for regional cookbooks, pamphlets from social organizations and churches, photographs of compatible households, or diaries with descriptions of activities as well as purchases such as furnishings, clothing, reading material, Christmas gifts, and products may prove valuable. The furnishings curator will have to evaluate when more generic information is useful and when it does not fit with realities of the household being interpreted.

Creating a Furnishings Plan

The curator has finished researching legal documents. He or she has scoured archives for letters, photographs, journals, diaries, receipt books, and other unpublished primary sources related to the family. With the assistance of an architectural historian, the curator has analyzed the material culture of the structure. Furnishings have been located and analyzed and have helped the curator understand the family's choices and tastes over a period of time. The curator has asked and answered questions related to the inhabitants' relationships and personal domestic activities. And the curator has consulted sources such as photographs, reminiscences, ladies' decorator books, and mail-order catalogs to help eliminate gaps in knowledge. At this point, the curator believes he or she has an intuitive understanding of the mind-set and circumstances of the historical characters whose lives are interpreted in the house. How is all of this information pulled together on paper to create a furnishings plan?

The outline that follows should help start the process. Rather than beginning with furniture, it requires the curator first to determine the big idea that he or she wants to communicate within the house and then identify the secondary stories that will help illustrate that one big idea. The worksheet then prompts the curator to layer in furniture based on what was known to be in the house, what one surmises was likely in the house, and what should be in the house to communicate the stories about the inhabitants.

For each room in the house (including hallways, porch, and basement if furnished), create a worksheet that includes the following layers of information and furnishings suggestions.

1. *The main idea you want to communicate to your visitors in this house.*
   Write down the main idea you want the scene re-created within the room to convey.

2. *Objects documented to have been in each room.*
   List all of the specific furnishings and accoutrements that you know were in the room and used by this family and that you have noted throughout your research. These include:
   - furnishings that your institution owns that have survived intact with the home
   - documented objects that another institution owns or the family retains
   - objects listed on inventories
   - objects disbursed through wills
   - objects clearly seen in photographs or other portrayals of the room
   - objects described clearly in letters, receipts, etc.

3. *Furnishings that are likely to have been here but that are not documented.*
   Using your understanding of period furnishings, information gleaned from generic sources, and knowledge and intuition about the family, write down those furnishings not listed above that you believe the family must have had in the room to assist with basic human needs, as well as to fulfill social and cultural needs. List furnishings necessary to fulfill basic human needs, including:
   - sanitary wares for personal hygiene
   - accommodations for these wares such as a dresser, washstand, or shelf
   - bedsteads or pallets for sleeping
   - furniture or peg rail for clothing storage
   - fireplace or stove for cooking and warmth
   - fuel and cooking utensils.

   Include ephemeral goods that might not have survived the generations or might not have been listed in an inventory because they were of no value or belonged to the widow, such as:

- rugs or carpets
- towels, bedcovers, pillows, linens
- clothing.

List other furnishings you feel this room should include because they fulfill important social or cultural needs—important objects that reflect the family's taste and sense of self. These are things your *intuition* tells you should be there. These may include stylish goods that are not essential to survival but may be important for social positioning:

- etageres or shelving for display of expensive and stylish knick-knacks
- accoutrements for visiting or guest accommodation
- special furniture largely for entertaining such as center tables or coffee tables.

4. *Character-specific objects and preferences.*
    These objects include carefully chosen props or collection items that will help you flesh out your characters' essential personality traits and interests. Develop a list of such items for every person to be depicted within the room. Include the following:

    - clothing you believe the character likely owned that would communicate what you know about his or her style, panache, conservatism, economic and social status, age, race, or ethnicity. Think of goods for dress, undress, sports, and hobbies.
    - appropriate books (artifact or reproduction), prints, pamphlets, or newspapers that communicate ethnicity, religious affiliation, political affiliation, training or formal education, mentors or personal heroes, or important local events
    - small objects such as items of personal hygiene or domestic decoration that are compatible with what you know about the inhabitants' presentation of self
    - photographs of mentors, heroes, or family members who had great influence on specific characters. Consider placing them prominently to help interpretation focus on the relationship.
    - reproductions of personal letters, photographs, notes, recollections, or diaries that speak of people important to the notable inhabitant

> - ethnic or regional foods. Develop scenes showing the preparation of foods that reflect the family's cultural traditions and tastes.
> - important relationships that should be implied. Think about how one might juxtapose individual characters' objects to imply relationships and interactions relevant to the characters.

5. *Activity-specific objects.*

   List activities that reveal something about the character whose presence should be apparent within this room. Should these activities be complete or in process of completion (fig. 7.4)? Think about whether reproductions or collection items will work best. List all objects associated with activities such as:

Figure 7.4. This scene illustrates an audiotape recording in which Kate Williams, servant at Sarah Jordan's Boardinghouse, complains about her endless work in a house full of bachelor boarders. She is prepping a bed for a new guest. Courtesy of Henry Ford Museum & Greenfield Village.

- domestic duties of inhabitants, including servants' work
- notable inhabitant's trade or profession
- children's schoolwork
- play, hobbies, and leisure activities for all inhabitants, as well as social and political activities.

Determine if this house should be neat or a bit unkempt. If the matron was known to be a meticulous housekeeper, are cleaning and mending chores evident in more private areas? Do many people live here? If so, ensure that the house looks as if it can accommodate the requisite number of inhabitants and reflects the bustle and objects associated with many coming and going. Consider the kinds of objects that are needed to get these messages across:

- cleaning buckets
- many work smocks on pegs
- undergarments on the floor
- schoolbooks piled on tables
- laundry baskets filled with the family's dirty clothes, and so forth.

Determine whether domestic traumas, rites of passage, or significant local events can or should be played out within this room. List all of the artifacts that must be included in order to complete such a scene. These types of activities could be suggested by ephemeral items such as:

- newspapers announcing important events (armistice, for example)
- invitations
- small gifts
- menus
- pamphlets for local events
- foodstuffs for rites of passage.

Think about the season in which scenes are set. Objects that reflect the season and related activities, such as maple sugaring, sledding, hunting, summer picnicking, national patriotic holidays, and religious holidays immediately set the time of year and connote appropriate activities and traditions.

6. *Final story layer.*
   This final layer entails objects included specifically to assist the interpreters as they make key points within their presentations. They are

important visual references that bolster the interpreter's story. Your intuition may tell you they were not likely to have been there; however, they do not seem out of place nor anachronistic. Use them sparingly—just enough to give your interpretation a push. A few strategically placed objects can be useful for generating discussion.

- A print of the Corliss Steam Engine that Henry Ford's father William saw at the Centennial Exposition and described to young Henry now hangs in the Ford sitting room. Curators do not believe the picture was originally framed and hung in the sitting room, but doing so now generates discussion of the engine's impact on Henry Ford, who was so galvanized by its description that he vowed he would leave the farm to work with machines in the city of Detroit.

- Portraits of family members who built the house or of the patriarch of the family may be included to talk about his or her importance. Amos Mattox's portrait hangs in his rural farmhouse to prompt discussions about his family, his resourcefulness, and his work on the farm.

- Symbolic objects sit on mantels in Greenfield Village, carefully chosen to represent traditions, social conventions, or issues important to a particular family. These choices are occasionally provocative. The Bible half hidden on the mantel in the brick Slave Quarters from Hermitage Plantation is useful in generating discussions on literacy and religion among the enslaved.

After listing the types of objects for each room, the curator must carefully choose the appropriate objects to fulfill the needs of the furnishings plan in terms of style, condition, color, age, and material. Again, use your intuition.

Finally, the curator must place the chosen objects within each room. Room use and object placement are culturally defined, so examination of period photographs or descriptions of similar period rooms can assist the curator in suggesting a relatively accurate arrangement. Think, too, of what is known about the physical nature of the character. How old is he or she? Sprightly? Infirm? Tall? Sit down and see what they could have reached, or stand at their approximate height and surmise the height of the mirror. Object placement requires delving into period preferences for use and arrangement of domestic spaces, understanding the peculiar circumstances of the specific activity, knowing the physical realities of the characters, and using one's own logic, imagination, and intuition. Realize that it is likely two curators will not come up with the same spatial arrangement using the exact same objects within a room.

A Word to the Cautious Curator

This fully furnished, theatrical method of interpreting the lives of a house's inhabitants is not for the faint of heart. It involves some risk taking. It requires the interpretive team to figure out what activities and relationships must be re-created visually within the house to bolster verbal interpretation, and whether or not they can be thoroughly documented. Indeed, sometimes the scenes that best tell the important stories are not precisely described in sources; however, the interpretive team may suggest setting them up to get the message across. In these cases, the curator must fill the void with educated guesses to successfully implement the vignettes. This may be difficult to do considering that most curatorial training emphasizes following documentation precisely and literally.

Needless to say, putting words in notable inhabitants' mouths, re-creating activity, or placing items in their rooms must be accomplished carefully and thoughtfully. Creating historical vignettes compels curators to imagine activities or events that likely occurred within the home but that are not documented. It then asks the curator, without knowing precisely what the characters would have chosen, to use insight and reason to furnish rooms in ways that seem compatible with the family's circumstances. It requires the curator to possess a *disciplined imagination* and an *intuition* about the characters whose lives are being interpreted.

What do these terms mean? Applying disciplined imagination is using one's deep knowledge of the period and domestic history and technology to place within the house objects that are implied by descriptions of characters or activity. We imagine it should be there, but it is not discussed. We are not indiscriminate in putting things in the house that we want to be there; instead, we are disciplined by our understanding of the circumstances of these historical characters and include only those artifacts and reproductions that do not misrepresent them, their relationships, or activities.

Years of research on their subjects help historic house curators know a house's inhabitants so well that they may feel comfortable filling in small details appropriate to illumination of the larger, three-dimensional picture. Extensive research and deep understanding of the historical characters and their circumstances help develop a gut feeling about what is appropriate to use and what must be left out. It is not unlike putting words into the mouths of historical characters when creating historical fiction. The script is often crafted to reveal a truth or send a message using words that we do not know that the characters ever said, but that the author feels are appropriate to hear from the character. Carol Kammen, whose regular column titled "On Doing Local History" is featured in the American Association for State and Local History's *History News*, relates the importance of taking risks and carefully crafting and using words, actions, or objects that are not documented but that can help us tell important stories. Ms. Kammen's statement below refers specifically to Colonial Williamsburg's controversial, re-created slave auctions and the activities and first-person interpretation that constitute living history:

> All of these events were drawn from the historical past and brought to life with words that cannot necessarily be quoted from the sources. After years of researching, learning, and reading, there are some things that the local historian knows about a place that are not documented and cannot be verified. . . . Local history must use every opportunity to meet myth with truth; to present the past with the complexity of life itself. Sometimes fiction provides an important way to speak truth about the past.[5]

If we do not take those risks, putting appropriate words in our historical characters' mouths or things in their rooms, we may be misrepresenting their lives yet again, perpetuating myths we all work hard to dispel.

Research about the Webster home and its inhabitants revealed that African-American servant Lucy Griffin was cared for in an upstairs bedroom on those frequent occasions when she took ill. Lucy and the mentally disabled Louisa Webster were loving companions, and it appears they shared the same room upstairs when Lucy was infirm (fig. 7.5). The interpretive team determined it would be valuable to show the family's care and concern for their beloved servant, and the interpretive plan called for a furnished sickroom. How does the furnishings curator accomplish this? We know nothing about the ministrations to Lucy. Was there a bedside table? Probably. If it was there, do we know what sat on it? No. If the curator wants to re-create the sickbed scene, it seems reasonable to install a table for the invalid near Lucy's bed. Genre paintings of similar scenes provide a starting point.

Genre paintings don't offer much information, so I use my disciplined imagination, based upon my knowledge of period objects, the characters involved, and the needs of invalids to paint the rest of the picture of what should be on such a table. After considerable thought, my "wants list" of furnishings includes a tablecloth, lighting device, tray, teapot, hot pad, cup and saucer, vessel for drinking liquid medicines, spoon, medicine bottles, pills, towel, and Lucy's personal items.

Figure 7.5. The sickroom is set up to accommodate both free black servant Lucy Griffin and Noah Webster's daughter Louisa. Courtesy of Henry Ford Museum & Greenfield Village.

Next, I need to implement the furnishings plan and choose the style and material of the objects. To do this, I call upon my intuitive understanding of the historical character's mind-set under such circumstances, including spending habits, personal style, age, ethnicity, race, regional availability of goods, and personal penchants that might affect their choice of goods. We do not know if we are right in our choices; instead, our intuition guides us in choices based on our deep understandings of these inhabitants. So, what does my intuition tell me should be on the bedside table in Lucy Griffin's sickroom?

Intuition suggests that Rebecca would have given Lucy Griffin things that were made decades prior (the Webster's married in 1789 and appeared to purchase few new things for their home in the 1830s), were well used and not the "best" goods (they're giving them to the servant), were not too fragile (Rebecca probably realized things could easily slip from reach across the bed), and were simple in form (the family was plain and practical). Any textiles should be the kind that Rebecca Webster, known as someone who "drove the needle," could make. Therefore, I choose a plain, early-nineteenth-century New England table, a handwoven check wool tablecloth, a pewter candleholder, a pewter tray, a simple late-eighteenth-century pewter teapot, a pieced and quilted hot pad, an older agate ware cup and saucer, a pewter cup, a horn spoon, glass medicine bottles, early manufactured pills in packages, a small linen towel, a wide-toothed wooden comb for thick hair, and a small handmade linen towel. I believe my intuitive understanding of the family, guided by extensive research and assessment of this particular scenario, has directed me in making the right choices (fig. 7.6).

Figure 7.6. Detail of the table next to the sickbed of infirm servant Lucy Griffin. Courtesy of Henry Ford Museum & Greenfield Village.

In sum, a historic house can be so much more than a period installation that is slavishly true to archival information but that reveals little about the important inhabitants. These environments instead can be layered with theatrical vignettes, carefully and imaginatively constructed to visually reveal ideas as complex as character, activity, and relationships. With the assistance of able interpreters, important messages have visual as well as verbal impact. The house interior then moves from a story about things to a home about people, communicating life as it was lived, not interiors as they were decorated. Such houses, accurately furnished and infused with character and activity, can take visitors to places they never imagined they could visit, capturing their hearts as well as engaging their minds. Do not be reticent about using your imagination and intuition—it is worth the risk. Create your own moments in time, and encourage visitors to peek in on those historical characters whose lives we have the responsibility and the honor to share.

Notes

1. Rebecca Webster to Noah Webster, New Haven, Connecticut, July 1824.
2. Rebecca Webster to Noah Webster, New Haven, Connecticut, n.d.
3. Noah Webster to Harriet Webster Fowler, New Haven, Connecticut, 27 June 1835.
4. Rebecca Webster to Emily Fowler Ford, New Haven, Connecticut, 5 April 1839.
5. Carol Kammen, "Truth and Fiction," *History News* 51 (Spring 1996): 4.

CHAPTER EIGHT

BALANCING OUR COMMITMENTS: ACCESS AND HISTORIC PRESERVATION

Valerie Coons McAllister

In a recent *National Register Bulletin*, interpretive consultant Ron Thomson and historian Marilyn Harper argue that "education is and always has been central to historic preservation in the United States. . . . [We] have cared about preserving historic places because they teach us and our descendants about who we are and where we came from." Providing opportunities to interact personally and meaningfully with historic properties and artifacts is key to fostering public appreciation for places and things historical and essential to continuing and expanding historic preservation efforts.[1]

To support their point, Thomson and Harper refer to the preamble of the National Historic Preservation Act of 1966, which states that "historic places are being preserved as living parts of communities nationwide in order that they can continue to teach *all* Americans [emphasis mine] about their past and help them better understand the present that has grown out of that past." The commitment to historic preservation in the United States, then, is based on a belief that historic places have something to teach and inspire everyone and that opportunities to enjoy and learn from historic places should be available to all who wish to pursue them.[2]

This inclusiveness and commitment to widespread participation is also at the heart of the Americans with Disabilities Act (ADA) of 1990. The ADA is far-reaching civil rights legislation that affirms the right of all people, regardless of disability, to equal participation in American society. With the law's passage, access to historic properties open to the public became a civil right.[3]

What does this mean for historic house museums and sites, whose architectural and historical integrity we are committed to preserve? Is it possible to achieve accessibility and maintain historic character and significance? The answer

168

is yes, if we know how to balance our dual commitments to historic preservation and access. As complex and challenging as it may be to strike that balance, it is essential to fulfilling historic house museums' and sites' missions as public educational institutions. We must address the needs of a broad spectrum of visitors representing a rich diversity of backgrounds, life experiences, interests, education, languages, learning styles, and communication preferences. Included among these are visitors with physical, sensory, and cognitive disabilities.

Meeting the needs of a diverse audience—creating opportunities for all visitors to make personal connections and enjoy meaningful experiences—is really the goal of successful interpretation, too. Many of the same tools, techniques, and teaching aids that improve access for visitors with disabilities make interpretation more engaging and effective for everyone. When embarking on the process of ADA compliance, such programmatic measures are an important part of improving access at historic houses and sites.

Compliance may also require making structural or physical changes, and these are naturally of great concern to historic preservation professionals. What types of changes does the ADA require? What impact will such changes have on historic character and significance? Before addressing these issues, it may be helpful to review the Americans with Disabilities Act and the National Historic Preservation Act to see what the two mandates require and how they relate to one another. As we do so, bear in mind that these federal regulations represent only one part of the picture. State and local access and historic preservation codes also exist, and it is important to be familiar with those that apply to your site. In several instances, state or local regulations exceed the federal requirements and therefore prevail over them.

The Americans with Disabilities Act of 1990[4]

The Americans with Disabilities Act prohibits discrimination against people with disabilities[5] in all major areas of life, including employment (Title I), state and local government services (Title II), public accommodations and commercial facilities (Title III), and telecommunications (Title IV).[6] Of these, Titles II and III are most relevant for museums and historic properties, with Title II covering sites overseen by a state or local government agency and Title III covering privately operated sites.

In contrast to past accessibility laws, which called for individuals with disabilities to prove discrimination, the ADA places responsibility for providing access squarely with employers and service providers. If discrimination on the basis of disability is charged, employers and service providers must prove that they have provided reasonable access.

Integration and independence are hallmarks of the Americans with Disabilities Act, reflecting another philosophical shift from previous legislation. Whenever possible, individuals with disabilities must be afforded independent access and accommodated along with nondisabled people. Assisted access and separate accommodations are no longer acceptable substitutes for inclusive, integrated services and programs, unless equal access can be achieved in no other way.

The ADA is clearly focused toward a future in which access is the rule rather than the exception. With regard to building and site access, for example, most ADA regulations apply to new construction and alterations and to plans for such. Existing facilities are covered in a more limited way. Very pragmatically, the law acknowledges the difficulty, cost, and complications often involved in retrofitting existing facilities, including the special challenges that historic properties present. It recognizes that individual circumstances demand individual solutions and therefore makes no attempt to mandate a single approach for all.

Because finding the best solution to access problems often requires exploring a variety of options, the ADA includes provisions to facilitate planning and decision making. For example, the law advises consulting people with appropriate expertise before finalizing or implementing access plans. With regard to historic properties, the ADA states that "interested persons should be invited to participate in the consultation process." Gathering input from individuals with expertise in historic preservation and in accessibility, including individuals with disabilities, increases the chance of finding access solutions that work.[7]

Another important recommendation (or requirement, in the case of Title II properties) is to develop a comprehensive plan for achieving access. Based on a thorough evaluation of current accessibility and on a clear understanding of ADA requirements and state and local regulations, such a plan enables a historic site to prioritize projects, target limited resources, and document decisions. A formal plan can also indicate a good-faith effort to comply with the law.

Voluntary compliance with the ADA, as opposed to litigation and court-ordered compliance, is strongly encouraged. To that end, the government agencies charged with enforcing the ADA[8] launched an extensive public education effort, making available a wealth of informational materials and establishing a network of technical assistance agencies. These resources offer valuable assistance and support, clarifying legal requirements and suggesting specific options and methods available to improve accessibility. Consistent with this approach, the Department of Justice and other enforcement agencies will respond to complaints by undertaking a thorough investigation and engaging in discussion and negotiation with the parties concerned. Litigation is not considered desirable or, in most cases, necessary.[9]

Title II: State and Local Government Services

Museums and historic properties administered by state or local government entities must comply with Title II of the ADA. These properties are required to provide program access, meaning they must ensure that people with disabilities are not excluded from services, programs, and activities because of inaccessible buildings or discriminatory policies or practices, unless doing so would result in a fundamental alteration or undue financial or administrative burdens.[10] "Fundamental alteration" means that the modification required for access is so significant that it alters the essential nature of the service, program, or activity being made accessible. "Undue burdens" are modifications that entail significant difficulty or expense, determined by carefully assessing each proposed modification and its impact in terms of cost, operations, and available resources.[11]

For existing facilities covered under Title II, program access need not require structural changes unless alternative methods, such as relocating the inaccessible program, prove ineffective. On the other hand, there may be instances when only structural changes will effectively achieve access. It is important to look at each program, service, or activity individually to determine the best means of making it accessible. Physical changes may be relatively simple and inexpensive, such as installing a ramp or adding a handrail, or they may be much more extensive and costly. All physical modifications must comply with the ADA Standards for Accessible Design (also known as ADA Standards or ADAAG, the ADA Accessibility Guidelines) or with the Uniform Federal Accessibility Standards (UFAS).

Title II also requires that covered entities conduct a self-evaluation of all programs, services, and activities to identify any physical or policy barriers that may limit or exclude participation by people with disabilities. From that self-evaluation, they must develop a transition plan outlining physical changes necessary to achieve compliance.

As noted earlier, new construction must be accessible, as must any alteration that affects the usability of the facility. Plans for new construction and alterations must comply with the ADA Standards or with the UFAS. All accessible features and equipment must be maintained in order to remain in compliance with the ADA.

Title III: Public Accommodations and Commercial Facilities

Privately administered and operated museums and historic properties, whether for-profit or nonprofit, are subject to the requirements of Title III. Under Title III, covered entities must:

1. Provide goods and services in an integrated setting—one in which people with and without disabilities can participate together—unless separate or different measures are necessary to ensure equal opportunity. To illustrate, a tour that is simultaneously presented orally and in American Sign Language (ASL) may accommodate the needs of deaf and hearing visitors together. Similarly, a tour that incorporates tactile or hands-on opportunities and vividly descriptive language may serve people with and without visual impairments equally well. On the other hand, if the tactile experience utilizes artifacts that are too rare or fragile for all visitors to handle, selected artifacts may be offered only to visitors who are blind or have low vision. When a separate or different program is the best means of ensuring equal access, no surcharge or special fee may be charged for the program, nor can a person with a disability be required to use the separate program rather than the standard program.

2. Review policies, practices, and procedures to determine if any of them exclude or limit the participation of people with disabilities. If identified, such practices must be reasonably modified, unless reasonable modification would fundamentally alter the nature of the goods, services, and programs offered. If a site has a no-animals policy, for instance, a reasonable modification of that policy would be to allow service animals such as guide dogs, hearing dogs, or other assistance animals. When "no touching" is the norm, offering tactile experiences for blind visitors would be a reasonable policy modification.

3. Provide auxiliary aids and services when necessary to ensure effective communication, unless such auxiliary aids and services would result in an undue burden or in a fundamental alteration. Sign language interpreters, captions, transcripts of oral or video programs, audiotapes, and large-print materials are examples of auxiliary aids and services that facilitate communication. This is a very flexible requirement in that the ADA does not mandate particular types of auxiliary aids for particular situations. For example, braille labels need not be installed alongside printed labels if effective communication with blind visitors can be achieved by an alternative method, such as audiotapes or other recordings.[12]

4. Remove physical barriers, if it is readily achievable to do so. Physical barriers include architectural barriers, as well as communication barriers that are structural in nature, such as signage and pay phones.

"Readily achievable" means "easily accomplishable and able to be carried out without much difficulty or expense"—in other words, cheap and easy.[13] Determining if barrier removal is "readily achievable" requires a careful assessment of cost, operational impact, impact on significant historical or architectural features, and available resources. Readily achievable barrier removal is a continuing obligation: what is not readily achievable today may become so in a year or two if cost, operational impact, program priorities, or resources change. As with Title II properties, physical modifications must comply with the ADA Standards.[14]

5. Provide readily achievable alternatives to barrier removal when barrier removal itself is not readily achievable. For example, an audiovisual tour of inaccessible spaces might serve visitors with disabilities in the short term until barrier removal becomes readily achievable and, under the continuing obligation provision, must be undertaken.

6. Comply with the ADA Standards to the greatest extent feasible when planning and implementing alterations that affect the usability of the facility. Alterations to primary function areas (areas where major activities take place) must include an accessible path of travel from the altered area to the entrance.[15]

7. Design and construct new facilities to comply with the ADA Standards.

8. Maintain accessible features.

The continuing obligation to remove barriers as their removal becomes readily achievable offers one convincing reason to establish a long-range access plan, which incorporates periodic reevaluation of barrier-removal projects. The process of developing a comprehensive access plan is also a very effective way to learn exactly how accessible a site and its programs are and what modifications or improvements are required to achieve compliance. Furthermore, it affords an opportunity to consult persons with expertise in accessibility, historic preservation, and interpretation and to gather input from individuals with various types of disabilities. Such advice and assistance are invaluable when determining which of several options for modification will work best in a particular situation, or when deciding among several methods of improving programmatic access. Given most museums' and historic properties' finite resources, compliance ordinarily must take place over several years. A formal, written plan, appropriately prioritized, offers direction and guidance throughout the compliance process and allows for careful allocation of money, staff, and time.

Title III recommends, but does not require, that public accommodations develop a long-range access plan. To assist with that effort, Title III suggests four priorities for barrier removal in existing facilities:

Priority 1: Getting in the front door. This includes parking, the route or path of travel from the parking area to the primary entrance, and the entrance itself.

Priority 2: Access to goods, services, and programs. Basically, this is "access to whatever happens once a visitor is in the front door."

Priority 3: Access to rest rooms.

Priority 4: Access to everything else.

In the early stages of planning for ADA compliance, it is easy to feel overwhelmed by all that needs to be accomplished. These suggestions can help public accommodations staff to focus on those areas that the ADA considers important to address first.

The National Historic Preservation Act and Historic Preservation Provisions of the ADA

Declaring that "the preservation of [our nation's] irreplaceable heritage is in the public interest" and that "its vital legacy. . . . [should] be maintained and enriched for future generations of Americans," Congress passed the National Historic Preservation Act in 1966. Among its provisions, the act established the National Register of Historic Places and the Advisory Council on Historic Preservation. It defined the historic properties and historic resources it preserved as "any prehistoric or historic district, site, building, structure or object included in, or eligible for inclusion on the National Register, including artifacts, records, and material remains related to such a property or resource."[16]

The National Historic Preservation Act protects significant features, materials, and spaces of designated historic properties—in other words, those features, materials, and spaces that define the properties' historic character. Physical alterations, for access or any other reason, that would threaten or destroy significant features should be avoided. This does not mean that the law prohibits all physical alterations to historic properties, however. To determine what is protected under the law, it is essential to know what features, materials, and spaces contribute to the property's significance and define its historic character.[17]

Much of the language of the National Historic Preservation Act (NHPA), as well as the process it established for reviewing and implementing changes to historic properties, were incorporated into the Americans with Disabilities Act.

As a result, the ADA shares with the NHPA a commitment to protecting the character and integrity of historic properties and mandates no action that would threaten or destroy historically significant features. Properties protected under the NHPA—in other words, those that are listed or eligible for listing on the National Register—or properties that are designated as historic under appropriate state or local law are termed "qualified historic buildings or facilities" under the ADA.

The ADA's General Rule regarding alterations to qualified historic buildings requires that they must comply with the same standards as alterations to nonhistoric properties unless it is determined that such compliance would threaten or destroy the historic significance of a feature of the building or facility. The review process through which such a determination may be made is based on the Section 106 process established under the National Historic Preservation Act. This process, which applies to federal, federally assisted, or federally licensed undertakings, requires that the Advisory Council on Historic Preservation be given reasonable opportunity to comment on the effects of the undertaking on properties listed in or eligible for listing in the National Register prior to the undertaking being approved. Under the ADA, proposed alterations to qualified historic buildings subject to NHPA Section 106 must follow that process, seeking comment from the Advisory Council on Historic Preservation or from the State Historic Preservation Officer (SHPO). Alterations to qualified historic buildings *not* subject to Section 106 follow a similar review process, seeking comment from the State Historic Preservation Officer. Other interested persons (state or local accessibility officials, individuals with disabilities, and organizations representing persons with disabilities) should also be invited to participate in this consultation process. If the Advisory Council or SHPO agrees that complying with the General Rule would threaten or destroy historic significance, less stringent alternative requirements may be used for the alteration affecting that feature of the building or facility.[18]

In very rare instances, even the alternative requirements may be found to threaten or destroy historical significance. When the Advisory Council or SHPO agrees that this is the case, structural changes need not be made. Instead, alternative methods may be used to provide access, such as an audiovisual presentation of the inaccessible space.[19]

Balancing commitments under the National Historic Preservation Act and the Americans with Disabilities Act amounts to providing the highest possible level of accessibility while minimizing impact on historically significant features and materials. The ADA's historic preservation provisions, so clearly consistent with the protections afforded under the National Historic Preservation Act, offer guidance and assistance to support these efforts. By becoming aware of what the ADA and applicable state and local laws require, carefully evaluating current accessibility, and planning necessary improvements in consultation with appropriate parties (including individuals with disabilities), striking that balance may be less difficult than originally supposed.

Case Study: Old Sturbridge Village[20]

For many years, Old Sturbridge Village (OSV) has made a priority of balancing accessibility with its living history mission and historic preservation concerns. Old Sturbridge Village is a re-created nineteenth-century New England town, where the landscape, roads and paths, gardens and fields provide a setting for historic buildings relocated from various parts of the Northeast. Within this setting, museum visitors engage in hands-on history, interacting with costumed interpreters to learn about traditional farming, craft processes, household and domestic activities, and early music and entertainment. The museum's mission to re-create a slice of history provides the context for determining how best to comply with federal, state, and local accessibility laws. In the language of the ADA, this mission defines the "essential nature" of the Old Sturbridge Village experience.[21] As such, it informs every decision about access within the historical environment, including the barrier-removal options OSV staff members consider.

The first two priorities for barrier removal, recommended by Title III, provide a useful framework for discussing several common physical and programmatic barriers to accessibility. Decisions about removing those barriers require careful consideration of several issues, questions, and possibilities, some of which are presented here within the context of Old Sturbridge Village.[22]

Priority #1: Getting in the Door

Enabling visitors with disabilities to get from the parking area to and through the entrance door is considered a primary objective for public accommodations. While historic preservation is not a concern when evaluating paved parking areas, other issues are very important to consider. Beyond the parking area, "getting in the door" becomes much more complicated, as does the challenge of balancing access with a living history mission. More than forty historical exhibit buildings situated on 200 acres make it necessary for Old Sturbridge Village staff to address this priority repeatedly and in a variety of ways.

Parking

Have accessible parking spaces (including van-accessible spaces) been designated in an appropriate location, as short a distance as possible from the accessible entrance? Are they clearly marked, with code-compliant pavement markings or signs? Are the spaces available in sufficient number? In addition to consulting the ADA Standards, it is important to check state and local parking regulations.

Accessible Route

The route connecting accessible parking spaces to an accessible building entrance may also be free of historical considerations, as is the initial route visitors must travel at Old Sturbridge Village. Level, well-maintained paved walkways with required curb cuts lead to the level entrance of the modern visitor center, the OSV's primary ticketing and orientation facility. Upon leaving the visitor center, however, visitors enter the re-created historical environment, where "accessible route" assumes a much more complex and challenging meaning.

Within the re-created village, roads are unpaved in keeping with a nineteenth-century environment. In most areas, the roads are level or gently sloping; in some locations, steeper grades can be found. Roads and paths are, of course, highly susceptible to weather conditions. In the past, they have presented a significant barrier to access, particularly for wheelchair users or others with limited mobility. In recent years, however, the OSV maintenance staff has experimented with a variety of road mixes and surface treatments and has made tremendous improvements in access. Today, the mix used is a combination of various size stone aggregates, sand, and stone dust, applied in layers to promote drainage and then "crowned" to facilitate watershed. The roads remain compact, firm, stable, and surprisingly accessible in all but the most severe weather conditions (fig. 8.1).

Entrances

Village homes, public buildings, and craft shops represent a range of access challenges, and each one must be addressed individually. One barrier that nearly all OSV structures share is entrance steps. Barrier removal has been accomplished in one of two ways: installing earthen inclines and constructing wooden ramps. Earthen inclines are generally the preferred solution because their visual impact is minimal—they accomplish access without calling undue attention to themselves. Because they are less steep than true ramps (having a slope of 1:20, versus the ramp's typical slope of 1:12), inclines do not require handrails, which increases their value within the museum environment. Furthermore, their initial construction cost is relatively low, though they require regular, lifelong maintenance.

Figure 8.1. Old Sturbridge Village staff developed new methods of constructing and maintaining the Village's unpaved roads and paths, improving their accessibility while retaining their historically accurate appearance. Photograph by Thomas Neill. Courtesy of Old Sturbridge Village [photo #120.Ac2p].

Wooden ramps, on the other hand, are more visually intrusive and more expensive to construct, though they are practically maintenance free once they are in place.

To determine which solution is most appropriate in a particular situation, Old Sturbridge Village staff members ask these questions: Which door(s) do visitors use for entrance and exit? How prominent is its location; in other words, is a ramp's visual impact a strong consideration? How many steps are there, and how high a rise to the entrance threshold? What surrounding landscape features must also be considered when making access decisions—entrance paths, adjacent gardens, fencing? How wide is the doorway? How easily can visitors open or close the door? (The door's weight, the force required to open or close it, and the accessibility of door hardware, which a visitor should be able to operate with closed fist and without twisting action, are important considerations.) Is it possible to open the door independently or is assistance required?

At one time, visitors entering through the front gate of the Salem Towne House, a large, impressive home situated on one end of the Village Common, encountered one step up to a bricked walkway leading to the front door. Following the walkway around the house where it adjoined a flagstoned courtyard, visitors entered the building through the stepped rear door, which served as the main entrance. In this case, two barrier-removal solutions were necessary, one for the single step at the front gate and another for the entrance door at the rear of the structure. The step at the front gate was eliminated by regrading—raising the road surface to the level of the top of the step, essentially burying the step in the road. The resulting earthen incline was distributed across the adjacent road surface to minimize the grade as much as possible, making the approach to the Salem Towne House barrier free.

At the rear entrance door, staff members constructed a wooden ramp, quite a rare solution within the re-created village. Why? A wooden ramp is slightly steeper than an earthen incline and requires less length to accommodate a comparable rise. It is therefore more space efficient. In this instance, an earthen incline would have had significant impact on the existing formal garden beside the house, requiring removing several plantings, reconfiguring some of the brick paths, and otherwise altering a traditional garden design. The wooden ramp, on the other hand, could be contained within the rear entrance courtyard, with minimal impact on the formal garden and minimal visual intrusion (fig. 8.2). The ramp is not visible from the front of the house or from the Village Common, an important consideration.

The rear entrance doorway at the Towne House is very wide—even wider than required under Massachusetts's access code, which far exceeds the ADA Standards' requirement for clear width of door opening. Throughout most of the year the rear door remains open, facilitating independent access. During the cold months, when the door is closed, most visitors have no trouble opening it without assistance, though an interpreter is available to help if the need arises.

The earthen incline installed at the Asa Knight Store is a much more typical example of barrier removal within the re-created village. In this exhibit building, also prominently located on the Village Common, two front doors serve as both entrance and exit doors. Both face the common; one gives access to the main room of the store, and the second enters the rear shop, a later addition to the building. In many respects, the two doors were equal candidates for accessible entrance. Each had two steps up to its threshold, with approximately equal rise from ground level; each door opening was sufficiently wide to meet Massachusetts's clear-width requirement; door hardware and ease of opening were comparable; immediately inside each door, clear floor space was sufficient to meet code

Figure 8.2. At the Salem Towne House, all visitors use the ramped rear entrance, which provides maximum access with minimum impact on the re-created historical landscape. Photograph by Thomas Neill. Courtesy of Old Sturbridge Village [photo #2830(28)].

requirements. Ultimately, to minimize visual intrusion, staff members constructed an earthen incline to the shop door, which is set back from the main
body of the store and slightly offset from the common (fig. 8.3).

As with all earthen inclines, a primary consideration is preserving the historic
structure. With frame structures, like the Asa Knight Store, it is important to minimize contact between soil and wood and ensure that the earthen incline drains well
and sheds water away from the building. To accomplish these objectives OSV's
maintenance staff established standard procedures for earthen ramp construction.
First, they create a foot-wide channel adjacent to the structure's foundation to facilitate airflow and minimize moisture accumulation. Next, they use large granite
retaining stones to edge the channel, keeping it clear and stabilizing the perimeter
of the incline. Finally, they construct the incline itself using a method similar to
that used on village roads. The materials (primarily sand and aggregates) are applied
in layers, with the largest aggregates in the lower layers to promote drainage. Each
layer is compacted for stability. The top layer, or dressing, must be regularly maintained to counteract erosion from weather conditions and visitor traffic.

On occasion, temporary barrier removal has been accomplished using a portable ramp. Before a permanent earthen incline was installed at the District School,
for example, an "off-the-shelf," standard-length metal ramp enabled students with
disabilities to visit the exhibit building. While portable ramps can serve a useful
purpose, they have several disadvantages. They are often heavy and difficult to
maneuver, they require staff to place and remove them, and they need storage space.
Also, a standard-length ramp may or may not suit the situation for which it is used.
To meet federal code requirements, a ramp must provide a slope of no more than
1:12; that is, for every inch of rise that it accommodates, it must be twelve inches
long. In many historic buildings, where a rise of two or more steps (fourteen or
more inches) is not unusual, a standard-length ramp may be too short, resulting in
a slope that is too steep for safe, independent use. It is important to recognize portable ramps as "stop-gap" measures; they are not acceptable for permanent use.

Priority #2: Access to Goods, Services, and Programs

Once a visitor is inside the door, can he or she participate in the programs
or services offered there? Within historic buildings, several common barriers may
make full visitor participation difficult. These may include narrow hallways and
doorways; high thresholds at room entrances, steps, or staircases; small rooms
with limited space to maneuver a wheelchair; and second-floor rooms.

Interior Access

Questions to consider when addressing first-floor interior access include: Are
there alternative routes through the building that would increase access to indi-

Figure 8.3.   Earthen inclines provide effective, unobtrusive access at many village exhibits, including the Asa Knight Store. Photograph by Thomas Neill. Courtesy of Old Sturbridge Village [photo #x2830(15)].

vidual rooms? Are narrow doorways or high thresholds alterable, or would alteration threaten or destroy historically significant features? If alteration is ruled out, what methods might be used to bring the program or experience to the visitor? Can the staff provide access through the use of artifacts, reproductions, or props? Might audiovisual programs or photographs be helpful?

At Old Sturbridge Village, interior access varies dramatically from building to building. At the Salem Towne House, wide hallways, wide interior doorways, and tight-weave carpeting ease access to first-floor spaces. At the Parsonage, though, narrow interior doorways pose problems for some visitors using wheelchairs. One such doorway is shared by the exhibit's two main program spaces, the kitchen and the parlor. By repositioning some nonhistoric door hardware, village staff members maximized the clear opening through that door without altering historic fabric. Currently, wheelchair users enjoy full access to the kitchen and full or partial (i.e., visual) access to the parlor, depending upon one's ability to navigate the narrow doorway.

Clear floor space is another important factor to consider when evaluating interior access. Can visitors using wheelchairs, walkers, canes, or other aids navigate the room easily and safely? If not, is alteration or rearrangement of the space possible? Can visitors participate more fully with staff assistance, tactile or hands-on opportunities, or other active involvement?

In the District School, the building entrance and vestibule are comfortably accessible, as is the entrance to the schoolroom, the exhibit's primary interpretive space. Within this room, however, the arrangement of furnishings limits clear floor space and wheelchair mobility. Benches are arranged in tight rows on three sides of the room, with little aisle space between. The teacher's desk and a wood stove stand close to the doorway, further crowding the space. The school is expected to undergo major maintenance in the next few years, including floor replacement and bench restoration. At that time, research, program, and maintenance staffs will have an opportunity to discuss possible access improvements. Might a row of benches be removed to increase clear floor space? How much would such removal reduce the total seating capacity of the room? Can that reduction be justified, particularly during periods of high visitation? Such questions address important operational considerations as well as issues of access, visitor service, and historical accuracy and preservation.

Second-Floor Spaces

Many of the same questions that help assess first-floor access apply to upper floors, as well. Only one is unique: How does a visitor get there? For most of us working at historic properties, removing a barrier as enormous as a flight of stairs is not readily achievable, and most historic houses are not equipped with an elevator as an accessible alternative. Still, modern technology does offer one way to physically transport visitors with limited mobility to the second floor without structural impact and with only temporary visual intrusion. Stair-Trac, a portable device that enables wheelchair users to "climb" stairs, is used at Drayton Hall in Charleston, South Carolina. Though it cannot be used independently, Stair-Trac allows visitors who use wheelchairs to enjoy second-floor displays and programs along with other visitors, instead of relying on programmatic alternatives to barrier removal.

Such alternatives are extremely important, however, and they are often the most readily achievable solutions. One popular alternative to barrier removal—videotaped tours of second-floor rooms—can provide an effective means of "bringing the program to the visitor." Old Sturbridge Village staff members explored this solution for several exhibit buildings but encountered another barrier: lack of suitable accessible spaces in which to unobtrusively install modern playback equipment. Ultimately, photograph books provided a very low-tech and surprisingly well-received solution. Using standard three-ring binders and a supply of clear vinyl sheet protectors, staff members compiled floor plans, eight-by-ten-inch color photos, and large-print text that together communicate the interpretive story of the second-floor spaces. Photos are organized room by room, from general to specific: an overall room view followed by photos of individual sections of the room and details of each section, such as significant objects or decoration. Whenever possible, they include images of the rooms in use—for example, costumed interpreters re-creating a period dance, sharing tea, or quilting together—to give visitors a clearer understanding of the rooms' multifunctional nature.

Line-of-Sight Issues

Photographs may also increase access at the Asa Knight Store, though for a very different reason. As described earlier, the store is largely accessible, but its high counters present a barrier for wheelchair users, visitors who are short, and children. Since altering the counters would be impossible, the OSV staff is exploring alternatives. Interpreters often use reproductions to make the store experience more accessible. When visitors have difficulty seeing over the tall counters, interpreters can show them objects that they might otherwise miss. Similarly, display cases situated atop the counters are inaccessible to many visitors. These closed cases have glass covers and can be viewed from the top only.

Possible access solutions include providing photographs of the objects within the cases, describing the objects in detail, and having the interpretive staff use a mirror to enable visitors to see items inside the case.

Effective Communication

Thus far we have discussed programmatic accommodations in the context of alternatives to barrier removal, but they are also important in the context of effective communication, an essential aspect of access to goods and services. Communication is, after all, the means by which we accomplish museums' and historic properties' educational mission.

Only two questions are necessary when considering this issue: By what means is communication with visitors accomplished, and what alternative forms of communication are offered? The second question is key to determining the level of communication access at museums and historic properties: the more alternatives offered—in other words, the greater the variety of available communication methods—the more accessible the experience or program.

If communication is primarily oral—through interpreters or guides, recorded tours, or other audio or audiovisual programs—is sign language interpretation also available, with or without advance notice? Are large-print transcripts of recorded tours or audio programs provided? Are other printed interpretive materials available? Are audiovisual programs captioned? Deaf and hard-of-hearing visitors find these alternatives especially helpful.

Are printed materials—exhibition labels, text panels, brochures, interpretive handouts—an important part of the museum's program? If so, are they available in recorded form? Large print? Braille? These alternatives especially benefit visitors who are blind or have low vision. Recordings and large-print materials often appeal much more broadly, as well.

Are hands-on or tactile opportunities available, using carefully selected artifacts, reproductions, or scale models? (Scale models are particularly helpful when interpreting buildings, outbuildings, and grounds or when presenting large objects in the collection.) Can staff members offer detailed descriptions to supplement such tactile experiences or to take their place? Again, visitors who are blind or have low vision find such opportunities helpful, as do visitors with cognitive disabilities and specific types of learning disabilities.

Have interpretive and teaching staffs received training in effective communication techniques? Skilled interpreters are accustomed to paying attention to how they say what they say: their vocabulary, volume and tone, clarity and diction, body language, and position in relation to visitors. They know how to ask questions and how to respond to them appropriately and sensitively. They have learned to leave quiet time, time for listening, for allowing visitors to look and ponder. The best interpreters know that people gather and process information in different ways and that varied presentation techniques make for a more effective learning experience. They know how to read their audience and adapt their presentations to the needs of their visitors, using whatever combination of techniques and experiences is appropriate to the situation. Regardless of age, education, experience, ability, or disability, many visitors respond positively to engaging, interactive, hands-on learning opportunities. These opportunities, facilitated by skilled interpreters, can enhance any museum experience, making a visit more meaningful and more accessible, in the broadest sense of the word (fig. 8.4).

Developing a Plan for Achieving Access

The advantages of developing a formal, written plan for achieving access have already been presented. Old Sturbridge Village took that step several years ago

Figure 8.4. Hands-on opportunities and lively interaction with costumed staff enhance interpretation and accessibility for visitors to Old Sturbridge Village. Photograph by Thomas Neill. Courtesy of Old Sturbridge Village [photo #x3466(1/1a)].

when staff produced the Access Transition Plan to guide access decision making. Based upon a comprehensive survey of OSV's administrative and public facilities and programs, the plan identified a wide range of projects that would improve physical and programmatic access throughout the village. The projects were prioritized and then categorized as short term, intermediate term, or long term, with target completion dates identified for each category. Appropriate staff members were assigned to oversee the projects, effectively distributing responsibility for access improvements throughout the organization. Because the document predated the ADA, an addendum was later produced to address new requirements and to revise plans and schedules for new and existing projects. These documents are regularly reviewed and updated as priorities and resources change. They are certainly living documents, as is appropriate for the ongoing process and continuing obligation of improving access.

In the mid-1980s, those who began that process at Old Sturbridge Village made several wise decisions that still support the museum's access efforts. The vision behind those decisions continues to guide the OSV staff, providing a sense of direction and focus. The following outline summarizes key steps taken at Old Sturbridge Village to plan for structural and programmatic accessibility. It incorporates ADA Title III requirements with which the village must comply. Staffs at other museums and historic properties facing similar challenges may benefit from OSV's experience.

1. Identify an ADA coordinator or access coordinator. This person will serve as a resource for visitors and staff and will oversee the development, implementation, and review of the ADA-compliance plan. Beware of seeing access as only the coordinator's job, however. Access is *everyone's* job, and the best coordinators are those who involve relevant others in decision making and in implementing access improvements.

2. Establish an advisory committee or similar vehicle for involving persons with disabilities in the access-planning process. It is extremely important for a user group to have input in access decisions. Making changes without such input can result in a dreadful waste of resources. However well intentioned the changes may be, if they prove ineffective, then time, money, and very possibly, staff energy and support, are lost—all resources that will be needed to correct what could have been done right in the first place.

   Advisors must fully understand and accept the museum's mission in order to effectively support and facilitate accessibility efforts and assist in developing a long-range access plan. That plan must, of course, support and be consistent with the museum's mission.

3. Conduct a self-evaluation, or comprehensive site survey. Identify all existing structural and programmatic barriers to accessibility, everything from entrance steps and narrow doorways to limited communication methods. Review policies, practices, and procedures for possible discrimination on the basis of disability.

4. Make reasonable modification of discriminatory policies and practices.

5. Provide auxiliary aids and services to ensure effective communication.

6. Identify barrier removal options. (Note the plural.) Again, input from a user group will help identify which options will work best for a particular situation, mission, and visitor community.

7. Determine which barrier removal options are readily achievable. Remember, "readily achievable" means cheap and easy. Consider the costs of the various options, available resources (monetary, personnel, time), impact on historically significant features, and effect on daily operations and revenue. When barrier removal is not readily achievable, identify readily achievable alternative methods of providing access.

   This step in the process needs to be broken down further for *qualified historic buildings:*

   a. Know what features, materials, and spaces convey historical significance and define historic character. Features of primary significance are those that cannot be altered in the process of barrier removal; features of secondary significance are potentially alterable.

   b. Identify barrier removal options using the General Rule (the same access standards that apply to nonhistoric properties and properties that do not fit the ADA's definition of "qualified historic buildings or facilities").

   c. If barrier removal in compliance with the General Rule may threaten or destroy the historical significance of a feature of the property, contact the State Historic Preservation Office (SHPO) or, for federal properties, the Advisory Council on Historic Preservation. A representative from the appropriate office must be involved in evaluating situations in which barrier removal may threaten or destroy historical significance and in determining what course of action is readily achievable. Be prepared to undertake a very thorough evaluation process, complete with meticulous documentation.

    d. If the Advisory Council or SHPO agrees that following the General Rule will threaten or destroy the historical significance of building features, evaluate barrier removal in compliance with the alternative minimum standards. In rare instances, even these minimal requirements may threaten or destroy historical significance.

    e. If the Advisory Council or SHPO agree that following the alternative standards will threaten or destroy historical significance, identify readily achievable alternatives to barrier removal to achieve access.

8. Prioritize all readily achievable projects (barrier removal as well as alternatives to barrier removal) and establish a time frame for them.

9. Identify the individuals responsible for implementing access improvements. It is important to have a museum-wide commitment to achieving access and to involve staff members from all appropriate administrative areas.

10. Get started—and keep at it! Remember to maintain the improvements made.

11. Reevaluate the access plan annually. Keep in mind the continuing obligation of readily achievable barrier removal. Revise and reprioritize the plan as necessary.

Maintaining the Balance

Access accommodations, as we have seen, can have structural as well as programmatic impact. By embarking thoughtfully and carefully on the path toward increased accessibility and by utilizing the many resources available, it is possible to successfully balance our dual commitments to access and historic preservation.

    The vast majority of visitors to historic properties, disabled and nondisabled, will welcome these efforts. After all, they too value the integrity and significance of historic sites; it is what brings them to a site's doors. And with these doors open and accessible, those who haven't felt welcome in the past may just give a historic site another chance—and bring their family and friends with them.

    Will this return justify an investment in accessibility? With at least forty-three million people with disabilities in the United States—not to mention people with temporary disabilities and an aging population experiencing natural sensory and mobility changes—there is a good chance that it will. This is a huge potential audience, even allowing for those people who may not be inclined to visit historic properties. Remember, too, that people with disabilities need to know they *can* visit our sites and that we are ready and willing to meet their needs. That is our mission—to share our historic and cultural resources with a broad and diverse public. Our commitments to accessibility and historic preservation are key to fulfilling that mission. And balancing our commitments will bring positive results in visitor satisfaction, community support, and audience development.

Notes

1. Ron Thomson and Marilyn Harper, "Telling the Stories: Planning Effective Interpretive Programs for Properties Listed in the National Register of Historic Places," *National Register Bulletin* (Washington, D.C.: National Park Service, 2000), available at www.cr.nps.gov/NR/publications/bulletins/interp/ (visited 21 March 2001).

2. Ibid.

3. Thomas C. Jester and Sharon C. Park, AIA, *Preservation Brief 32: Making Historic Properties Accessible* (Washington, D.C.: National Park Service, 1993), available at www2.cr.nps.gov/TPS/briefs/brief32.htm (visited 21 March 2001).

4. Public Law 101–336: The Americans with Disabilities Act of 1990, enacted 26 July 1990, available at www.usdoj.gov/crt/ada/adahom1.htm (visited 21 March 2001). Title II regulations published in the *Federal Register*, 26 July 1991. Title III regulations published in the Code of Federal Regulations (28 CFR Part 36), Department of Justice, 1 July 1994. Unless otherwise noted, all ADA references are from these publications and from *The Americans with Disabilities Act Title III Technical Assistance Manual*, U.S. Department of Justice, November 1993 and 1994 Supplement.

5. The ADA defines individuals with disabilities very broadly, as individuals "who have a physical or mental impairment that substantially limits one or more major life activities; . . . who have a record of such impairment; and who are regarded as having such an impairment, whether they have the impairment or not." See *Title III Technical Assistance Manual*, 9.

6. In addition to these major areas, "Title V: Miscellaneous Provisions" covers subjects as diverse as life and health insurance, accessibility of Congress and Capitol buildings, and dispute resolution.

7. 28 CFR Part 36 (Title III), 4.1.7: Accessible Buildings: Historic Preservation, 2(c).

8. Title I is administered and enforced by the Equal Employment Opportunity Commission and the Department of Justice (employment by state and local government), Titles II and III by the Department of Justice and the Department of Transportation (transportation provisions only), Title IV by the Federal Communications Commission.

9. Former attorney general Janet Reno, cited in *Section 504 Compliance Handbook*, Supplement 102 (Washington, D.C.: Thompson Publishing Group, September 1995), 2.

10. John P. S. Salmen, *Everyone's Welcome: The ADA and Museums* (Washington, D.C.: American Association of Museums, 1998), 20.

11. "Available resources" includes resources of a parent entity, if any.

12. Since braille is not universally used by people who are blind, recorded materials are often a better choice to make printed information accessible. Furthermore, recordings serve a much broader audience, not limited to visitors with low vision.

13. *Title III Technical Assistance Manual,* 31.

14. Unlike Title II properties, Title III sites do not have the option of using UFAS.

15. In addition to providing an accessible route between the entrance and the altered area, the accessible path of travel requirement encompasses the bathrooms, telephones, and drinking fountains serving the altered area. See *Title III Technical Assistance Manual,* 52.

16. Public Law 102–575: National Historic Preservation Act of 1966 (as amended through 1992), available at www.cr.nps.gov/local-law/nhpa1966.htm (visited 21 March 2001).

17. Jester and Park, *Preservation Brief 32,* 1–2. When considering alterations to historic properties, consult "The Secretary of the Interior's Standards for the Treatment of Historic Properties." This document, used by State Historic Preservation Officers all over the country, presents a series of concepts related to maintaining, repairing, and replacing historic materials as well as designing new additions or making alterations.

18. These provisions apply to alterations that trigger the ADA Standards' requirements for exterior and interior accessible routes, ramps, entrances, and toilets. The alternative requirements, when approved for use, provide a minimal level of access. For example, a ramp may be steeper than that permitted under the General Rule. See *Title III Technical Assistance Manual,* 55.

19. *Title III Technical Assistance Manual,* 55–56.

20. The author gratefully acknowledges the support and assistance of former colleagues from Old Sturbridge Village, including Alberta Sebolt George, Phyllis Portier, Colleen Couture, Nancy Johnston, Brad King, David Simmons, and Eric White. Their review of the manuscript and assistance with photographic images were invaluable.

21. *Title III Technical Assistance Manual,* 29.

22. Old Sturbridge Village has a well-deserved reputation for sympathetic barrier removal within its re-created historical environment. The village's longstanding goal has been to provide the highest level of accessibility possible within the mission of re-creating an early-nineteenth-century New England environment. Access solutions reached at Old Sturbridge Village may or may not be appropriate at other historical settings.

CHAPTER NINE

HISTORIC HOUSE TOURS THAT SUCCEED: CHOOSING THE BEST TOUR APPROACH

Barbara Abramoff Levy

Tours are among the most common interpretation tools used by historic house museums in the United States. It is possible to travel from state to state taking hundreds of tours. However, tour implementations—and therefore tour experiences—vary widely from site to site. Tour types fall into a few basic categories, but a wide variety of creative and personalized tour implementations exist within each category. The unique qualities and limitations of individual museums dictate the choice of tour type and guide museum staff members in shaping a tour to fit their needs.

Despite the differences that exist between the tour types, good historic house tours have some important things in common.

- *They are based on a thorough knowledge of history.* It is essential that a tour, like all interpretations, have intellectual integrity.

- *They are organized around the site's three to five most important themes.* Themes provide a structure that helps visitors learn and remember.

- *Perceptible evidence at the museum supports the themes.* As the tour progresses, interpreters use the material culture to illustrate and reinforce the themes.

- *The interpretation is tied to the most important biographies.* Most visitors are interested in stories about the people connected to the history of the site. Good tours link the people's stories with the evidence and use both to communicate the themes.

- *The tours include historical context.* Understanding the historical context in which the site existed is essential to gaining a clear and accurate picture of the past. It is also a good framework for understanding how the past relates to the present.

- *They are part of a carefully thought-out, well-planned visitor experience.* From start to finish, the museum staff must create a smooth, comfortable, and friendly visitor experience.

Whether guided or self-guided, tours must have a shape, too—an introduction, a body with transitions, and a conclusion or summary. The time frame for the tour should be reasonable, not too long or too short. The standing area in each interpreted space must be large enough for visitors to be able to hear and to see. Good traffic flow is also essential, as are polite and pleasant business dealings with visitors. Last, and perhaps most importantly, all staff members—not just interpreters—must be well informed, well trained, and engaging.

Third-Person Interpreter-Led Tours

The most common type of tour at historic house museums is the third-person interpreter-led tour. In the third-person tour, an interpreter, docent, or guide leads a group of visitors through the site. The interpreter talks *about* history without representing herself as part of that history. These tours occur at regularly scheduled intervals and for predetermined lengths of time. Generally, visitors are not free to wander on their own; they must stay with the tour group. In the purest form of the third-person interpreter-led tour, the interpreter wears her own (modern) clothing and speaks as herself. Most often, she does not portray a historical character or wear a period costume, although third-person guided tours conducted by costumed interpreters speaking as themselves do exist.

A third-person interpreter-led tour is never successful without a good interpreter. This requires a careful interpreter selection process and a well-designed training program. A successful tour also provides a physical tour experience that helps visitors get as close as possible to seeing the house in its historical perspective. This, in turn, requires a strong and consistent collection, a furnishings plan that supports the storyline, and evidence that is clearly visible. Also, the story has to be within the reach of the visitor's imagination. For this to happen, the tour environment should replicate to the greatest extent possible the conditions of the interpreted period, so that the whole space contributes to and enhances the visitors' comprehension of the information they are hearing.

Third-person interpreter-led tours usually work best with no (or minimal) barriers, because it is the space itself that speaks in the first person. If the interpreter is acting in the third person, the space needs to be as evocative as possible—the fewer modern intrusions or barriers the better.

Likewise, third-person interpreter-led tours are best kept as small as reasonable so the visitors can come close to the interpreter to hear and to see. This way, they also have enough room to experience the site without a crush of people making it impossible to "feel" the space. The best tour outlines for guided tours are flexible, allowing interpreters to personalize and alter their tours without straying from the content objectives. The tour outline acts as a kind of skeleton, embellished and personalized by the interpreter to suit the audience. Interpreters can, in these situations, think of the tour as a method of storytelling in which the space and the collection help them unravel the mystery of the site.

Strengths and Weaknesses

One important asset of a third-person interpreter-led tour is that the museum is able to control the interpretive content; all visitors are exposed to the same basic ideas. In addition, a good tour outline in the hands of a skilled interpreter leads to a tour that is consistently educational and entertaining. Interaction with an informative and engaging interpreter is a real pleasure; it also provides visitors an opportunity to ask questions and otherwise interact with a knowledgeable staff person. Interpreter-led tours enable visitors to experience the actual space and collection. The power of the real is no trivial thing. Historically accurate spaces filled with objects used by real people evoke the past like little else.

There are, however, weaknesses. In the hands of an unskilled interpreter, the tour experience can be truly terrible. A good interpreter selection process and a well-designed and ongoing training program are essential tools for ensuring a high quality tour experience for visitors.

Because time, information dissemination, and access to the historical spaces are highly controlled, visitors have a limited ability to influence the guided tour experience or shape it to their own interests. They are captive, required to follow the interpreter through the rooms listening dutifully to the spiel. This problem is lessened when interpreters take time to learn something about each group before the tour and use the information to tailor the experience to visitors' interests to some extent. Allowing quiet time for visitors to experience the spaces and encouraging questions from them also help to mitigate these liabilities.

The fixed content of a tour—which is a pedagogical asset—is also a handicap. Why should visitors return if the tour is essentially the same all the time? Creating a flexible tour outline, offering a variety of different tours, and supplementing the tours with programs, exhibits, and publications are ways to lessen these problems.

Finally, the interpreter-led tour can be difficult for interpreters. It is hard to stay animated and fresh when you have been giving the same tour all day. Providing a flexible tour outline rather than a script allows interpreters to vary tours and avoids boredom. It is also helpful to limit the number of tours required of interpreters to no more than five in a given day, if possible.

Case Studies

Gropius House

The tour at the Gropius House in Lincoln, Massachusetts, uses the collection skillfully to illustrate Gropius's design philosophy and bring the Gropius family's story to life.[1] Gropius House is a relatively modern historic house built in 1937 and 1938 by the architect Walter Gropius for himself and his family. The house has small rooms, very modern collections, and themes that largely have to do with Gropius's design approach, style, and family life as illustrated by the house and artifacts.

Gropius believed that architectural design should be collaborative; that the users and the architect must work together closely to find the perfect design solutions. This philosophy is amply illustrated in the house. For example, a spiral staircase was added to the front elevation of the house at the suggestion of Gropius's daughter who wanted to be able to bring her friends directly to her room. Placed in front of a large window, the adults could easily see the children enter. Dirt from their shoes was scraped off by the treads, and the harsh front elevation was softened by the gently curving stair (fig. 9.1).

The house was designed for maximum efficiency, simplicity, and utility, and the elements that make it work are also evident throughout. Objects displayed effectively connect the design concepts to the family's daily life. Numerous famous Bauhaus designers who were friends and colleagues of Gropius in Germany designed and produced much of the furniture and artwork. These objects allow the interpreter to widen visitors' understanding of the Bauhaus style and of the architect's world. Because the artwork often generates questions by visitors, interpreters can customize or expand the tours.

With all of the family possessions still in place and the design philosophy clearly evident, the house makes a strong impact on visitors. In a way, it speaks for itself. Part of the success of the Gropius House traditional third-person tours is a result of this very characteristic; interpreters allow the house to work its magic without undue interference. The tour, while thorough, is as clean and focused as the house. One lesson we can take away from the Gropius House tour is that sometimes less is more. If the house or collection speaks for itself, the interpreter does not need to speak for it.

Figure 9.1. **The design of architect Walter Gropius's house illustrates Gropius's belief that good design was the result of a strong collaboration between the architect and user. The spiral staircase was added to the front elevation of the house at the suggestion of Gropius's daughter who wanted to be able to bring her friends directly to her room. Placed in front of a large window, the adults could easily see the children enter. Dirt from their shoes was scraped off by the treads, and the harsh front elevation was softened by the gently curving stair. Photograph by David Bohl. Courtesy of the Society for the Preservation of New England Antiquities.**

Cliveden

Cliveden, in Philadelphia, Pennsylvania, also uses a third-person interpreter-led tour, but it has an interesting twist.[2] It was built in the 1760s as the Chew family country house. Extensive research and self-study led to the decision to focus the interpretation on how and why the Chew family preserved the house's colonial history in the nineteenth century. The revised interpretation required a new installation of the furnishings. To help visitors discriminate the nineteenth-century overlay from the eighteenth-century artifacts and spaces in the context of the third-person interpreter-led tour, the museum's staff had to change the tour as well. One theme the tour now explores is the creation of national symbols and myths in general, and Chew family myth making in particular. Artifacts effectively support these ideas. For example, a memory painting displayed in the house depicts the battle of Germantown, which took place during the Revolution. The painting, made in the 1870s by E. L. Henry, is an example of nineteenth-century mythologizing of history (fig. 9.2).

Historical photographs taken in the 1930s of Cliveden's entrance hall show how the family clustered photographs and objects, supporting their own interpretation of colonial history. (See chapter 10, fig. 10.2.) The current installation adapts this idea. Interspersed among the eighteenth-century furnishings are groups of artifacts, photographs, and prints that enable interpreters to tell stories about the nineteenth-century Chews, their lives, and their points of view. (See chapter 10, fig. 10.3.) These stories make it possible for interpreters and visitors to slip comfortably back and forth between the nineteenth and the eighteenth centuries. Within the tour framework, then, the interpreter can choose among a variety of stories, adapting the tour to meet the needs and interests of the visitors, and the stories hang together because of the consistency of the themes.

Drayton Hall

Drayton Hall is a plantation house in Charleston, South Carolina, built in 1738.[3] It has survived nearly intact with very few alterations and it is exhibited completely unfurnished and unrestored. (See chapter 12, fig. 12.1.)

Figure 9.2. This "memory painting" of Cliveden during the revolutionary battle of Germantown, made in the 1870s by E. L. Henry, reflects the late-nineteenth-century impulse to mythologize colonial history. Courtesy of Cliveden, a property of the National Trust for Historic Preservation in the United States.

This site consists of an architectural artifact and landscape, yet its goal is to interpret 300 years of life and work in the South Carolina low country. In order to interpret the empty house, interpreters use the architecture and the space as evidence to support a storyline that goes beyond architectural history. The Drayton Hall tour strives to help visitors learn how to see and imagine the history in the place themselves. Interpreters give basic background and contextual information and then ask directed questions, such as "Where are you? How was this room used? Where have you seen this form before in your hometown? How would you use this room in your house today?" Student tours are almost completely inquiry tours. With adults, interpreters use questioning judiciously so as not to make visitors feel uncomfortable.

Interpreters focus visitors' attention on specific elements and relate them to the work that went on in the house. While looking at a fireplace, they might ask, "What kinds of work would be required to use and maintain this fireplace? Who would do it?" Building on visitors' knowledge, these questions enable the interpreter to evoke a picture of work in people's imaginations, and they open doors for discussion about other activities and issues, such as the role of slaves on the plantation (fig. 9.3). As the tour progresses, questions help visitors compare and contrast what they have seen. Directed questioning is one of the easiest ways to skew the tour to the interests of visitors based on responses to the questions.

Flexibility is a primary strength of the Drayton Hall tour. The tour approach keeps interpreters interested and allows them to customize the tour for visitors. It also encourages visitors' own abilities to furnish and people the house in their imaginations. The main drawback is that this tour method does not work easily with narrow time constraints. It is difficult to maintain a tight schedule when interpreters are asking people questions and eliciting their answers. In these circumstances, Drayton Hall interpreters revert to lecture. Another challenge with this third-person tour style is that extensive interpreter training is required. No one can fully anticipate the precise direction the questioning is going to take. Most importantly, the interpreters have to be very good teachers, and they have to be able to encourage responses from those people who are comfortable, without making those who are not feel inferior or out of place.

Self-Guided Tours

Another popular tour type is the self-guided tour. These tours can be handled in a number of ways. Interpretive information can be disseminated through brochures, interpretive labels, or text panels. Historic sites often use interpreters—sometimes in costume, sometimes not—stationed on tour routes to answer

Figure 9.3. Interpreters at Drayton Hall use the architecture of the site and directed questioning techniques to interpret 300 years of life and work in the South Carolina low country. Looking at the fireplace in the great hall, for example, an interpreter might ask, "Who might have built and tended the fire? Who might have cleaned the fireplace?" Courtesy of Drayton Hall, historic site of the National Trust for Historic Preservation, Charleston, South Carolina.

questions and interact with visitors. When a tour is not guided, security becomes a bigger issue, and areas may need to be cordoned off with ropes, railings, Plexiglas, or some other suitable barrier.

Strengths and Weaknesses

The strengths of this kind of tour are significant. Because it works well for a large volume of people, heavily trafficked sites frequently use some form of self-guided tour. The self-guided tour naturally gives visitors control over the experience as well, allowing them to shape it to meet their needs. Consequently, it is ideal for groups of mixed ages and interests, like families. Self-guided tours guarantee that the experience is different every single time the visitor comes, so the chance that a visitor will return is greater.

One drawback to the self-guided tour is that it restricts the visitor's engagement with the space. Because there frequently are barriers for security reasons, visitors cannot enter spaces to get a sense of how they feel. If crowds of visitors are on hand, pushing into small viewing areas, barriers also have the effect of restricting the amount of time that visitors interact with a space.

The self-guided tour format often has an impact on the consistency of the message being conveyed. If visitors are making their own choices about their experience, it is hard to know if the museum's interpretive objectives are being met. In addition, because the staff cannot be sure what experiences the visitor has already had at the site, it can be difficult to help visitors make connections between the things they've seen. These problems can be mitigated by adding stationed interpreters who consistently engage the public in conversation, or by supplementing the tour experience with demonstrations, special programs, changing exhibits, and written materials.

A danger of the stationed interpreter format is that interpreters can and often do very easily fall back into describing, instead of interpreting. Guide training must include lots of practice drawing out questions and creating an environment where visitors want to engage in conversation with the interpreter.

Case Studies

Noah Webster House

At the Noah Webster House, built in 1825, the interpretive themes cover Webster, the famous intellectual and prolific author and lexicographer, his family members and servants living in the house, the rearrangement of the house to accommodate Webster's increasing infirmities, and the women of the family as typical of middle-class American women in the early nineteenth century.[4] The drawing room door has a rope barrier, and the space is used as a look-in room only. Because the family seldom used the drawing room, this interpretive approach is consistent with the message of formality the room conveys. In contrast, the family regularly used the parlor as a sitting room. Visitors can walk directly into this room and view the activities suggested by artifacts and reproductions. They can get relatively close to the artifacts, even though a floor-to-ceiling, clear Plexiglas wall protects the collection. In Webster's study/bedroom, where the author finished his dictionary, a waist-high barrier provides protection and holds labels, which help visitors interpret for themselves.

Sarah Jordan Boardinghouse

The Sarah Jordan Boardinghouse uses another variant of the self-guided tour format. It employs some stationed guides, some barriers, and an audio loop.[5] The boardinghouse was established in Menlo Park, New Jersey, to accommodate the bachelor employees of Thomas Edison's nearby laboratory. The interpretation of the house, however, highlights the roles of the women who ran the place, and it explores gender roles by comparing the women's lives with those of their male boarders. In the gents' sitting room, for example, the table is set for men's leisure activities, stereopticon viewing, chess, and gazing at pictures of pretty actresses. The ladies' sitting room, on the other hand, depicts a much more feminine space that the boarders never entered. Upstairs are the boarders' bedrooms, one complete with men's "drawers" under the bed, dirty shirts strewn about, and unmade beds. When visitors enter, their motion activates a recording of an Irish servant woman talking about her work:

Oh, I don't know if washin' or cleanin' tires me out more. But it is the day to clean, and I'd best get finished. Already tidied up Mr. Griffith's room at the top of the stairs. Oh, he's a nice man, neat in his ways.

Now, this room. I'll pick up after these three, but it's the last time. Heaven only knows what I'll find on the floor. In the room next door, it's Mr. Houser. You can tell which things are his, girly pictures and fancy Bay Rum. And one day, I even saw a knife on the dresser. He's a bit wild next to young Mr. Hipple and smart Mr. Lawson, but they all seem to get along, most of the time.

Now, what's left? Finish the last bedroom. Try to get this all done in the forenoon. But there's still the floor in the small bedroom that needs scrubbin' and the bed to do up. Then, tomorrow's wash day. Pump the water, heat the water, boil the clothes, rinse the clothes, and hang 'em out in the yard. And, then, the next day, it's the ironin'.[6]

Firestone Farm

Instead of barriers, text labels, and tapes, the interpretation at Firestone Farm uses costumed interpreters at stations.[7] This kind of blended interpretation—with interpreters in costume performing period activities but speaking primarily in the third person—is sometimes called second-person interpretation because it is neither first-person reenactment nor third-person narration, but something in between. Costumes and period activities help to pull the visitor into the period, and the interpreter connects the past with the present by using the third-person point of view. Many midsize or larger open-air history museums, like Old Sturbridge Village, Colonial Williamsburg, Conner Prairie, and others, use this technique.

Although the farmhouse was built in 1828, it is interpreted to 1882, when the house was renovated. Visitors enter through the kitchen as the family would have, and the activities of the interpreters encourage dialogue (fig. 9.4). Some rooms, such as the formal parlor, which was infrequently used by the family, are look-in rooms. The family sitting room, in contrast, is not only a walk-in space but is furnished entirely with reproductions and artifacts that may be used by visitors. They can sit down, pull up to the fire, knit, and read reproduction newspapers. The interpreter in this room is engaged in an activity and always interacts in some way with the visitors. In both rooms, the interpretation matches the reality of room usage in the period.

Recorded Tours

Third-person tours can also be conducted by means of recordings. Audio tours can be simple, using a single interpreter speaking as though she were giving the tour in person, or complex, with multiple tracks, a variety of narrators and actors, quotes from primary sources, music, and ambient sounds.

Figure 9.4. Costumed stationed interpreters in the kitchen of Firestone Farm perform period activities but speak in the third person. The activities are engaging for visitors and make it easy for them to initiate conversations with interpreters by asking questions about the work. Courtesy of Henry Ford Museum & Greenfield Village.

Strengths and Weaknesses

A recorded tour solves interpreter training and other personnel problems, and it allows the museum to maintain complete control over the message and its delivery. Current technology has made it possible to offer the visitor many choices on recordings. This encourages visitors to customize a tour to their own interests and needs. For example, tracks suitable for families, collections or architecture buffs, landscape lovers, and more can be included along with a standard house tour on a single player. Visitors have control over what and how much they listen to and when.

Recordings have a significant downside, however. Because they are even more rigidly fixed than interpreter-led tours, once the visitor has heard what the recording has to offer there is little incentive to return to the site. Moreover, visitors miss the opportunity to ask questions and interact with a knowledgeable, living person who can animate the experience. Recorded tours must be carefully researched, have well-written scripts, and be artfully produced. Once completed, they cannot be easily altered. Recordings should be used judiciously and should be accompanied by other, more flexible, forms of interpretation like interpreters stationed around the property to engage people in conversation, changing exhibits, programs, and supplemental written materials.

Case Studies

Franklin D. Roosevelt National Historic Site

In fortuitous circumstances, interpretive recordings of actual historical characters may be available. In the past, the Franklin D. Roosevelt National Historic Site, in Hyde Park, New York, sometimes used a simple tour of the museum recorded by Eleanor Roosevelt in which she shared her memories of the house, its furnishings, events, and anecdotes.[8] These tours were offered off-season, when visitors had the option of renting the taped tour or taking a self-guided tour. Eleanor Roosevelt's insights, her distinctive voice and speech, and her presence provided an extraordinary experience for visitors. The following excerpts offer a sense of what the interpretation was like:

> Now, the two chairs on each side of the fireplace, to your left, are the chairs given to the governor of the State of New York, which is used as his desk chair in his office while he's been there. Since my husband served two terms when he was governor—it was only two years for each term—so he had two chairs. He always sat on the left side; my mother-in-law sat in the one on the right side.

And when he did not have cocktails before dinner in the little study he would have a card table put in front of him here and would have them here. On the night the king and queen of England were here they drove up after a full day at the fair. They were quite late for dinner and there were people here waiting for them. My husband said, "Oh, they will be tired. They will want a cocktail." My mother-in-law firmly said, "I'm quite sure the king would prefer a nice, hot cup of tea." So when they came in, my husband said to the king, "I have cocktails, but my mother thinks that you would rather have a hot cup of tea." The king looked at him and said, "My mother would have said the same thing, but I will have a cocktail." And so that has always remained a tale in this house. . . .

When the king and queen of England stayed here, the king had the pink room. Prime Minister Mackenzie King, who came down from Canada with them, had the little green room, which you can see at the opposite end of the pink room. In the morning when the king came to breakfast, he said, "I felt very much at home last night, because you have the same prints that my grandmother has in the room I have when I visit her." Of course, they're just old English prints, so this was quite natural. But the night that he was here after dinner, the president kept him downstairs with Mackenzie King, and they discussed the coming war, which everybody knew pretty well was on the way. When he came upstairs, he knocked on Mackenzie King's door, and he said "Come in Mackenzie, I must talk to you." When he came in, he told my husband afterwards, that the king said, "Why cannot my ministers talk to me as the president did? I've learned more tonight than I've ever known before." That was very interesting because it showed that people who are in a position of being dependent on you, of course, are never quite as frank, never quite as able to tell you exactly what they think.[9]

Lyndhurst

Most historic houses do not have such an august person as Eleanor Roosevelt to narrate a tour tape. Nevertheless, recorded tours can work with good scripts and effective narrators. Lyndhurst, in Tarrytown, New York, has recently moved from using third-person interpreter-led tours to employing recorded tours.[10] Their recordings offer many options for visitors, allowing them to customize their tours, choose what to see, and get additional in-depth information about subjects that interest them. The Lyndhurst recording offers three different tracks for visitors to use. One track contains the main tour, which includes the overall history of the site, including the social history. The second includes more in-depth information about the architecture, objects, and landscape features. The third track contains a family tour that is to be used in conjunction with activity cards. Following are two excerpts from the Lyndhurst recorded tours.

Narrator (music and sound of ladies conversing in the background):
Here's Lyndhurst's most richly furnished room, the drawing room. The drawing room was a formal room designed primarily for entertaining. During the day, ladies received callers here, or family members might sit around the table to read, talk, and sew. In the evening, guests gathered here before dinner. After dinner, the gentlemen would remain in the dining room while the ladies withdrew to this room. The name drawing room comes from the word withdraw. The drawing room was a feminine space where one could enjoy a peaceful and very refined respite from the world outside. . . .

Narrator:
This small room is called the cabinet room. It marks the beginning of the addition made to the house in 1864. It connects to the library at the left, but it could also be closed off with sliding doors. Jay Gould and his family used this room as a small intimate sitting room. Like the library, its well-stocked bookshelves and comfortable chairs encouraged reading and relaxation. As a businessman, Jay Gould may have been known as the "skunk of Wall Street," but his family knew him as a loving husband and father. His letters to his wife Helen when they were apart are full of solicitude and warmth.

Actor (train sounds in the background):
August 15, 1881. My dear wife, Not hearing from you today, I began to worry about you, and finally telegraphed Mr. Williams to send up and reply my telegraph. Am just in receipt of the welcome news, all well at home.
July 31, 1899. I wish I had you here with me now. I would give all this beautiful scenery for a few kisses and embraces. . . . *(train whistle)*[11]

Mount Auburn Cemetery

Although Mount Auburn Cemetery, a historic picturesque cemetery opened in 1831 in Cambridge, Massachusetts, is not a historic house, their interesting audio tour is instructive. The Mount Auburn recording—which is designed for "windshield" touring—mixes audio technology, ambient sound, music, acting, and third-person narration, combining them smoothly to convey the interpretive message. The recording makes excellent use of primary source material, like this quote from the cemetery's dedication speech by Joseph Storey:

Actor (music and bird sounds in the background):
All around us there breathes a solemn calm as if we were in the bosom of a wilderness, broken only by the breeze as it murmurs through the tops of the forest. Or, by the notes of the warbler, pouring forth his matin or his evening song. Ascend but a few steps and what a change of scenery to surprise and delight us. We seem in an instant to pass from the confines of death to the bright and balmy regions of life. We stand as it were upon the borders of two worlds,

and we may gather lessons of profound wisdom by contrasting the one with the other, or solace our heart by melancholy meditations.

Narrator (music and bird sounds in the background):
On September 24, 1831, with these words, and quite a few others, Joseph Storey, associate justice of the U. S. Supreme Court, addressed a crowd of some 2,000 at Mount Auburn's dedication in the wooded dell before you. On that day, what we now call Consecration Dell, looked pretty much as it does today. Only fifty-two, Justice Storey knew all too well the pain of bereavement. For all his worldly success, he was a man weary with melancholy caused by the deaths of his parents, his first wife, and, weeks before he wrote this speech, his ten-year-old daughter—his fifth child lost in fifteen years.[12]

First-Person Interpretation

First-person interpretation is more of an interpretive technique than a tour type. Nevertheless, because first-person interpretation is often used in conjunction with tours, its unique issues merit special attention. In first-person interpretation, interpreters completely assume the roles of historical characters; they are actors who do not acknowledge the "future" beyond the period of interpretation. The technique may be used in the interpreter-led format or in self-guided tour formats that use stationed interpreters.

Strengths and Weaknesses

A great advantage of first-person interpretation is that it can be exceptionally entertaining. Like going to the theater, it captures people's interest and engages their imaginations. Because it can be so captivating, it is often extremely effective pedagogically as well. Creating this type of fantasy helps to overcome the limitations of a weak collection, which is used more as a stage set. Using illusion in this way is especially well suited to sites where the story is inherently dramatic or vastly different from the visitors' backgrounds and experiences.

The weaknesses of this type of interpretation, however, are significant. If the actors are not good, the tour can be terrible, even embarrassing, for visitors. In addition to requiring good talent, the interpretation must be based on excellent, wide-ranging research, and the interpreters must endure intense and repeated training. The Beechwood Theater Company actors (at the Astor's Beechwood Mansion), for example, must do copious background reading. They go through weeks of daily training, which includes a twenty-four-hour period when all of the actors live together in the museum part of the house, acting completely in character all day and all night, including during meals.

First-person interpreters have to internalize character traits, vocabulary, mores, gestures, stances, and period history—local, regional, and national. Even if the actor is well prepared and the acting done well, there is a danger of straying from defensible reading between the lines to far-flung fictionalizing.

Occasionally, visitors are unwilling to suspend disbelief. When faced with skeptics who do not want to engage in the fantasy, the interpreter has to be resourceful enough to bring them into the fold or figure out how to keep them from poisoning the experience for the others. Overall, first-person interpretation is a big investment, and it has big risks, but when it is done well, it can be fabulously successful.

Case Study

The Astor's Beechwood Mansion

At the Astor's Beechwood Mansion, the summer home of the Astor family in Newport, Rhode Island, the interpretation re-creates late-nineteenth-century Newport high society through portrayals of the Astor family, their friends, and their servants. Servants greet visitors at the door, and their only diversion from character comes when one of them explains the tour rules and provides basic information. All interpreters have acting training and are members of the Beechwood Theater Company. Through their comments and questions, actors bring visitors into the fantasy by giving the tour group a "role" to play. Visitors come to understand that they are members of the "Four Hundred," the social register created by Mrs. Astor, and that they have been invited to dinner the next evening. They have come to preview the house.

Interpreters follow a fixed thematic structure and incorporate a changing daily storyline, but they improvise the tour based on these. Each actor plays two roles: one "upstairs" person (a family member or friend of the Astors), and one "downstairs" person (a servant). After the servant's introduction, the tour group is handed over to a family member or family friend who gives the tour of the more formal public rooms. An encounter with a servant near the bedrooms enables the "downstairs" actor to hand the group back to a servant who finishes the tour of the bedrooms and service wing. As the tour progresses, other actors periodically come through the house and interact with the tour group or interpreter. In this way, the house is peopled. The actors use body language, speech, and action—all in character—to advance the interpretation.

Technology-Based Tours

Many historic house museums use video to supplement their tours. These videos often provide contextual background or set the stage for the historic house visit.

Although videos can be useful complements to tours, they are not generally successful substitutes. The one exception, however, is the use of video to provide a tour for spaces that are otherwise inaccessible. For example, an interpreted video tour of a second or third floor is extremely helpful for visitors who cannot manage the stairs.

Increasingly, virtual tours are available on Web sites. These tours are useful for introducing people to a site and piquing their interest. Virtual tours are also available on CD-ROM. This software can be incorporated into the actual tour, used to supplement the tour, or sold.

Although computer-based technology holds much promise for the museum field, the jury is out on the benefits and liabilities of computer-based tours. In the last analysis, however, a historic house museum's greatest asset is its real stuff. As such, bringing people to the site should be central to the interpretive mission.

While the formula for a good tour is not complicated, it does require making a serious and ongoing commitment to making the visitor experience the best it can be. Given the competing demands on staff time, the brushfires that always seem to arise and need immediate attention, and existing tours that are deemed good enough, it is all too easy to let work on improving the tour slide. This is a dangerous choice. In the end, the quality of the visitor experience is tightly linked to visitation, which, in turn, influences funding and viability. A good tour not only helps convey what is important and interesting about a site, but it also illustrates that the site cares about and respects its visitors. When historic house museum staff members have done their tour homework, visitors come away from the tour experience with smiles on their faces. Presenting a great tour is one of the most important things a historic house museum can do.

Notes

1. Gropius House is a property of the Society for the Preservation of New England Antiquities (SPNEA).

2. Cliveden is a historic site of the National Trust for Historic Preservation.

3. Drayton Hall is a historic site of the National Trust for Historic Preservation.

4. The Noah Webster House is a property of Henry Ford Museum & Greenfield Village.

5. The Sarah Jordan Boardinghouse is a property of Henry Ford Museum & Greenfield Village.

6. Excerpt from audio recording used in the Sarah Jordan Boardinghouse (Dearborn, Mich.: Henry Ford Museum & Greenfield Village, 1988).

7. Firestone Farm is a property of Henry Ford Museum & Greenfield Village.

8. The Franklin D. Roosevelt National Historic Site is a property of the National Park Service.

9. Eleanor Roosevelt, excerpt from interview with National Park Service, 21 November 1959. National Park Service, Home of Franklin D. Roosevelt National Historic Site.

10. Lyndhurst is a historic site of the National Trust for Historic Preservation.

11. Excerpt from audio tour of Lyndhurst, a historic site of the National Trust for Historic Preservation (Washington, D.C.: National Trust for Historic Preservation, 2000).

12. Excerpt from "Reflections: An Audio Tape Driving Tour of Mount Auburn Cemetery," produced by Michael Schaffer for the Friends of Mount Auburn Cemetery (Cambridge, Mass., 1995).

CHAPTER TEN

CREATING MEMORABLE VISITS: HOW TO DEVELOP AND IMPLEMENT THEME-BASED TOURS

Sandra Mackenzie Lloyd

Imagine yourself back to the Dark Ages when you were a child dragged by your parents or teacher to some historic site. Recall that blurry memory? The impression of seeing a lot of dusty old stuff? Hearing the guide drone on *forever* about chairs you couldn't sit on, events you couldn't see, and bed bolts you couldn't tighten? Much like cod liver oil, these historic site visits were supposed to be good for you. Somehow inspire you to love history, George Washington, and apple pie. But your thoughts were on escape. How much longer would you be trapped in this boring old place? What the heck did this have to do with your life? And when were you going to be able to play basketball?

Imagine yourself today, at your historic site. You have just given a pleasant tour to four adults who clung to your every word about rococo revival chairs, Sam Houston, and sleeping tight courtesy of those bed bolts. You and your visitors had a good time. Your tour was a success! But yesterday was a different story. You had a group of ten people with different interests and different degrees of interest. You tried everything you knew—gave them all your stuff—but by the end you thought, "Why ever did they come; they didn't even pay attention!"

Sound familiar? Lots of guides have been there.

Schoolchildren, group tours, families, folks who just wandered in—historic houses get quite a mixed bag of visitors. Of these, only a few people just *love* historic places. Most folks are, at best, mildly interested in history and, if educational theory and exit surveys are accurate, they remember just three to seven bits of information they hear during their whole visit. Pessimists might say, "This is really depressing. All they'll remember is that we have peeling paint and smoke alarms on the ceiling." Optimists would say, "What a challenge! How can I make sure they remember the three or five best *ideas* about our property?"

Given these two options, be optimistic! Historic houses can and should develop and implement strong, memorable, interpretive tours that appeal to a broad public. These are tours that tell the important stories associated with a site—stories so fascinating that people listen attentively. Even better, they likely will remember a few key ideas that make a site significant.

To create memorable tours, historic sites must move beyond tours filled with facts—whether it's smoke alarms, drapery fabrics, names, dates, or a jumble of jargon. People simply can't remember all the facts that guides so carefully memorize then dutifully present to visitors. Each of us knows how long it took to master this information. How can we expect visitors, hearing it once, to remember all they have heard? We can't. So it is our responsibility at historic houses to do the hard work by creating good tours, so that our visitors have an easy time seeing and absorbing what is truly important about our sites. Lest there be any question, we should *not* do watered down history. In fact, creating excellent tours requires tremendous research, scholarly input, and testing. It must take into account new ideas about women's history, multicultural issues, educational theory, learning styles, and new technology.[1] In summary, we must do hard work *and* hard history. Then we must do what is harder yet—figure out how to present sophisticated history in a comprehensible and engaging way to the general public.

Thematic Tours: What They Are and How to Create Them

To create excellent tours, historic sites must rethink what they do, top to bottom, on a fairly regular basis. This will involve interpretive planning, addressed earlier in this book. An effective way for historic sites to implement this planning is to create thematic tours. Thematic tours are not special subject tours, such as "The Furniture of Smith House" or "Celebrating the Holidays at Hanson Mansion." Thematic tours are built on the central facts and ideas illustrated by a site, its people, and the events that occurred there. Thematic tours convey important information about a site then place it within a larger historical context of significant local, national, and even international events. They also provide links with contemporary experiences to assure that visitors understand history in intellectual, emotional, and ultimately personal ways. To create thematic tours, sites should follow four steps.

Step #1: Start with the *facts*. Facts include the names of people and important dates, together with all of the information that a site has collected and will continue to collect. Facts are found in manuscripts, books, newspapers, diaries, oral histories, maps, photographs, and many other materials. Facts also include the site's physical resources: the house, its landscape, the collections of objects and art. Sites should identify a great number of facts about the buildings, the people who lived, worked, and visited there, and the collections. Over time, sites must weigh those facts, sift and rearrange them, then set aside most while keeping the cream. Those that survive this scrutiny are the most important facts about your site. A fact to keep, for example, is "this house was built in 1869 and is the oldest in town."

Step #2: Take these important facts and use them to identify and develop a few key *themes*. These themes are well-interpreted ideas that make it clear why a site is special and memorable. Sometimes a site's major themes are obvious, but sometimes it takes time to conceptualize them. Here is an example of a well-developed theme that offers engaging information and ideas: "As the oldest house in Beaumont, the John Doe House illustrates early settlement in East Texas that was an important frontier in America's westward expansion in the nineteenth century."

Step #3: Take these key themes, which should number from about three to five, and use them to write a narrative *storyline* for the site. This need not be long; several pithy sentences are often enough. This storyline should resonate with the themes that make the historic site special and integrate its unique physical resources: the house, gardens, and collections. It should also be alive with the stories of the people connected with the site. As an example, a storyline for the John Doe House might state,

> The John Doe House tells the story of a family who left their small farm in South Carolina for the new opportunities available on the East Texas frontier. Over three generations they moved from a small frame house on a struggling farm to a grand mansion financed by new oil fortunes. Their storied energy, prosperity, and occasional adversity—and their Texas pride and spirit—come to life in their house and its furnishings. Theirs is a genuine American story.

Step #4: The site has chosen the strongest facts, developed excellent themes, and written an interesting storyline that is well amplified by physical evidence and good people stories. This storyline is the interpretive foundation for the site. It will shape public programs, brochures, videos, and exhibits. It also is the foundation on which to build memorable *thematic tours* that can engage a reasonably broad audience.

Completing these steps requires time, money, and commitment, so the process can appear daunting. It is fair, then, to ask whether a site must do *all* of this work to develop good tours. Can't a site just do some good guide training?

The answer is maybe, particularly if the site has a good interpretive plan in place. Lacking that, sites should take a deep breath and stir up some of that old house dust, because the process of developing an excellent thematic tour will benefit the institution and help make it more meaningful to the general public.

Using Interpretive Planning to Develop Thematic Tours: A Case Study

Cliveden, a historic house that is a property of the National Trust for Historic Preservation, offers a good case study to examine the process of developing thematic tours.[2] Variations of this strategy have worked successfully at other historic sites interested in improving their overall public interpretation, including their guided tour. This case study then is intended to illustrate a process that other sites can use or adapt to suit their particular needs.

Background: From Family Home to Historic House Museum

Cliveden is a grand stone mansion located in the Germantown section of Philadelphia. Benjamin Chew, a wealthy Philadelphia lawyer, built it between 1763 and 1767 as a country house. For all but twenty years, the Chew family owned Cliveden until the National Trust acquired it in 1972. The family still owned nearly all of the mansion's furnishings, too, including outstanding examples of Philadelphia craftsmanship. Added to these riches are some 200,000 Chew family papers that document the collections and life in the house from the eighteenth through the twentieth centuries (fig. 10.1).

The unquestioned authenticity of Cliveden's architectural significance, well-documented family history, and original decorative arts is amplified by its one great day of fame. On October 4, 1777, it was the primary site of the Revolutionary War battle of Germantown. On that fateful morning, a British regiment occupied Cliveden and used its sturdy stone walls as a shield while they sniped at the Continental army, led by George Washington. Washington commanded his troops to launch their cannons directly on the house, but neither it nor the British fell, sealing a British victory. Still, four years later the Americans won the war and gradually, battle-scarred Cliveden achieved fame for its role in the Revolution.[3]

This combination of resources assures that Cliveden has the main ingredients, or facts, needed to underpin a historic house museum. It is an old house with interesting architecture. It has a great collection of objects and documents. It has good people stories documented by the collection of family papers. And it

Figure 10.1. Exterior view of Cliveden. Cliveden, located in Philadelphia, was built between 1763 and 1767 for its wealthy owners, lawyer Benjamin Chew, his wife Elizabeth, and their children. Its sophisticated and well-preserved architecture, original furnishings, and extensive collection of family papers reflect the residence of seven generations of the Chew family. Cliveden also was a central location of the Revolutionary War battle of Germantown. British troops barricaded themselves inside the house on October 4, 1777. George Washington led the Americans in a full assault that failed and eventually led to his retreat to Valley Forge. Though the British won the battle, later generations of the Chew family celebrated the role their house played in an important engagement of the Revolution. Cliveden now is a historic house museum and co-stewardship property of the National Trust for Historic Preservation. Courtesy of Library of Congress, Prints and Photographs Division, Historic American Buildings Survey, HABS, PA, 51–GERM, 64–4.

has a great event: something important happened here. Most historic sites can identify similar ingredients that are the key resources and facts to be developed.

Sites use these resources in various ways. At Cliveden, when the Chews transferred its ownership to the National Trust in 1972, the Trust proudly proclaimed it "our Colonial crown jewel." The jewels in this colonial crown included the battle, the architectural significance of the house, and the collections, especially the extraordinary Chippendale furniture. The National Trust saw Cliveden as its showcase for colonial history, so the first curator converted Cliveden from a family home to a colonial historic house museum. Using practices popular in the 1970s, he installed the decorative arts collection in period rooms whose style is best described as a tasteful intermingling of objects made between 1760 and about 1840. With few exceptions, he banished nearly all of the later family furnishings to the attic.

This installation assured that Cliveden looked gorgeous when it opened in 1976. People came to see the Chippendale sofas and hear about the battle. No doubt there was the added allure of getting inside an exclusive house once owned by people listed in the Social Register. Tours emphasized the glories of particular objects, the white male who built the house, and battle lore and gore. This first flush of success is probably similar to the experiences of many historic sites newly opened to the public. But by the late 1980s, Cliveden's initial cachet faded and fewer people came. It became clear that the status quo didn't have much of a future and changes were in order. Not change for change's sake, but change predicated on a comprehensive plan that followed the four steps outlined above.

Step #1—Collecting the Facts

To find the right way to change, Cliveden began by conducting a lot of research. This took a lot of time and money, both of which required budgeting. The site's staff did certain work while hired consultants did much of the rest as outlined below.

The first project was to prepare a Historic Structures Report.[4] An HSR, as they are usually called, examines the physical fabric of a house, its outbuildings, and the surrounding landscape. It requires research in manuscript and other resources, and usually involves archaeology. The variety of skills required means that an HSR is a team effort.[5] At Cliveden, historians combed the Chew family papers to discover what craftsmen worked at the site, how much they were paid, and when certain features were built or altered. Architects probed the fabric of the house, looked under floorboards and climbed on the roof in the process of preparing detailed drawings. A paint analyst figured out what colors of paint were used and when. Graduate students from the University of Pennsylvania examined the stucco while archaeologists explored several rich sites near the house.

After four years of work, the HSR confirmed much of what was already known about Cliveden, but it also revealed much new information. This is typical for an HSR. Also typical is that all of this research made things complicated, some might say messy. For example, the team found that the main part of Cliveden was largely unchanged from its initial construction in 1763 to 1767, but it had a big wing added in 1867 to 1868. Plus, the eighteenth-century farm was gone, but there was a vaguely nineteenth-century garden with distinctly twentieth-century plants.

Though the findings proved complex, the HSR put careful documentation, findings from the physical evidence, and a narrative interpretation at our fingertips. We now had numerous facts, ready to use.

The problem, though, was that the HSR raised a big and basic question. Was Cliveden in fact the "Colonial crown jewel" touted by the National Trust? The HSR clearly indicated that this was not accurate, or at least was too simplistic a description. The research demonstrated that Cliveden is actually a well-preserved eighteenth-century house with a nineteenth-century addition sitting in a vaguely nineteenth-century landscape, the whole of which sits in a decidedly urban late-twentieth-century cityscape. This means that all of this research turned the "Colonial crown jewel" upside down. We had a far more complicated situation, which sites should expect, because history is rarely tidy (fig. 10.2).

Just to make things more complicated, Cliveden's staff actually searched for more facts. As architects prepared the Historic Structures Report, a social historian plumbed the Chew papers to learn more about the people who had lived there for two hundred years. Diaries, letters, account books, scrapbooks, photographs, and other memorabilia fueled her efforts, and she wrote a detailed site history that fleshed out Cliveden's people over two centuries.[6] It reads rather like a soap opera, but a *true* soap opera filled with stories that have the genuine ring of human experience. Good research in family papers and other sources will likely uncover similarly interesting people stories at most historic sites.

Cliveden now faced the enviable problem of figuring out what to do with all of this information, for the Historic Structures Report and the site history together gave enough data to develop and present a two-week tour of the site. Recognizing reality, it was time to cull this research to develop a tour that took less than an hour. This was easier said than done.

Step #2—Finding the Themes

Cliveden needed to find the significant themes that lurked within this multitude of facts. To do this the site conducted an institutional self-study to explore Cliveden's future as a museum. The director wrote a successful proposal to the National Endowment for the Humanities, which permitted a comprehensive and admittedly costly approach. This process proved crucial, so even if your sites can't do everything Cliveden did, find ways to take some of these steps.

Figure 10.2. Entrance Hall, 1931. By the early twentieth century, the Chew family intermingled their eighteenth-century furnishings with Victorian furnishings and a healthy dose of potted palms. They also created a "Battle corner" (left wall) where they clustered prints and paintings of the Revolutionary War battle of Germantown and the people associated with it. Courtesy of Cliveden, a property of the National Trust for Historic Preservation in the United States.

Cliveden's self-study began with a two-day brainstorming session that brought together staff members, scholars, and museum professionals with different but pertinent areas of expertise including colonial history, the landscape, and historic house interiors. Over two days, this group generated an abundance of ideas, using the wealth of facts they had at hand. As should be expected, many great ideas later got eliminated because they were impractical or somehow didn't use Cliveden's resources to best advantage. For example, Cliveden was once a farm so one consultant urged bringing back animals such as cows and sheep. That idea got thrown out because the noise and smell of farm animals would be controversial in Cliveden's residential urban neighborhood.

Still, many brainstorms lingered in our minds as we moved to the next, and ultimately invaluable, step of the self-study. Six people—three staff members, a board member, and two guides—took two week-long trips to visit museums large and small in New England and Virginia. This admittedly was expensive but proved highly enlightening. We also attended conferences and visited sites closer to home, which was more economical but equally useful.

As we traveled near and far, we discovered what's happening in the museum field. Some of it is good, some is not, and some is truly inspiring. We got ideas about public programs, interpretive themes, historic house installations, research, school tours, publications, and exhibits. We met many skilled and enthusiastic people who later fielded phone calls and answered questions. Seeing places and meeting colleagues fed our minds and generated more ideas. And, like magpies, we picked pieces from different places and brought them home to Cliveden to start thinking about what we could be.

This process gradually led us to the development of a variety of themes that seemed central to the history of Cliveden and its interpretation to the public. After considerable discussion among the staff, buttressed by public responses solicited during tours and focus groups, we arrived at these key thematic ideas:

1. The architectural significance of Cliveden is matched by the integrity of its family-owned collections of decorative arts and manuscripts. These are local and even national resources worthy of continued preservation, research, and interpretation.

2. The battle of Germantown—a significant moment in the American Revolution—occurred in and around Cliveden on October 4, 1777. A British regiment occupied the house and George Washington directed his regiments to fire directly on it. The house stood, the British won, and Washington was forced to retreat, ultimately to Valley Forge.

3. The Chew Family lived at Cliveden for all but twenty years from 1765 through 1972. Their stories are documented and illustrated by the house and its furnishings. Among the most fascinating stories is the one that revolves around their decision in the 1860s to preserve Cliveden as a monument to colonial history. This decision affected their family life for a century but also placed them in the vanguard of the colonial revival movement.

The question remained about how to link and reinforce these themes to assure a coherent, stimulating, and informative tour. To do this we chose to write a storyline for the site and its history.

Step #3—Writing the Storyline

The single phrase that shaped how we coalesced our research, scholarly input, museum visits, and development of themes came from Massachusetts. At the Society for the Preservation of New England Antiquities, educator Peter Gittleman told us to "sing the song the house sings best." That became our goal. With all of the facts and the new themes in hand, we tried to find the song—or storyline—that Cliveden sang best. This proved deceptively hard. We struggled to find a compelling way to integrate the themes in ways that would energize the stories we wanted to tell. To further the process, we devised an exercise. We tried to finish the sentence that began with, "Cliveden tells the story of . . . ."

Once again, answering this was easier said than done. For six months we grappled with different ideas because there was no obvious, single answer to this simple phrase, which is the case at most historic houses.

For example, we thought about building on the third theme—the family's ownership of Cliveden over time—by saying, "Cliveden tells the story of a summer house enjoyed by many generations of one family." This is true and is potentially interesting. But this focus presented one big problem. What would we do with the battle of Germantown, which happened in October when the family did not live there? Not talk about it? We knew this was impossible because it was both bad history and bad for visitors who came to Cliveden to learn more about it. This event was too central to the history of the house. So while this summer house idea was interesting, generally, we realized it was not our best song.

At the other end of the spectrum we considered presenting Cliveden just as it was when the family gave it to the National Trust in 1972. That way we could talk about the full spectrum of the site's history and its residents, add the 1959 Formica kitchen to the tour, and place a few provocative ashtrays around. While tempting and even trendy, and perhaps desirable down the line, we eliminated that approach as well because we weren't convinced that this was Cliveden's *best* song.

We continued asking ourselves, "What is the story of Cliveden?" The wagons kept circling around certain information we knew we had to communicate, chiefly the battle of Germantown. This was Cliveden's defining moment and visitors expected to hear about it. We learned from focus groups how crucial it is to take visitors' expectations into consideration.[7] Historic sites must take seriously what visitors expect to see and hear. As a result, the combination of historical significance and visitor expectations placed the battle high on our interpretive list.

Our site history and our museum visits also convinced us that we had to tell people stories, so we needed to develop both the stories and ways to communicate them. Plus we had all of this stuff, our gorgeous and original collection of decorative arts that were part of the resource and story. This meant we had to address the furnishings plan as well.

With all of these givens and needs—the battle, the people stories, and the collections—we asked more questions with the goal of finding our best song. Why, for example, did seven generations of the same family choose to live at Cliveden? Why did the family keep all of this old stuff? Why did they decide Cliveden was so important nationally that it could no longer remain a private home? Why was it worthy of becoming a museum of the National Trust for Historic Preservation? These questions were bringing us closer to answering, "The story of Cliveden is . . . ." Which means all sites, just like Cliveden, must keep asking questions until they find the best answer.

The more we thought, the more we realized that Cliveden's story has two key features: *the family* who chose to preserve it, and *the battle*, which is the primary reason why they preserved it. We discovered these two stories converged in the nineteenth century when Cliveden became both a family heirloom and a national relic. Specifically, by 1876 and the Philadelphia Centennial Exposition, the Chews consciously chose to preserve Cliveden as the visible symbol of their family's history and social status. To achieve this, they focused on the obvious: their house, the Chew House (as it appeared in period books), survived a Revolutionary War battle. Honoring this decision demanded financial and personal sacrifice by the family for more than a century. It also affected how people lived in the house. For example, Anne Chew reluctantly agreed in 1867 to add a wing with a heated bedroom and an indoor bathroom, as long as it was not visible from the front of her "grandfather's house." As she said (and as we discovered during the research for the site history), "I have always wanted these accommodations for myself but should have lived and died without them rather than tear away the old landmarks." This preservation mantra, expressed in 1868, guided our thinking.

Also starting with the Centennial, the Chews marketed Cliveden as a Revolutionary War site worthy of patriotic recognition by the public. They exhibited the original front doors, pitted with holes left by musket and cannon balls, in Independence Hall. They had photographers take pictures, which were mounted and sold as stereopticon card souvenirs of colonial Philadelphia. They encouraged the publication of Cliveden in children's history books, emphasizing its link with the Revolution, if not the loss suffered there by Washington. Over time, these efforts paid off and helped Cliveden achieve status as an important colonial relic, which ultimately assured its long-term preservation.

The most intriguing aspect of these decisions is that they required the nineteenth-century Chews to rewrite their eighteenth-century history to better suit patriotic American needs. The Chews, in fact, were Tories during the Revolution, and Benjamin Chew, Cliveden's builder, was actually imprisoned by patriots. More alarming in a sense was that his daughter, Peggy Chew, cavorted with British soldiers who occupied Philadelphia during 1777 and 1778. They even managed to skirt the problem that the Americans lost the battle of Germantown. The nineteenth-century Chews downplayed these eighteenth-century facts quite effectively by eliminating the Tory connections in written accounts of the family and emphasizing that their heroic house survived a battle, not that it defeated Washington.

This nineteenth-century story of preservation, family pride, and rewriting history opened an unusual interpretive opportunity to Cliveden. By focusing on this nineteenth-century story, Cliveden would in fact emphasize the eighteenth century and the great event that was the Chew family's claim to fame. The nineteenth-century story also allowed looking forward to the twentieth century to explain why the family stayed for generations in their old-fashioned house. This was the interpretive fulcrum we needed in order to develop our rather complicated themes. So, hooray, we thought. We've found our story!

But how could we tell this story? It was complex and loaded with detail. We had an eighteenth-century event, crucial nineteenth-century preservation, all in a twentieth-century museum. We recognized that flexibility was imperative as we considered our interpretive plans. We knew we had to balance the overarching storyline with the need to explain a broad sweep of time in ways that visitors would understand and enjoy. This balancing act is one that many sites share.

It was with all of this information and these concerns that we at last wrote our storyline for Cliveden. These few sentences reflect several years of research and several more of thought:

> Cliveden tells the story of a stone house that stopped George Washington's army and sheltered one family for two centuries. Cliveden's one day of fame—October 4, 1777—shaped the war that made America free and the lives of the people who called it "home." At this rare place, original architecture, artifacts, and family papers converge with a great moment in history to create a vivid picture of the past.

This new storyline established Cliveden's key theme that a family made a conscious decision to preserve their house because an important event happened there. This storyline would underpin future interpretive planning for the site as a whole and in all formats including installation, publications, special exhibits and public programs, and guided tours. After a lot of work, we liked what we had. Now we needed to breathe life into the storyline and find ways to present it to the public.

Step #4—Testing the Themes and Storyline by Developing a Thematic Tour

Knowing that full implementation of the interpretive planning project would take time, money, and potentially, reinstallation of the house, we decided to test the waters with a few experiments. By doing this we embraced the philosophy that historic house museums are not frozen in their exhibits or their presentation to the public.

For our experiment we targeted some guinea pigs—all of those wiggly schoolchildren trapped on class trips. With the dual aim of improving our school programs and testing ideas that could lead to the overall reinterpretation of Cliveden, we developed several thematic school tours. We also began modifying the installation of the house, initially to improve school tours, but it ultimately affected regular tours, as well.

The most influential thematic tour we developed was based on a relatively new approach to history pioneered at places like Colonial Williamsburg. This approach is called "perspectivistic history," which actually translates into a very understandable idea. Perspectivistic history is history that looks at particular events from the perspective, or point of view, of particular people at particular moments in time. For example, this approach takes into account that the Civil War experience was different for Robert E. Lee than it was for a black private in the Union infantry. But as Ken Burns demonstrated in his Civil War series developed for the Public Broadcasting Service, each of these men has a story, an interesting and important story to tell.[8]

Perspectivistic history works magnificently at historic sites. First-person tours, or tours presented by costumed interpreters who speak in the present tense about life long ago, offer well-known and excellent examples of it. Colonial Williamsburg has been a leader in this type of interpretation and interaction with the public. Visitors may encounter a historic person such as Thomas Jefferson, who offers his views on political liberty, or take a tour with a female hatmaker, who shows her town from her point of view as a single woman supporting herself in a trade. Visitors also encounter representatives of fifty percent of Williamsburg's historic population—its enslaved African Americans. Through first-person accounts, these remarkable interpreters present compelling counterpoints to the stories told by "Jefferson" or "Patrick Henry." This first-person approach is challenging, but when done well, it encourages visitors to interact with the interpreters because it carries the potential of making history personal.

Chews for a Day

Our self-study experiences, specifically at Colonial Williamsburg, encouraged us to try a little perspectivistic interpretation at Cliveden. As a pilot project, we culled information from our Historic Structures Report and site history and developed a thematic school tour called "Chews for a Day." The program focused on 1777, the year of the battle of Germantown, and assembled primary source information about the family members, servants and slaves, household costs, and the battle. We chose four characters, real people from the site's history, and developed their biographies. In doing this, we, as staff members, started to think in new ways about how each of these people would have used the house. We developed tours that presented the house from each character's point of view. We based the tours on real stories of real people, each of whom had a somewhat different experience at Cliveden during the Civil War.

We also developed curriculum materials geared to grades four through seven, trained a small corps of highly experienced guides, and then called several local schools to see if they would be interested in bringing a class or two for a free tour. Free tours are popular, several schools booked, and our pilot was under way.

"Chews for a Day" had three parts. The first part took place in Cliveden's classroom space and introduced the students to Cliveden in 1777. The lesson presumed that the Revolutionary War was something less than two years in duration with an outcome still unknown. It also introduced aspects of daily life by analyzing how much shoes, flour, and tea cost in terms that helped students understand the colonial economy. After this introduction, the class was divided into four groups. Each group received an autobiography that told their life history to that point. As part of the directions, the students were encouraged to think in the first person and "become" this historic person. After reading the autobiographies, guides took groups to the house for a tour given from the perspective of that historic person. As much as possible, guides and students were encouraged to think in the first person.

Some students toured the house as Cliveden's owner, Ben Chew, Senior. He was a rich and powerful Loyalist who had just been exiled by radical patriots.

Others saw Cliveden as his wife, Elizabeth, who was left behind to be a single parent to eight children during the British occupation of Philadelphia. A third group saw Cliveden through the eyes of the eldest son, Ben, Junior, who is of army age but serves in neither the American nor British forces. The fourth group (by all accounts the most fun) became Ben's flirtatious sister, Peggy. She dates British soldiers, including Major John André, who two years later got the noose for his dastardly collaboration with the American traitor, Benedict Arnold. Four different tours presented the stories of these four characters within Cliveden's evocative historic environment. The tours and the related stories offered compelling perspectives of wartime experiences. And as we learned, because the stories of these four characters engaged the students personally, the students absorbed surprising amounts of rather sophisticated material.

"Chews for a Day" proved popular because children liked imagining they were real historic people living in this real environment and experiencing real events. By assuming the character of Ben Chew, Senior, for example, students had to think about the choices that faced colonial Americans during the Revolution. Was it safer to remain tied with England? Were the patriots well-intentioned but overzealous malcontents who threatened the rule of law? Was it just to be imprisoned for loyalty to the Crown, as Chew was, and to be removed from a loving family and beloved home? Elizabeth Chew faced worries about her husband and caring for her many children. She also had to tend to the aftermath of the battle of Germantown, which shattered Cliveden's windows, battered doors, and set the roof on fire. Ben, Junior, held the role as the male head of household, even though he was just seventeen years old. Given that, and given the politics of his father, would he join the military, and if so, on which side? Peggy Chew was by all accounts beautiful, charming, and very smart. For her, war opened opportunities for romance, especially when thousands of young British soldiers, far from home, occupied Philadelphia. Would she sit out the war or take advantage of these unusual opportunities? As the students learned, charming Peggy took advantage of the situation and danced her way through the British army. Her most prominent beau, Major John André, presented her with a beautiful book, still at Cliveden, that described the magical "Mischianza" ball that he choreographed for the British army and Tory Philadelphia.

Wartime difficulties—and romance—made a strong impression with most kids who took part in "Chews for a Day." This energy and personal connection with history came through in the third part of the program when each group prepared and presented information about their character for the rest of the class. Some of these presentations came in the form of a short play, which continued the first-person approach to Cliveden's history. Other presentations took a more contemporary format and ranged from game shows to talk shows that offered tidbits about the character and their take on their life. Students typically left Cliveden energized, and teachers reported back positively that the trip had been an effective way to present lots of different information and several different viewpoints about the Revolution. Perhaps the most telling expression of how students connected with the site and this program occurred several months later when a young girl came up to me in a grocery store and declared, "Remember me? I was Peggy Chew!"

Still, "Chews for a Day" required a great deal of extra work. First, we had to train the guides in ways that were new and with expectations that were different. Like the staff, they had to learn the biographies of the historical characters, then begin thinking about the house from that perspective. Guide training involved lectures, room studies, and tour demonstrations. Not everybody liked the program, but those who did embraced it because, like the students, they found the stories intriguing. And, like many of the students, the corps of guides who led this program ended up connecting in very personal ways with the different characters. So overall, this extra work invigorated many guides in a good way.

The most unexpected result of this experimental tour was that it influenced regular adult tours as well. The stories we developed for the students proved equally effective with adults, offering rather sophisticated ideas in an appealing package. For general tours and school groups two stories stood out: children and adults loved hearing about the blood and gore of the battle as well as the romantic and traitorous flings of Peggy Chew. This made us think about how to reinforce these stories visually.

That's when we began rearranging the house.

Furnishings plans and the research required to produce them are important foundations for historic house installations. Old photographs, inventories, and other documentation must be consulted. Still, rigid adherence to furnishings plans can risk creating a sterile environment that speaks more to curators than the general public. Cliveden chose a different path that built on the spirit of collaboration among a staff that had navigated through the HSR, the self-study, the development of the storyline, and the launch of "Chews for a Day."

With a team that included the curator of collections, the museum educator, the historian, the director, and guides, Cliveden's new installation followed a nontraditional route that favored the stories we had developed over curatorial purity. Simply stated, we rearranged the collection, clustering objects so they told a story visually. For example, we installed a "battle corner" in Cliveden's sweeping entrance hall. Paintings, engravings, rifles, and battle-scarred walls, when grouped together, permitted telling the story of the battle with a beginning, a middle, and an end. Though these exact objects were never together at any point in Cliveden's history, the overall appearance is similar to that of late nineteenth-century photographs. This compromise favored the interpretive potential of objects over curatorial purity (fig. 10.3).

The battle corner proved so effective that we installed similar vignettes throughout the house to trigger key stories linked to our interpretive themes. There was, for example, a "Mischianza corner," which grouped objects from the actual eighteenth-century event with nineteenth-century photographs that showed Chew family members re-creating it. This grouping reinforced our interpretive theme that a nineteenth-century family chose to preserve its eighteenth-century history, and it presented wonderful opportunities to describe the glorious excess that was the Mischianza, as well as the curious amnesia that the nineteenth-century Chews had about their Tory forebears. This rearrangement helped both guides and visitors: guides could now relay complete stories in one place, while visitors heard a well-developed story once and enjoyed the visual reinforcement of related objects (fig. 10.4).

This new approach also encouraged us to plot the house by creating tour routes that allowed stories to unfold and develop. Coherent stories, effectively told and visually reinforced, help engage a broad public accustomed to the storytelling media of television and movies. This now seems obvious, but to understand this, Cliveden literally had to turn its house upside down and inside out. Which, simply, is what historic houses *must* do if we are to have a future. We must turn our houses upside down, do good history, and find effective ways to connect with our twenty-first-century public.

As historic houses face the future, keep these four ideas in mind. First, do a lot of research. Second, use this research to identify the themes that make your site special. Third, find the "song your house sings best" and use the new themes to develop the storyline you want your public to experience and remember, whether by guided or self-guided tours, videos, publications, demonstrations, or school programs. Finally, develop, experiment with, and implement theme-driven programs that bring life to the storyline. Discover what works with your public and what doesn't. Keep improving your product. Connect in personal ways with your public. In the process, if your experience is like that at Cliveden, you will shake out some historic house dust, reinvigorate your staff and guides, and retrieve visitor surveys that say, "What a great tour!" Best of all, great themes and great stories encourage surprise assaults in grocery stores by children who say, "Remember me? I was Peggy Chew!"

Figure 10.3. Entrance Hall, 1995. Using early-twentieth-century photographs of the entrance hall as inspiration, Cliveden's curator installed a "battle corner" filled with paintings, photographs, and objects linked to the story of the battle of Germantown. This installation reflected a historic appearance of the space (see figure 10.2). At least as important, it facilitated presenting a cohesive interpretation of the battle story by clustering relevant objects from the collection. Photograph by Ron Blunt. Courtesy of Cliveden, a property of the National Trust for Historic Preservation in the United States.

Figure 10.4.   Bedroom, 1995. The "Mischianza corner" introduced a collection of photographs, prints, and a dress to tell the romantic and controversial story of Peggy Chew. Peggy, the teenaged daughter of Benjamin and Elizabeth Chew, attended the grand ball organized by the British army during its occupation of Philadelphia in 1778. Major John André escorted her and later presented her with a book describing the event and illustrating the white gowns Peggy and other Tory girls wore. The exhibited dress is a copy made ca. 1896 by Peggy's great-niece, Bessie Chew. Bessie and her brother, also in costume, posed for photographs that re-created the Mischianza. By then, the scandal of Peggy's dancing with the British had evolved into pride of the Chew family's colonial roots. The story of the Mischianza offers rich opportunities for interpretation about romance, treason, and, ultimately, how different generations understand and even manipulate history for particular purposes. Photograph by Ron Blunt. Courtesy of Cliveden, a property of the National Trust for Historic Preservation in the United States.

Notes

1. Many books and articles address issues of interpretation at museums and historic sites. The newsletter the *Docent Educator* published by Alan Gartenhaus generally includes short, pithy articles that address a variety of these issues. Selected other sources include Alison L. Grinder and E. Sue McCoy, *The Good Guide: A Sourcebook for Interpreters, Docents, and Tour Guides* (Scottsdale, Ariz.: Ironwood Press, 1985); John H. Falk and Lynn D. Dierking, *The Museum Experience* (Washington, D.C.: Whalesback Books, 1992); Sam Ham, *Environmental Interpretation: A Practical Guide for People with Big Ideas and Small Budgets* (Golden, Colo.: North American Press, 1992); and William J. Lewis, *Interpreting for Park Visitors* (Philadelphia: Eastern Acorn Press, 1988).

2. Susan Schreiber, formerly director of interpretation for the National Trust for Historic Preservation, developed this strategy and has employed it at Trust sites including Montpelier in Virginia and the Woodrow Wilson House in Washington, D.C. Barbara Levy served as a consultant on several of these projects and has implemented similar interpretive planning strategies at non-National Trust properties. The strategies presented in this discussion are the product of close collaboration with them over the last ten years. I have adapted and employed this process at sites such as Pennsbury Manor, the reconstructed home of Pennsylvania's founder William Penn, and the Betsy Ross House to develop videos, landscape interpretation, self-guided tours, and historical research for exhibits.

3. For more information about the battle of Germantown, see Thomas J. McGuire, *The Surprise of Germantown, October 4, 1777* (Gettysburg, Pa.: Thomas Publications and Cliveden of the National Trust, 1994). The battle and Cliveden's role in it are also discussed in general histories of the Revolution.

4. Martin J. Rosenblum, R. A. and Associates, "Historic Structures Report: Cliveden," 4 vols. (report prepared for Cliveden of the National Trust for Historic Preservation, June 1994).

5. The National Park Service (NPS) helped establish the guidelines for a Historic Structures Report (HSR). Models of NPS HSRs are typically on file at NPS sites. Many other historic sites, often ones that have either Historic Landmark or National Historic Site status, have undertaken these considerable projects. Architects usually serve as the supervisors of an HSR and work with a team of historians, technicians, and archaeologists. State historic preservation offices can provide the names of reputable architects skilled in the production of these reports. HSRs assure thorough documentation of the physical fabric of historic buildings and their change and development over time. They are used as reference for a site and its preservation and interpretation. Historic Landscape Reports (HLRs) offer the same comprehensive study and analysis of the landscape in which a building sits. Features included in HLRs range from gardens to farmyards. They sometimes include buildings related to the landscape such as garden houses, barns, or sheds. Both HSRs and HLRs are valuable for their historical record of change over time, and

the presentation of the site as it exists at the time of writing. An excellent HSR and HLR provide the benchmarks for understanding, preserving, and interpreting the site.

6. Nancy E. Richards, "Cliveden: The Chew Mansion in Germantown" (manuscript prepared for Cliveden of the National Trust for Historic Preservation, November 1993).

7. Cliveden conducted several focus groups during the interpretive planning project. Advertisements appeared in local papers offering a free tour and small stipend in exchange for a follow-up discussion about the site and its presentation. These relatively informal conversations revealed that local residents cared deeply about the beautiful open space that characterizes Cliveden's landscape, that they enjoyed the annual re-creation of the battle of Germantown, and consequently that they knew that the house played an important role in the American Revolution. In fact, Cliveden's connection with the Revolution proved so dominant in people's knowledge of the site, both before and after visiting, that it became clear that this story must be central to the interpretation. This was an important story, people enjoyed hearing it, and even more important, many *expected* to hear it. The lesson from this is that historic sites must fulfill visitor expectations, which often requires providing information about the obvious. What sites must do, however, is make sure that they start with this expectation, then expand visitor knowledge and interest by integrating strong research and compelling stories.

8. Ken Burns, *The Civil War*, narrated by David McCullough, written and produced by Ken Burns, PBS special (Florentine Films, September 1990).

CHAPTER ELEVEN

ENGAGING VISITORS THROUGH EFFECTIVE COMMUNICATION

Margaret Piatt

Historic houses immediately focus visitors' attention on the concept of home. Home is a universal experience and all visitors, to some degree, bring to every historic house their own understanding of house and home. They automatically respond from their perspectives and wonder what it would be like to live in the house. Would they be comfortable? Could they maintain it? How would they change the furnishings? Historic house museum interpreters skilled at engaging visitors through effective communication are well aware of these personal reactions and they integrate them into their interpretation.

I will be forever shaped by the first historic house that I ever knew and by the first house museum in which I worked as a tour guide. Both experiences took place in a building that was also my home. I have come to understand that this was an unusual childhood—to live in a house that was also open to the public—but the oddity of it has given me a lifelong fascination with communication and a sense of destiny about interpreting history through historic houses. Since my days as a child living in a historic house museum, I have gone on to manage Sunnyside (Washington Irving's home administered by Historic Hudson Valley), to coordinate domestic history programs and interpreter staff training at Old Sturbridge Village, and to consult for many historic house museums all over the country. Each experience has given me insight into the process of interacting with visitors in historic house museums. My communication skills have improved through study and practice, but I learned the key principles of the process when I gave my first tours of my own home.

My Piatt family great-great-great-grandparents settled in central Ohio in the early nineteenth century. They came from Cincinnati where they were involved in a variety of endeavors. Elizabeth was a social reformer and abolitionist and Benjamin was an entrepreneur and circuit court judge. He and his brother accumulated a decent fortune in property and money from their flatboat trade down the Ohio and Mississippi Rivers. Benjamin continued to invest in farming and milling so that by the time he died mid-century, he had a prosperous estate. These holdings were divided among his many children. The youngest, Abram, my great-great-grandfather, operated the farm throughout his early adult life. In 1864, when he was in his mid-forties, he decided to build a new house (fig. 11.1).

We have never really known why Abram chose to construct his house in the way he did. Some said that he selected limestone from the Piatt quarry and native wood from the family land because it was expedient. In a romantic sense, they said that Abram wanted to build a monument to the land. Clearly the family loved the land as they all wrote poetry about it, painted and drew landscapes of it, and continued to name every new structure on it with an adaptation of the original Shawnee name for the place, Mackachak. Others suggested that Abram

Figure 11.1. Mac-A-Cheek Castle, built for Abram Sanders Piatt in 1864 in West Liberty, Ohio. Courtesy of Piatt Castles.

wanted to impress his new wife, and still others said that he built his odd house because he had the money and he could. In any case, Abram spent much of his capital on a large stone structure with a five-story tower that he named Mac-A-Cheek. In the spirit of practical whimsy, he adapted the channel that had once been a millrace into a moat that curved around the north side on the crest of a hillside overlooking fields and meadows. Before long, local people began calling the place Piatt's Castle.

When Abram died in 1908, his son William inherited the building and eighty acres around it. The other brothers were more sensible and wished to own greater pieces of farmland, but William loved the house that he had helped his father build. They hadn't hired a designer; they developed its look by themselves and William continued to enjoy tinkering with the building, which he used as a farmhouse and place to invent farm machinery.

The story is told that in 1912, William had grown tired of the people coming to gawk at the big, stone castle, so he said, "If I charge admission, they'll go away." It didn't work. Instead it began the tradition of the Piatt family as farmer–tour guides. William created a cabinet of curiosities. He brought his grandmother's spinning wheels out of the attic and placed them in the drawing room—a large lavish room, rarely used. On tables, he set out all of the early war memorial items and guns, shell boxes, musical instruments, and old shoes. A Chickering piano originally belonging to his grandmother, Elizabeth, and the best furniture from each generation completed the setting. William added his own favorite chair made of horns. He also bought a huge walnut case from the Masons, took off all the Masonic symbols, put on symbols of nature, and filled it with his favorite things, including what he called his "Indian relic" collection, and he conducted every single tour. He did that for quite a long time and the tradition continued through the next two generations.

Like most families in the United States, the Piatts encountered difficult times from about 1917 through the 1940s. The 1918 flu epidemic took the lives of many in the family, including William's wife, son, and daughter-in-law. The latter were my grandparents. World War I took other family members and then the depression hit. Shortly thereafter William died and two of his daughters inherited the house and the care of their orphan nephews. They had no money left, but they could still plow fields, raise chickens, and give tours. Over time, the sisters opened more rooms and lived in fewer until they resided in an apartment that had once been the servants' quarters. The years after World War II brought a new prosperity to the country and a rise in tourism. My father was a natural salesman who preferred talking to farming, so very gradually he shifted the priorities and became a tour guide–farmer. That is the life into which I was born.

Lessons Learned While Giving Tours

I was a tour guide prodigy. When I was five years old, my Great Uncle Cricket came to stay for a while. I loved Cricket. He was real shiny and kind of round, and he was funny. I liked to hang around Cricket who liked to hang around the refrigerator. Mother became annoyed by this habit so one day she said to me, "Peggy, go take Cricket on a tour." The very thought of spending that much time with Uncle Cricket sounded pretty good, so I agreed. Then, I encountered a problem. I didn't have the foggiest idea how to give a tour. I did know one thing: you don't start a tour in the kitchen. So I told Uncle Cricket to go out the kitchen door and to enter through the front door. He did so while I ran through the building and met him in the entrance hall. That is how Daddy always started a tour, at the front door.

I invited Uncle Cricket into the drawing room, which is what Daddy always did, and I remembered that Daddy always used some kind of a big sweeping gesture to draw attention to the magnitude of the space. I walked right to the middle of the intricately patterned parquet floor and stood in my favorite spot, the diamond shape, and I said with wide outstretched arms, "This is the drawing room!" Well, you know, Cricket looked at me like he expected more. I panicked. I didn't know anything more. I looked around frantically until I spied the Chickering piano. I boldly gestured with an extended arm and a pointed finger and firmly declared, "That is a piano." He looked at the piano and he looked back at me as if he still expected me to say something else. In desperation, I added, "It's old." That seemed finally to satisfy him so I sighed with relief and escorted Cricket out of the room.

Once in the hallway I showed Uncle Cricket my favorite feature in the castle. The stairs had grooves running along the sides, and Daddy said they were dust channels. I had often heard him explain, "There are no corners on the stairs to trap the dust so all one needs to do is simply sweep the dust from either side, and it comes right down the dust channels." Cricket reacted with interest to this explanation from me and we pondered that if this was such a good idea, why didn't everybody put dust channels in their homes? Our conversation was so comfortable that I began to relax. I took a gamble and decided to confide something to Uncle Cricket. I told him when nobody was around my brother and I came out and raced our toys down the dust channels. I thought this confidence pleased him as he leaned back and chuckled.

My first tour progressed upstairs to see bedrooms and back downstairs where we looked at dining rooms and the library until finally we ended up in my great-great-grandfather's office. In this room, we kept a very precious and important object. It was the Mac-A-Cheek Press, not a printing press but a newspaper. In addition to farming, Abram Piatt dabbled in journalism. He wrote and edited a journal "Devoted to Politics, Literature, Agriculture, Science, Art, and General Intelligence." We have all the volumes and one of them was open to the same week, over a hundred years ago. I knew Daddy valued the paper so I pointed it out saying, "That's a newspaper. Read it." I, of course, could not read, but Cricket looked down dutifully at the 1860s newspaper and said, "This is really pretty interesting." He became quite absorbed and read a couple of articles. As he did that, I realized that I had completed the tour and it was time for me to usher him out of the office door. As I opened it, I mimicked Mother's words when she gave tours, "This is the end of your tour." A thought occurred to me so I held out my hand and added, "That will be a quarter, please." Uncle Cricket chuckled again, dug into his pocket and gave me a quarter.

A popular author claims that everything he needed to know, he learned in kindergarten.[1] In the field of historic house interpretation, that is true for me. By the time I was five years old I had gained many lessons from my first tour. I discovered that when interpreting, it is not enough to just name rooms or to name the objects within the rooms or to brag about how old or beautiful the objects are. It is more effective if we actually take the time to explain how people used objects and why. It's even more effective if we show how objects work and share something personal about them. But, it is even more effective when we give the visitor something to do. No matter what, somebody pays for the experience.

I didn't give another tour of the castle for ten more years, but when I turned fifteen, Daddy told me it was time for me to be a tour guide. I didn't want to do it. I was self-conscious and obsessed with my appearance. I was certain that I didn't look good enough to talk with strangers. I still had braces and I wore funny glasses. Everything was awful. I also didn't want to be the boss's daughter. But I didn't get any preferential treatment. I was trained just the way everybody else was trained. We were each given a tour that Mother wrote and we memorized it. Then we started giving tours. Sometimes Daddy took new guides on a tour, which wasn't too much help because he told totally different things than were in the written tour, and we weren't allowed to say the things he said; we had to say what was in the script. That is how my parents controlled the length of the tours and the information shared.

As I began my new job as a paid tour guide, I encountered a problem similar to the one I faced at the age of five. I didn't understand most of what was in the script. Despite growing up in the building, surrounded by the objects and overhearing thousands of tours, I didn't really understand the meaning of many of the words or references. That summer when I was fifteen, I made a powerful discovery—if you assume an uninterested and slouching posture, mumble words in a monotone, and look down at the ground, no one asks any questions. As this was my goal, I was delighted with my discovery and that is how I survived my first summer of guiding tours.

By the second summer I'd studied American history in high school and realized that I now understood many of the statements in the script. Furthermore, I was growing interested in the topic, not just because there were some members of my family connected to ideas in American history, but also because the region where I lived was connected to these ideas. Ohio was beginning to seem more interesting than I had imagined and I was excited by this knowledge. I had another experience that was even more significant. During my junior year, I had taken a speech class and through it I began to find my voice. Even though I had to give the memorized tour, I spent the whole of my sixteenth summer practicing. I practiced how and where to stand. I discovered I could see people better if I stood in certain places, and, therefore, they could probably see me better. I began experimenting with pacing and volume and inflection, and it was really fun. I watched the people. I paid attention to what they looked at. I decided if Mother or Daddy were not listening, that I would change the order of the information to coincide with what the visitors seemed to notice. I changed the words to a vocabulary that was more compatible with the way I naturally spoke. I enjoyed giving tours that summer, and by the end of it I was good. I was really good! People nodded when I spoke, smiled at me often, laughed at my jokes, and gave me tips!

The next summer I was not as effective because I had fallen into two typical traps. I had become arrogant and I had become bored. I no longer thought actively about what I was saying or paid much attention to what the visitors were doing. I still knew how to stand and when to smile, but I had lost my inner drive. I imagine that I appeared much like flight attendants who are giving life saving instructions for the millionth time. I went through the motions. That last summer before going off to college, I dragged myself, day after day, tour after tour, through that building, telling the same old blah ba blah ba blah. I knew how to get people to react. I just stopped caring, until the day that changed my life.

On one very hot day in mid-August, I had an experience that affected my entire career, not only as a tour guide but also as a public speaker, a stage director, and a teacher. I can honestly say that in the more than thirty years that have followed, I have never again been bored in any work requiring verbal and nonverbal communication.

I was giving my fourth tour of the day and I was standing across from the stairs on the top floor. This was the worst place to be as the visitors were tired from the last climb of stairs, the objects and information were the least interesting, and it was a very hot and humid day. It was the type of day in August when the sky turns white, the grass is brown, and no air moves.

Visitors were slogging through the hallway aimlessly looking at stuff while I propped myself against a door and blabbed the words of the tour. My mind drifted but my mouth kept moving. I don't know how long I talked before I noticed them, but in a jolt, I suddenly realized that two people were not looking around. Instead, they were standing right in front, looking directly at me. One was a man who looked much like the then-young astronaut, John Glenn, dressed in vacation garb. He had on red plaid Bermuda shorts and a yellow shirt with a collar. I remember this vividly. He wore tennis socks and tennis shoes and had a blond crew cut. Actually, he also looked somewhat like a grown-up Ken doll. Right next to him was a little boy who looked just like him. As they stood there they did something that seriously frightened me. They were listening to me! They seemed to be particularly interested, but I had no idea what I was saying. Do you know what it is like when you are driving down a familiar highway and suddenly you don't know how you got there or where you are going? To find my way, I started trying to think about what I was saying, and I watched them. They looked back at me, smiling, nodding, and acting interested, and it was the first time I began to wonder why. Why are they interested? Why did they come here? Who are they? Where did they come from? It became pretty clear that the man was not John Glenn so I decided he and his son came from Michigan. I began to wonder what they were going to do when they left and what they were going to say to others about their tour, and if they often visited historical places.

On that hot August day in 1969 I started to care about visitors and I've never been bored again. I also experienced humility and that was much different from the anxiety I had felt two years before. Insecure public speakers fear they will fail. Humble public speakers know they can fail and that it takes constant effort to maintain quality. The formula for effective communication is really that simple. Effective communicators need to know what they are talking about. Content is important, but knowing and understanding information is not enough. Effective interpreters must be equally interested, if not more so, in their visitors. They must care about their visitors, what they're like, why they are in their museums, and what they want to explore or learn. They must then work to master teaching and speaking technique in order to help visitors connect with the content.

A Model of Communication

Most of us were asked to study models for the communication process in some course in high school or college. The standard model helps us visualize communication as a process in which a sender transmits a message to a receiver (fig. 11.2). The senders and receivers can be individuals, groups, or organizations. Senders and receivers are affected by all of their life experiences. These certainly include their age, gender, race and ethnicity, economic status, educational background, political leanings, and religious beliefs as well as their personality, interests, and feelings about their companions. Other factors include their health, their current comfort, their most immediate experience, and things that happened to them as children. Out of this filter of life experiences, the sender creates a message to send to the receiver. The message might be simple or complicated and it can be delivered through multiple channels. The message is decoded through the receiver's filter of life experiences and usually generates immediate feedback. At that moment the sender has become the receiver and the process continues.

In a historic house museum, the sender in the communication process can be the trustees and staff. They shape messages about their historical site and visitor program that they send through channels such as advertising, signs, visitor comfort areas, exhibits, tours, special events, and films. The sender can also be an interpreter who uses language, posture, facial expression, gestures, vocal tone, volume, intonation, and articulation to send messages. In both cases, the receiver is the visitor. Sometimes mixed messages are sent—when I was a teenaged tour guide, for instance, and looked down at the ground while I mumbled, "If you have any questions, I'll be glad to answer them." My spoken language offered an invitation while my body language slammed the door in the face of anyone wanting to accept the invitation.

A Model for the Communication Process

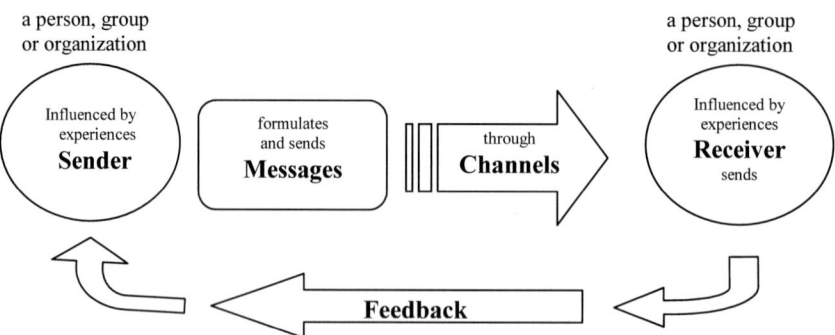

Figure 11.2.   A model of communication.

When we consider that messages are multiple and complicated, and the channels are varied, it is easy to understand why communication often fails. Furthermore, if the life experiences of the sender are vastly different than the life experiences of the receiver, it is a challenge for the first to construct a message that the latter can reconstruct. This is why we must never lose interest in our visitors' past experiences in historic house museums and their motivations for visiting ours. Do their life experiences suggest to them that these museums are dull and that the presentation will be condescending and rude? Did they come here today to receive a particular message, but did their human interaction with interpreters make it clear that no one cared?

Even if the sender and receiver have complementary life experiences, communication can fail if the message is confusing or the channel is ineffective. There are so many places within the model that barriers to communication can occur. Breakdowns happen if the sender does not select a channel that works for the receiver, when interpreters use words that visitors don't understand, or if the message is not appropriate for the receiver.

Another personal experience—in which I was the visitor, not the tour guide—illustrates these points well. When my daughter was a child, she was enrolled in a class at an art museum that I quite love. I was delighted because I could take her to the class and then wait for her by spending pleasurable time in the museum looking and learning about art. One day, as I was walking through the galleries, I noticed that there was a tour in progress. I decided to see if I could join. I was a perfect visitor. I wanted to be there, I was interested in the subject matter, and I had time. I joined the end of this tour group just as I heard the tour guide walk into a gallery space and say in a high, fluty voice, "As you enter the gallery, note the Whistler." I thought, "Does she always use that tone or is that her tour guide accent?" I walked into the gallery prepared to look at the Whistler, but here I encountered a problem. There were more than ten paintings and I didn't know which one was the Whistler. I am not ignorant about art, but I certainly don't know every work by every artist and in this case, I could not tell which painting was Whistler's. Since the labels were far away and I couldn't see them, I looked to the guide for a clue. This is what I saw. Like a figure in an Egyptian drawing, she was walking sideways, around the walls of the gallery. She wasn't looking at the people, and she wasn't looking at the art. She was looking at the ceiling, and I couldn't easily hear what she was saying. I stopped looking at her and started looking at the visitors. They were lounging on gallery benches, looking miserable with shoulders bent and glum faces. One of them was viewing a painting on the other side of the gallery and I started to feel sorry for the guide. I thought, "Well, this is a tough group." My heart is always out there with tour guides. I've been through it. So I looked back at her and thought, "I'm really going to listen hard to her." And I did. I listened really hard, and I wish I could tell you what she said. I wish I could remember the words she selected to describe this art. I can't remember the words because I didn't understand most of them and the sequence of her phrases seemed archaic at best. I don't think she actually said anything meaningful. I think she spoke in an affected babble meant to make her sound educated. I turned my attention back to the visitors and started listening to them. I noticed that they were speaking French. They were! It was not evident if they even spoke English. Here is our challenge. We must all ask ourselves: How often does this happen? How often do our museums create complicated and meaningless messages that we deliver to people who are not paying attention and who couldn't understand the words even if they tried? You want to say "never," but honestly, you know the answer is "sometimes," and you fervently hope it is not "often."

Strategies and Techniques to Improve Communication

Every one of us is capable of being an effective communicator and each of us sometimes fails. My decision to become a museum educator forced me to consider my own strengths and weaknesses as a communicator. When I was in graduate school, my advisor came to watch me teach a combination class of fifth- and sixth-grade students. I was nervous and became even more so as I watched her sit silently in the back of the room taking notes. After class, she told me to call her on the telephone when I knew what I had done well and what could be improved. I went home and lamented that I had done nothing well. Finally, I called to confess this to her and to expand on the ugly details of my failure. She told me that I was absolutely correct, that I had not done well in the described areas. She then surprised me by telling me how important it was to realize these weaknesses. When she asked what I had done well, I claimed, "Nothing." She replied by telling me to call her again when I knew what I had done well. After much soul searching, I made that call. Since then, I have come to see how useful this painful exercise had been. If we can't acknowledge our strengths, how can we use them when we need them? If we can't recognize our weaknesses, how can we improve them? I encourage you to periodically consider your own. Try to improve in areas where you are weak, but also use your advantages to compensate for your limitations. Think of your strengths as a talent savings account that you can draw upon when you need it.

In workshops, I often ask participants to list their communication strengths and weaknesses and to share those insights with a partner. I offer certain ground rules: include both strengths and weaknesses; don't tell anything that you are not comfortable sharing; both people must take a turn talking and each person must focus their concentration on listening; when one listens, he or she should also watch the speaker.

Improving Vocal Skills

When I asked attendees at the 1998 McFaddin-Ward House conference on historic house museums[2] to participate in the exercise, the room erupted in noise as one hundred individuals began speaking with each other. I watched as they worked to overcome the increased noise in the room. They faced each other, leaned in to be closer, and made eye contact. They focused on each other and they adjusted the way they spoke and how they listened. This contrasts sharply with how they sat and the way I had to manage my volume, pitch, diction, and energy when I spoke to the complete assembly. Interpreters in historic house museums frequently shift from talking with a few visitors to speaking to large crowds. It takes mental and vocal dexterity to make those transitions. Sometimes people are very effective when communicating with a small number of visitors, but they don't adequately increase their volume, accentuate their diction, or magnify their energy when they are in a bigger space with a larger number of people. I have seen other interpreters who are quite comfortable speaking to large crowds, but they are too loud when trying to use a less formal style with smaller groups in more intimate settings such as the rooms in historic house museums.

For some interpreters, the difficulty in adapting to different types of speaking situations is attitudinal—they can't imagine speaking to a large crowd. They manage the situation by pretending it is not happening. In other cases, their struggle comes from not knowing how to adapt the instrument of their voice to play a wider range. This latter problem can seem more complicated although it is actually easier to solve. If interpreters are not already familiar with the principles of how to breathe to control volume and pitch and how to improve their tonal sound and diction through correct use of their resonating chambers and articulators, they should be given training and encouraged to practice as part of their training. Professional singers, actors, and public speakers know the importance of caring for their voice so that they have the greatest flexibility in using it to convey meaning. The same is true for interpreters.

If we pay attention, we hear examples every day of speakers who use their vocal characteristics to convey meaning. In a conference presentation on disaster planning, Arthur Dutil spoke of the damage that water can cause historic structures; he lowered his pitch and added a frightening quivering sound as he described water as "the enemy."[3] The crowd reacted, and I actually felt scared. I could feel fear, not only because I could imagine how water could destroy a historic structure, but also because when Mr. Dutil said the words, he sounded like he was going into battle against a fierce enemy. His words conveyed his message, but his tone gave the message its emotional power and force.

At an interpreters' conference in 1991, interpretive specialist Dale Jones and I identified a list of six qualities that most speakers want in their voice.[4] They are:

1. Vocal expressiveness. Controlled by the use of pitch, volume, and speed, the human voice is capable of subtle nuances and shades of meaning.

2. Articulate diction. Using the lips, teeth, and tongue to shape words, this quality creates a clear and distinct manner that is easily understood and easily heard.

3. Pleasing tone. Effected by the way sound resonates through our nasal and mouth cavities and off the bones in our head, clear round tones invite people to listen and are easier to hear.

4. Personality. This unique quality identifies each of us as individuals and incorporates our pronunciation and dialect.

5. Projection. Both volume and energy are controlled by the release of air from our lungs to create a voice that suggests enthusiasm and liveliness.

6. Sincerity. The most effective voices sound honest and reinforce the meaning of the spoken words.

Interpreter training materials should include books on the care and use of voice including exercises for warm-up, flexibility, and control. One that I often consult is *Freeing the Natural Voice* by Kristin Linklater. Most vocal exercises emphasize breathing control. This not only aids in proper use of the voice, but it is key to helping calm the nerves and providing a positive attitude about speaking.

Comedian Jerry Seinfeld addressed fear of public speaking in his stand-up routines on his popular television show. He reported that recent studies list public speaking as the number one fear among Americans, followed by death. Can that be true? Imagine the conversation: "Would you give a speech?" "No, I'd rather die please."[5] Although most interpreters are comfortable speaking in front of the public, some are not. I've known many professionals who came to their positions because of their love of the museum's subject matter or skill in a craft, but they really did not want to talk.

As a young man, my husband was one of these people. He was a highly skilled potter at Old Sturbridge Village and many stood in wonder at his speed and technique at throwing pots on a kick wheel. However, he found that the concentration needed to succeed at the craft and his own natural reserve made it very difficult for him to talk. At first, he avoided speaking as much as possible, causing some people to conclude that he was aloof or unfriendly. These incorrect conclusions were reinforced when he did speak. The feeling that people were waiting and he should talk to them made him nervous. Unfortunately, his tension translated into rudeness when he tried to use short sentences to say that he would explain more about the process as soon as he removed the pot from the wheel. Eventually, he learned how to pace his demonstration with conversation and how to use warmer tones and simple gestures such as smiling when communicating with visitors. One day, the audience applauded when he finished making a pot. On that day, he discovered the excitement of actually connecting to an audience instead of just transferring information.[6]

Most people hate to watch anyone fail. It is embarrassing to watch someone struggle and it is thrilling to witness anything done well. Therefore, most visitors are totally prepared to encourage historic house interpreters to succeed. They want the communication to be effective, engaging, and fun. I mention this because many people list one of their weaknesses in communication as fear of judgmental audiences. Certainly audiences who are harsh or indifferent are a challenge to the most accomplished speakers, but my observation and experience has convinced me that the vast majority of people interacting with interpreters are seeking a positive exchange and are thrilled to experience one.

I like to think of the audience as a kind of mirror. I can tell how well I am communicating by how well the audience responds. Audiences unconsciously mimic speakers. When speakers are animated and interesting, audiences look alert and engaged. They smile and react with open and friendly body posture (fig. 11.3). A speaker who uses a monotone voice with little vocal pacing and no physical movement inspires listeners to act the same way. In contrast, interpreters who speak with a pitch that is irritating to most ears or use distracting gestures such as twitching, tapping, and meaningless pacing, often cause audiences to feel tense or nervous. It is not possible for anyone to hold the interest of every visitor all of the time, but interpreters dedicated to effectively engaging visitors will use the facial clues, body language, and gestures of their visitors to help them adapt their presentational style.

Figure 11.3. A costumed interpreter at Old Sturbridge Village gestures to a plant as she watches the reactions of a young visitor. Photograph by Thomas Neill. Courtesy of Old Sturbridge Village [photo #90.V82gc.15.2.]

Using Gestures

The communication model (fig. 11.2) illustrates that speakers have multiple channels available to them as they send their messages. As important as the selection of words and the quality of the voice may be, both can be reinforced with effective use of gestures. Gestures help give meaning to words as they offer images that stimulate visual learning. Just as volume should be amplified for bigger crowds and larger spaces, gestures should be increased in size if the audience is far away or in a large venue. Overly large gestures can seem inappropriate or threatening in smaller rooms. In either kind of location, effective gestures reinforce meaning.

There are four basic types of gestures: indicative, imitative, emphatic, and autistic. If I raise four fingers while making that statement about gestures, I am using an indicative gesture. These gestures indicate or illustrate, creating a vivid image to help visitors remember what was said. Tour guides should find these gestures helpful when outlining information or giving directions. Since more people will watch than listen, it is important to use indicative gestures that are clear, concise, and correct. It is confusing when speakers say, "Turn right," while pointing to the left.

I witnessed a skillful use of the second type of gestures when I attended a keynote address given by Rex Ellis, an accomplished speaker and museum professional. Imitative gestures imitate, or mimic, movement and Dr. Ellis demonstrated two different ways to use this gesture. While telling a story about a small child looking at a handful of balloons, Dr. Ellis reached out and mimed the action of a vendor holding balloon strings. With that simple action he sparked my memory of actual balloon vendors and I saw a handful of strings held in Dr. Ellis's tight fist while the helium-filled balloons tugged against his hold. In the story, young children bought the balloons and released them one by one. As Dr. Ellis described that action, he utilized another type of mimicking gesture. His hand made a light, wavering gesture as he raised it above and away from his body causing me to see the balloons float away. The last balloon to float away was a black balloon that represented the spirit of the main character. As that balloon floated up, Dr. Ellis used his hand gesture to let it rise, then he shifted and let his eyes follow it, and finally his body followed it, and everyone in that room sat and watched that balloon float high. Dr. Ellis took some time to execute this effect, but in doing so, he superbly used gesture and body language to reinforce our understanding of the words spoken by the balloon vendor to the little boy in the story: "You see, it's not what's on the outside, it's what's on the inside that makes the balloon fly."[7]

Emphatic gestures are less realistic. They are usually an accentuated movement that gives emphasis to a specific word or phrase. These are effective attention grabbers and are often used as an expression of intense feeling. A few years ago, I watched a political candidate on television use an emphatic gesture of bending his arms at his elbows, thereby moving his hands from shoulder to waist height to give emphasis to key words. This simple gesture helped to reinforce a point as important. Unfortunately, the candidate repeated the gesture multiple times in every sentence. It became ridiculous to watch and the power of the emphasis became irritating and meaningless. The candidate lost the election. Perhaps it was politics, but I always suspected he lost because of poor communication.

The last kind of gesture is a secret one, called autistic. This is a gesture that we give to ourselves, often to manage strong feelings that we want to keep private or don't even realize we are feeling, such as anger or tension. Twirling head and facial hair, thumping knees and feet, clenching fists, and tightening shoulders are examples of autistic gestures. These gestures can become useful to us when we become aware of them and understand what they mean to us. Occasionally when engaged in public speaking, I discover myself using an autistic gesture that tells me I am nervous. When I was younger, the tension was often a result of my fear that people would not like me or that I did not know my material well enough. At this point, my tension is more often connected to the fact that I can't figure out how to manage my time and I am getting nervous that I did not plan my content appropriately. For whatever reason we feel tension during speaking, we should control it before it controls us and causes us to behave in ways that send unwanted and inappropriate messages to our listeners.

Releasing Tension

Several techniques can enable us to manage our fear of public speaking and ensure our success when giving tours. The first and perhaps most important relates to our attitude. Fear of failing causes tension. We should all counteract this by replacing negative thoughts with positive affirmations. Physical exercises aid in the mental process. I often try to calm my nerves before speaking by stretching my shoulders, arms, and hands. Other effective strategies are to massage your face and neck and to yawn a huge, impolite yawn. As you repeat the yawn, vocalize the sound "Aaah." If you feel tense while in the presence of your audience, hide your hands behind a podium or a piece of furniture and focus the tension by clenching your fists. Release the tension as you release the clench and relax your hands.

These physical exercises help to calm the mind and prepare the body for effective communication, but nothing is more effective than breathing. As you breathe, release the air in your lungs by exhaling through your mouth. Replace the air by inhaling very slowly through your nose. If you place your hand on your stomach you should feel it extend as your diaphragm lowers to make room for your lungs to fill with air. These deep breaths will help you gain greater vocal control as they help you relax.

Organizing the Message

A relaxed tour guide with effective speaking skills will not necessarily conduct an effective tour of a historic house museum if he or she has not constructed a message that is appropriate and meaningful for the visitors. The following are questions that can help any speaker consider how to plan a presentation or an interpretive experience:

1. What do you know about your audience?
   Age, learning styles and needs, interests, motivations, etc.

2. What are your presentational goals?
   What kind of experience do you want your audience to have?
   What kind of atmosphere do you want to create?

3. What are your learning goals?

   What do you want your audience to know or be able to do when they leave?

   Why do you want the audience to learn this?

4. How will you focus the content of your session or tour?

   What concepts do you plan to present?

   What are the main points or questions?

   Is there an implied hierarchy of ideas?

   What are subquestions or secondary ideas?

   Are these new ideas for this group?

   Is the group ready for these ideas? If not, what can you do to prepare them?

   Is it possible to work with all of these ideas within your time limits?

   How will you reinforce your most important messages?

5. How will you structure the presentation to reach your goals?

   What strategies do you plan to use?

   How much time will you need for each strategy?

   Is there variety in your different strategies?

   Why are these strategies effective for the nature of your audience and your goals?

6. How do you plan to involve your audience?

   What will you ask them to do, say, or consider?

   Does each question or activity build on previous knowledge or skills?

   How will you use transitions to connect ideas?

7. What materials will you need? Objects, documents, media, etc.

8. How will you evaluate or assess the results of your presentation?

   What went well or was effective?

   What was less effective or a problem?

   What would you change for the next time?[8]

Receiving Messages

I began using the communication model in staff training at Old Sturbridge Village to help interpreters analyze their own powers as communicators and to better understand their successes and their failures at engaging museum visitors. One time, as I explained the idea of how both senders and receivers, or interpreters and visitors, are affected by their life experiences, a college-aged interpreter said, "Do you know what you're asking? You're asking me to be a really good human."⁹ I don't know about the "good" part, but I am asking that we each take stock of our own humanity so that we can recognize how our attitudes and beliefs affect the ways in which we share information with other people.

Sometimes our life experiences are so different that it is very hard to understand other people's intentions even if we do understand the meaning of their words. In communication workshops I often engage participants in sharing an experience with a partner and then repeating to each other what they have heard. Few repeat every word. Most participants summarize, paraphrase, or interpret what they have heard. In some cases, individuals discover that their partner misunderstood the meaning of their message. Sometimes this give-and-take process is essential to discovering if we understand others and if we have been understood. Interpreters should never assume that visitors understand or could possibly remember everything they have said.

Our responsibility as effective communicators is not just to organize and deliver information, but also to receive the messages visitors are giving to us. To do that, we need to focus most of our concentration on paying attention to the actions and reactions of our receivers. Have you ever wondered how therapists, salespeople, and palm readers are so knowledgeable about people? They're listening and watching. They draw from their training and experience to make educated guesses based on the information communicated to them. They then ask questions to confirm or counter their observations. They offer us models of how to be expert receivers of messages. They remind us that to be effective communicators in museums, our subject to master is not just the content of the museum, but also the people visiting the museum.

Supporting Interpreters so They Can Be Effective

For some museum staff members, interaction with the public is infrequent, but they still have an indirect impact on visitors' experiences by conducting or organizing interpreters' training sessions. These individuals need to consider what kind of example they are setting when they speak publicly or when they make selections of public speakers to include as part of interpreter training. I've met many extraordinarily intelligent and knowledgeable museum professionals who were phenomenal writers but inexperienced public speakers. Despite this, they are asked to give lectures or tours to interpreters and sometimes to visitors—without training, practice, or defined standards. They represent their institution, but no one seems to care if they do it ineffectively. Few museums publish written materials that have not been reviewed or edited, but they will schedule training lectures and public programs for which the speakers are not coached or rehearsed.

Effective training programs model the behavior they want interpreters to learn. If you are planning interpreter staff training, avoid featuring poor public speakers and using passive methods like lectures to teach active interpretive techniques such as inquiry-based tours.

Interpreters need knowledge and experience in all the areas that I've described here—understanding visitors, shaping messages, using voice and body language. They also need time to practice with positive and useful feedback. If we are committed to effective interpretation, then we must be committed to the time it takes to develop and maintain it. Effective communication is never constant. Each of us is capable of shaping interesting and appropriate messages and conveying them with skill. To maintain our skills we need time to develop our material and to practice our delivery.

By the very nature of life and communication, some practice will happen on the job and some away from the workplace. Each of us has opportunities to observe and participate in effective and ineffective communication every day, with our friends and family, our colleagues, our visitors, and the people we meet in the world at large. We can gain much from these experiences if we remain open to our own growth and are constantly interested in the people around us. We must never forget that communication is about sharing. Effective interpreters engage visitors because they share their knowledge, they share their enthusiasm, and they share their respect.

Notes

1. Robert Fulghum, *All I Really Need to Know I Learned in Kindergarten: Uncommon Thoughts on Common Things* (New York: Ivy Books, 1993).

2. *Historic House Museums: Issues & Operations II* (McFaddin-Ward House Conference, Beaumont, Tex., 6 November 1998).

3. Arthur Dutil, "Disaster—A Public Place, Museum, or Historic House without a Disaster Plan" (presentation made at *Historic House Museums: Issues & Operations II*, McFaddin-Ward House Conference, Beaumont, Tex., 5 November 1998).

4. Dale Jones and Margaret Piatt, "Planning Effective Living History Performances, Vocal Training" (presentation made at *A Union of Spirits: A Conference for Interpreters*, the Farmer's Museum in Cooperstown, N.Y., 1991).

5. Jerry Seinfeld, *Seinfeld*, NBC, 1995.

6. Conversation with James White based on experiences as an interpreter at Old Sturbridge Village in the 1970s.

7. Rex M. Ellis, "The Importance of History to a Community" (presentation made at

Historic House Museums: Issues & Operations II, McFaddin-Ward Conference, 5 November 1998).

8. Margaret Piatt, "Effective Communication in Museums" (presentation made at the New England Museum Association Conference, 1998).

9. Conversation with David Magnante in introductory staff training at Old Sturbridge Village, 1982.

CHAPTER TWELVE

BUILDING A TOOL KIT FOR YOUR INTERPRETERS: METHODS OF SUCCESS FROM DRAYTON HALL

Meggett B. Lavin

Though there may be as many ways to manage interpretive programs as there are historic sites, there is one goal that we all share: we expect our interpreters to happily step into the role of educator, entertainer, diplomat, historian, policeman, public relations expert, salesperson, and 911 operator. Are they ready? How do you know? How do they know? Have you given them the tools to do the job?

At Drayton Hall, a historic house museum in Charleston, South Carolina, everyone knows that staff members who assist visitors are as important as the site (fig. 12.1). To guests participating in tours and programs, the interpreters *are* the site. The interpreters also represent the National Trust for Historic Preservation, the site's parent organization. Rain, shine, or crying babies, the museum depends on them to convey its mission and message to more than 65,000 people a year. This is a tremendous responsibility that Drayton Hall strives to balance with equally high rewards. Working in an aesthetic and historically important environment is a good start, but it is just the beginning. The process of recruiting, hiring, and retaining interpreters is serious business that requires considerable staff time and funding to ensure they are enthusiastic and educated about their work.

Drayton Hall's interpretation program is managed and directed by the education and research department; however, the museum believes that everyone on staff needs to be involved in the education of an interpreter. It also believes that every staff member should be able to give an abbreviated tour (easier said than done). Everyone is invited to participate in interpreter training and continuing education sessions. Conversely, a senior interpreter represents the interpreters at property management meetings. This firmly establishes the importance of the

Figure 12.1. Drayton Hall (built ca. 1738), Charleston, South Carolina. Photograph by Gene Heizer. Courtesy of Drayton Hall, a property of the National Trust for Historic Preservation.

interpreters' role in the organization and develops an appreciation for their daily challenges.

Drayton Hall's interpreters are part-time paid staff. The site originally depended on volunteers, but Charleston has numerous nonprofits that all compete heavily for volunteers and there is a thriving tourism industry that pays very well. As the interpretive program developed and the training commitment increased, it became more effective to invest time and money in a few people who would work several days a week. The museum now averages sixteen part-time paid interpreters for a full-time, year-round schedule of tours and programs.

Would Drayton Hall's interpreter tool kit work for an all-volunteer organization? Yes. All you need is commitment, consensus, enthusiasm, and plenty of perks. You can also expect the training time to take longer.

Getting Started

Whether your interpreters are paid or volunteer, you must decide the qualities and minimum qualifications they need to participate in your program. Drayton Hall, like most house museums, is looking for a person who is outgoing, articulate, resourceful, and able to learn. He or she should also view unscheduled buses as an opportunity, and appreciate that at least one fourth of the visitors touch everything in order to learn. It is quite helpful if a candidate has an academic background in history or a related field, but someone with a passion for the site's history and an ability to teach is an equally great find.

Ideally, the criteria for recruiting and hiring your interpreters are stated in a written job description crafted specifically for the position. The job description includes the general qualifications and specific duties for the job, and usually relates the position to the overall mission of the site. If this is not the case, it's time to brainstorm with everyone on staff who will be working with your interpreters and create a job description. Prioritize your criteria and use the list as a guideline for culling through resumes and preparing interview questions. Take the time to devise open-ended questions that will help a candidate reveal his or her abilities. Get beyond resume information with questions such as, "How would your colleagues describe your work on a good day?" The most effective questions pose a problem or situation. For example: "We don't allow smoking around the historic buildings. You are leading a tour group to the main house and one of them lights up a cigarette. How would you handle this?" Make sure that the questions are fair and do not require specific knowledge of your site or its policies. Ask every candidate the same set of questions and keep a chart rating their responses. The chart not only records your evaluation of the candidate, but also the effectiveness of the question. Over time you will be able to streamline the interview process down to a few key questions that quickly identify the skills and qualifications your program requires.

One of the greatest disappointments for all programs is losing new interpreters during or shortly after training. To ensure that your careful recruiting and hiring process is not in vain, consider using a contract. Keeping in mind that any contract must be drafted for review with legal counsel before adopting it as policy, a basic contract should contain three sections: the first describes the organization and lists the training and services provided, as well as the length of training and any trial period; the second lists the commitments and responsibilities the new interpreter will fulfill; the third consists of a grievance clause that states the new interpreter's options in case of problems with his or her supervisor. The contract is discussed, signed, and dated by the new interpreter and the program director. The purpose of this formal arrangement is to underscore the seriousness of each party's commitment and cut down on dropouts before you invest a lot of time, energy, and dollars in training. It has helped Drayton Hall reduce its rate of trainee loss to almost zero.

Once your interpreters have signed on, the real work begins. You have limited time to prepare your interpreters to inspire visitors with your site's story and to manage any variety of visitor situations. This is especially true at Drayton Hall where our interpreters must bring two-and-a-half centuries of history to life with an unfurnished, unrestored house and its surviving rural landscape. "No furniture? No costumes? No exhibits?" No kidding. The challenge is enormous, but as many great craftsmen say, "You can do anything if you have the right tools."

Tool #1—A Plan

In building a tool kit for your interpreters, the first tool to provide is a plan (fig. 12.2a&b). While some programs have a yearly training course and a syllabus to prepare interpreters, Drayton Hall does not. The education and research department hires a limited number of candidates twice a year and tailors its training program to each new interpreter's background. Trainees are provided with a set of self-study guidelines and educational materials that will take them from their first day of work to their first practice tours and beyond. The guidelines feature a checklist of every requirement, such as filling out personnel cards and meeting with department heads, as well as a prioritized list of tours, workshops, readings, and videos to absorb (fig. 12.3).

Interpreters also receive a notebook with detailed interpretive and operations information and a copy of the museum's *Written Tour for Hearing-Impaired Visitors*. The notebook has multiple sections that include the mission statement, interpretation guidelines, policies and procedures, safety and security protocols, fact sheets, and education program materials. The *Written Tour* provides a visual reference and inventory for each interpretive area and also serves as a workbook. After an initial review of all the materials, each interpreter works with the education and research department to draft a personal schedule for successfully completing the training plan and giving approved tours within two to three months. Once interpreters have been approved to give tours, they continue to follow the training checklist for learning specialized programs and developing professional expertise.[1]

DRAYTON HALL
MUSEUM EDUCATOR TRAINING GUIDELINES

NAME_____   DATE _____

CHECKLIST   **DATE**

I.   Fill out personnel cards and turn in to Financial Administrator (Paula Marion)
     (by the end of the first day)   _____

II. Follow and take notes on each tour. (please stick to this list only)
     Tim Chesser (first three weeks)   _____
     Stephanie Thurman (first three weeks)   _____
     Peggy Reider (first three weeks)   _____
     Holly Watkins (first three weeks)   _____
     Kerin Murtagh (first three weeks)   _____

III. Observe *Connections* and take notes on each program. Use this as an opportunity to gather information
     for your house tour. After you've been approved for your house tour, you may observe these again to
     help you craft your *Connections* program. (please stick to this list only)
     Judy Johnson (first four weeks)   _____
     Peggy Reider (first four weeks)   _____
     Tim Chesser (first four weeks)   _____
     Holly Watkins (first four weeks)   _____

IV. Meet with Lauri Lechner for instruction
     in membership sales. (before first practice tour)   _____

V.   Meet with Superintendent of Buildings & Grounds (John Kidder)
     for instruction in security and maintenance procedures (after approval but
     before first tour with the public).   _____

VI. Museum Shop orientation with Shop Manager (Renee DeVane) (after
     approval but before first tour with the public).   _____

VII. Observe student education programs: (dependent on seasonal schedule)
     Student House Tour   _____
     Archaeology   _____
     Diaries in the Dirt   _____
     Preservation   _____
     Student Connections   _____
     Games Day   _____
     Marsh Madness   _____

VIII. READING
      Drayton Hall History:
          Drayton Hall Written Tour   _____
          Interiors (DH newsletter back-issues on staff library shelf) _____

Drayton Hall Education & Research Department
Education/ Orientation Materials/ h Training Guidelines.doc   *revised 4/01*

Drayton Hall provides guidelines (fig. 12.2a, this page) and checklists (fig. 12.2b, next page) for each phase of interpreter training. Courtesy of Drayton Hall, a National Trust Historic Site.

ORIENTATION MATERIALS

For phase one of Drayton Hall Museum Educator Training

- Paperwork for Business Office
  - NTHP Employment Application
  - NTHP Employee Profile
  - NTHP Direct Deposit Authorization Agreement
  - W-4 Form
  - INS Form (attach a photocopy of Drivers License & SS Card)
- Interpreter Position Description & Requirements
- Employment Agreement
- Levels of Achievement for Drayton Hall Interpreters
- Mentor/Interpreter Responsibilities
- Mentor Checklist (for mentor)
- Interpreter Training Guidelines
- Review Process for Interpreters
- Tour Information Framework
- House Tour Training Evaluation
- Interpreter Performance Standards
- Self evaluation for Interpreters
- Written Tour
- Drayton Hall Self-Guided Walks brochure
- Employee Manual
- Schedule
- Staff List and Phone Numbers
- Current *Interiors* Newsletter
- PR folder
- National Trust tote bag
- Rice spoon

Drayton Hall

Drayton Hall Education & Research Department
Education/ Orientation materials/ a Orientation Materials check list.doc

revised 4/01

256

Interpreter Training Videos

Drayton Hall has a collection of videos that will be helpful for learning social history and interpretation techniques. Many of these videos were made during actual training workshops held over the past ten years. Plan to set aside time on a regular basis to view the following list of programs. Make notes and list questions to discuss with the education staff.

- *When Rice was King* (105)

- *"I'd Like to See What's Down There"* (99)

- *Family Across the Sea* (22)

- *The Strength of These Arms: Black Labor, White Rice* (108)

- African American Interpretation- Dorothy Redford (20)

- *This Obsolete Finery: How do we Make Sense of Historic Sites* (36)

- *Cultural Gifts: Carolina Gold Rice* (102)

- Clothing Styles and Textiles – Rosemary Brandau (2 tapes: 92, 93)

- Room Use/Interiors – Betsy Garrett (88)

- Tea Ceremonies – Elizabeth Gussler (76)

- Garden and Landscape – Peter Hatch (77)

- Palladio – Mario di Valmarana (101)

- Foodways – Rosemary Brandau (23)

- Eighteenth Century Music and Musical Instruments (71)

Drayton Hall Education and Research Department

Figure 12.3. Drayton Hall supplements its reading requirements and practice sessions with an extensive collection of videos that provide content and demonstrate a variety of interpretive techniques. Courtesy of Drayton Hall, a National Trust Historic Site.

Tool #2—Expectations

It is critical to establish expectations from the beginning. This prevents surprises for either the interpreter or the organization. The recruitment and hiring contract, a copy of the mission statement, and a written set of performance standards leave no doubt about what the interpreters and the organization are striving for. Drayton Hall's performance standards were adapted from interpreter evaluations developed by Sunnyside, a property of Historic Hudson Valley. They quantify six levels of performance, from excellent to unsatisfactory, in seven areas of the job: depth of knowledge; presentation; appearance; public interaction; reliability; initiative; and staff relations. For example, under depth of knowledge, excellent performance is defined as follows:

> This interpreter has full command of the interpretive materials. S/he uses these materials and others to interpret in breadth (historical context) and in depth (site specific/subject area specific), i.e., s/he makes two types of relationships: connections between the site and what was happening around it locally, nationally, and globally, and connections between the site and the world today.

Good performance is:

> This interpreter has full command of selected portions of the interpretive materials and other readings. S/he has either great breadth or depth of knowledge, but not both. Examples: s/he has good general knowledge of architectural history, but can not connect that knowledge to other events of the time; s/he has extensive knowledge of national or world history but uneven knowledge of the site itself.

Unsatisfactory performance is:

> This interpreter simply repeats what s/he has heard from other interpreters. S/he does not have command of the interpretive materials. This interpreter may or may not serve more as a host(ess) leading visitors through the site, rather than as an interpreter.[2]

The goal is to have interpreters reach the level of good performance by the end of their trial period and excellent performance by their second year. A series of steps for training and evaluation allows both the interpreter and the education and research department to monitor individual progress. These steps include self-tests, self-taping (audio), self-evaluations, and peer review. Videotaping is available for the brave, though the timid survive the experience as long as the tape is reviewed in private. These milestones are designed to positively reinforce the interpreter's accomplishments, but also let staff members know if the relationship is not working out. It is far better to find out early that the person you hired or recruited is not the right match, rather than to have your visitors discover it for you later. This will give you time to evaluate whether there are other opportunities for your trainee to work with your site and take the necessary steps to channel his or her talents.[3]

Tool #3—Directions

While Drayton Hall's training program is self-paced and self-study, interpreters are not alone. The education and research department assigns mentors to guide new interpreters through the training requirements and interpretive materials. An interpreter and his or her mentor sign a contract that outlines how they will work together for six months. Mentors help the new interpreters become familiar with the training materials and daily operations of the site (fig. 12.4). They listen patiently through nervous practice tours and offer constructive criticism, insider tips, and encouragement. Their primary goal is to help new interpreters become part of the staff as quickly as possible.

Mentors also assist the senior staff from the education and research department in conducting a variety of specialized workshops to introduce trainees to all of the interpretive programs. The topics covered include influences on the architectural, economic, and social history of Charleston; African-American history before and after emancipation; archaeology; construction techniques; historic landscape interpretation; the general house tour; the student programs; and methods for accommodating disabled visitors. Workshop instructors provide the program content, model teaching and questioning strategies, and encourage new interpreters to make their own connections with the lessons of the site.

The first mentors were staff members from the education and research department, but over time the department invited senior interpreters to take on this role. This has meant setting up a checklist system to mentor the mentors and keep up with everyone's progress. Though time-consuming initially, in the end, the mentor system reduces the demands on a very busy office and provides a great opportunity for the senior interpreters to be recognized for their expertise.

Recognition may come in a variety of forms, depending on the site. Drayton Hall used the abilities required for mentorship to create an achievement scale for pay increases. Volunteer organizations might provide incentive through merit certificates, special badges, preferred scheduling, additional shop discounts, exclusive events, or educational travel. Whatever honors you choose, make sure

MENTOR CHECKLIST   Trainee: _____

_____ Gather all orientation materials and Employee and Interpretation manuals. Check to make sure that paperwork has been turned into the Financial Administrator.

_____ Read, discuss, and sign (where necessary) Mentor/Interpreter Responsibilities agreement, Self Evaluations, Training Guidelines list with trainee.

_____ Discuss sign-in, lunch, and pay procedures.

_____ Introduce trainee to all staff and volunteers, including shop staff. Review ground-rules for kitchen use, shop behavior, schedule changes, etc.

_____ Tour office building (including library and video library); review check-out procedures.

_____ Review Employee Manual; flag important memos and pages for careful reading (i.e., memos on security, memberships, kitchen duty, etc.).

_____ Review basic tour techniques (engaging the public, three topics per stop, including the NTHP in each stop, etc.).

_____ Review what to do during "down time," i.e., help Education & Research Department, PR Department.

After Trainee has gone on several tours:

_____ Look through old photographs to point out and explain changes.

_____ Tour the property, explaining inland rice cultivation, the rice fields and reserve pond, the nature trail project with PRT, African-American cemetery, Bowens' house site, location of slave houses (colonial and antebellum), Nipper's grave, the revetment, orangerie site, barn, chimney.

_____ Review information on handicap accessibility. Show how to use written tour for hearing-impaired visitors, make sure Trainee knows what is touchable for blind and sight-impaired visitors. Assist in training on use of StairTrac™. Make sure Trainee knows what can and <u>cannot</u> be done to accommodate handicapped visitors.

_____ Explain how to deal with special requests from visitors, i.e., , education programs information, public relations information, etc.

_____ Talk about SPU behavior (i.e., not eating before guests, excessive drinking, etc.).

Drayton Hall Education & Research Department
Education/ Orientation materials/g Mentor Checklist.doc   *revised 6/01*

Figure 12.4.   The Mentor Checklist assures that every trainee gets the same level of preparation and support during training. It is also used to evaluate the mentor's progress. Courtesy of Drayton Hall, a National Trust Historic Site.

that they are sincere and relatively easy to award. Rewarding people for their accomplishments and willingness to assume more responsibility should be a pleasant task.

Tool #4—Ownership

Think of what you entrust your interpreters with when they take visitors through your property. Not only must they be knowledgeable, entertaining, and represent the mission of your site, they must also be responsible for the security of the collection and safety of the group. Interpreters who feel they have ownership in the property and its programs will be motivated to fulfill the museum's educational mission and protect the collection as much as the curator.

The first step in adding ownership to the tool kit is to treat interpreters as professionals and team members. This attitude should be present in every aspect of your program, from the recruitment, hiring, and training process to daily management, continuing education, evaluation, and recognition. It is demonstrated in the wording and the quality of all your materials and in the priority of your expectations and concerns. It is seen and heard in the emphasis on "we," not "I." It is fostered through a team approach to management that includes interpreters in the decision-making process for issues that affect their work. It is supported by an interpretive program director who encourages and facilitates open, two-way communication on a daily basis and through creative team problem solving during interpreter meetings and special projects. Individual and group contributions are purposely sought out and are highly valued. Everyone has the opportunity to make a difference and is responsible for the result.

The advantage of this approach is most evident during times of major change. A program that has open communication and a team approach to problem solving will more readily find the opportunity in change, rather than balk at the threat. For example, Drayton Hall faced a major change in the interpretive program when it first contemplated a formal annual evaluation. Instead of announcing a new program, complete with evaluation forms and procedures, members of the education and research staff discussed the need for formal evaluations as a group and reviewed possible options. The department then invited interpreters to volunteer for a committee to do a thorough study and create a model for review. Everyone volunteered. Everyone wanted a say in the outcome because it directly affected his or her work. Each time the committee met, there were intense discussions and debates over definitions before there was agreement. No one thought there should be an "unsatisfactory performance" level on the interpreter review because they set high standards for themselves. It took quite a bit of explaining to convince them that an evaluator needs a low mark for comparison. It was worth the time and effort to work through, because in the end, they adopted a document that reflected their high professional expectations and they were willing to be measured by it. They truly owned it.

Drayton Hall's education and research department consistently finds the synergy approach to program development and management to be the most effective way to share and expand the talents of the group while pursuing excellence for the organization. It recognizes everyone's abilities, bridges differences, and builds a team that has confidence in itself and the institution. It does take more time and sensitivity, but this priority investment in the people of your site will be reflected in the positive, professional attitude they convey to the public.

Tool #5—Authority

With ownership comes authority and the ability to solve problems on one's own—this is crucial at a small site. Anything can happen and your interpreters need the confidence, skills, and good sense to handle a sudden turn of events and still keep smiling. What do you do when an alligator lumbers out of the pond toward your group? What's your first response when a visitor faints? What do you say when a journalist asks for your comments about another site? How do you ask a movie star or head of state to keep their hands off the collection? Interpreters need to know exactly how much authority they have, and when and how to get help.

Guidelines are usually the result of past experiences—good and bad. Review all of the current policies and procedures for your site to see how many are relevant for interpreters. Policies and procedures may be found in any number of resources, including operations manuals, employee handbooks, disaster manuals, interpretation manuals, safety and security notebooks, departmental memos, and office newsletters. Use these as a baseline for compiling guidelines for your interpreters. Involve seasoned interpreters in the process and review the results with every department. You will probably find that there are more policies and procedures known through oral history than through actual documentation. New interpreters, as well as seasoned ones, need to have written policies to learn from and support their actions.

Of course, reading about policies and procedures is not enough. Interpreters actually need to practice implementing them to be prepared. Plan workshops that give interpreters opportunities to role-play typical situations. Seasoned interpreters love to share war stories and how they successfully handled difficult people and logistical problems. There is nothing better than a session of outrageous stories and most embarrassing moments to get everyone ready for high season. Work with your safety and security officer to provide ongoing hands-on training for emergencies that require first aid, CPR, police, firefighters, and other disaster preparedness. It is also very helpful to require new interpreters to meet with each department to learn who is responsible for what within the organization. This gives them a greater understanding of the operation as a whole and how their actions may affect others.

Tool #6—Opportunities for Personal Growth and Professional Development

Perhaps the most important tool to provide interpreters is the opportunity for personal growth and professional development. Though it represents a big investment of time and money for the site, continuing education is one of the greatest joys of working in the history field. There can never be enough. Drayton Hall provides a steady stream of resources for interpreters to learn from, such as books, fact sheets, lectures, newsletters, primary research, professional journals, workshops, and videos (fig. 12.5). Interpreters are directed to learn more about the mechanics of their profession through publications such as *The Docent Educator, The Good Guide, Interpreting Our Heritage,* and Colonial Williamsburg's *Interpreter.*[4]

For most sites, the vehicle for ongoing education is the monthly interpreters' meeting. At Drayton Hall, this is an opportunity to work on specific issues and strategies as a group. Typical topics include tour techniques, adapting tour material for different audiences and learning styles, site-related research, organizational updates, policy reviews, or problems du jour.

All Drayton Hall staff members benefit from a reciprocal pass program they participate in with museums and nature centers in the Charleston area. They also take staff trips beyond Charleston to learn about other sites and their particular challenges with preservation and interpretation. Once a year, Drayton Hall brings in nationally known speakers for a cooperative training series with three other house museum organizations: The Charleston Museum, Historic Charleston Foundation, and Middleton Place. Together, these institutions have been able to pool their funds to offer lectures and hands-on workshops by authors and experts on the topics of architecture, African-American history, eighteenth-century foodways, costume history, customer service, decorative arts, historic landscapes, interpretation techniques, period music, transportation history, travel, and more. The strength of the programs is not only in the speaker's knowledge, but also in the use of one of our sites and its collections for demonstration and appli-

Since You Asked

History and Information from the Education & Research Office

ANOTHER CHARLES DRAYTON

Compiled by Peggy Reider

In 1822, Denmark Vesey of Charleston, a free black carpenter and a member of the African Methodist Church, planned a slave revolt so extensive that it may have involved hundreds of blacks.

The first alarm came on May 30 when a house servant reported a plot and one man was arrested. He implicated three others who were questioned but not held. The plot had been scheduled for July 14 but the date was moved up to June 16 as a result of the first alarm. Less than 72 hours before the plot was to take place it was again reported. The government activated the militia and a special tribunal was formed. Charges were brought against 117 blacks. Of those, 35 were sentenced to death and 37 to deportation. Denmark Vesey was convicted on June 28 and hanged July 2. Four weeks later another 22 people were hanged.

Charles Drayton was a slave and cook belonging to the Honorable John Drayton (former governor of South Carolina and William Henry Drayton's son) who lived at 24 Friend Street in Charleston. Charles was a member and a class leader in the African Methodist Church where Denmark Vesey was also a member. As such, his role was to attend to the spiritual welfare of his class members – advising, reproving, comforting, and/or exhorting to ensure that they worked on their own salvation.

At the June 21 trial of accused conspirator Peter Poyas, "Y" (a slave belonging to Colonel George W. Cross) testified that Charles Drayton had told him that he "commanded the country-born company" and that he had "prepared for himself a gun and a sword."

Charles Drayton was arrested July 2, 1822. He had previously pledged with others not to tell even if threatened by death. However, after being sentenced to death on July 10, he called for the Warden and agreed to tell all he knew in exchange for having his sentence commuted from death to deportation. He subsequently testified in the trials of 24 people and exonerated only three.

On January 20, 1823, Charles Drayton died in the workhouse while waiting to be deported to another colony.

Bibliography

Designs Against Charleston: The Trial Record of the Denmark Vesey Slave Conspiracy of 1822 by Edward A. Pearson, University of North Carolina Press, 1999.

He Shall Go Out Free: The Lives of Denmark Vesey by Douglas R. Egerton, Madison House, 1999.

South Carolina, A History by Walter Edgar, University of South Carolina Press, 1998.

July 11, 2001

Figure 12.5a. (this page) and 12.5b. (opposite page) Drayton Hall's education and research department produces fact sheets on site-specific topics for ongoing interpreter education. Courtesy of Drayton Hall, a National Trust Historic Site.

Archaeology at Drayton Hall

1974-1976	**AREA AROUND MAIN HOUSE, SOUTH (KITCHEN) FLANKER, BASEMENT FLOOR, DRIVEWAY, MOUND**
Drive/mound	The **driveway** originally went straight up to the house, and had a return located approximately under the second tier of the mound.
	• A **graveled courtyard** existed between the carriage return and the land-side steps.
	• Ruts and potholes in drive were filled with trash thrown out from house.
	• From soil samples and artifacts found, the **mound** was constructed during dredging/construction of the reflecting pond, confirming family stories.
Basement	From organic matter and rodent burrows, the **northeast room in basement** was used for food storage, and was once paved. Currently has dirt floor.
	• **Stone paving** in central basement area dates to about 1820, evidence of brick was found underneath.
S. Flanker	Entire **foundation** was uncovered, fireplace opened on one side.
	• Evidence indicated the building was cleared out and razed, as opposed to collapsing.
	• From artifact dates, **construction date** appears to have been 20-25 years after the main house.
	• Bone and waste parts of animals indicated food preparation conducted there.
	• Kitchen wares and fine wares located, also indicating food preparation use.
	• Prior to Civil War its use may have changed from kitchen/bake house to storage.
	• Course of bricks excavated between flanker and house to determine how they were connected. Corresponds to Gibbes drawing.
Oct. 1979	**UNDERWATER ARCHAEOLOGY ALONG RIVERBANK PRIOR TO INSTALLATION OF REVETMENT**
	• Few artifacts were found, determined that there would be **no adverse impact** on resources if revetment were installed.
1979 – 1982	**NORTH FLANKER, PRIVY, WELL BEHIND SOUTH FLANKER, FLOOR SW ROOM OF MAIN HOUSE BASEMENT, TESTING PRIOR TO INSTALLATION OF WATER MAIN**
SW Basement '79	**No indication** this room was used as a doctor's office.
Well '80	5' X 5' well lined with wooden boards located to the south of kitchen flanker. Contained 19th century artifacts indicating it was no longer in use and was being filled.
Privy '81	Artifacts in the builder's trench revealed a **construction date** near to that of the main house.
	• Discovered **brick drainage system**. Brick trough runs the full length of back wall where seats were located. Brick "pipe" underground runs from NW corner of privy (see arch near ground level) out into yard, an early attempt at a septic system.
	• From Gibbes sketch we know the **roofline and flooring was changed** sometime after 1840s, and fireplace was a later addition. Flooring was removed during excavation revealing the joists had been changed, new joist pockets were broken into the N and S walls.
North flanker '81	**Shallow foundation** may mean building was constructed quickly and cheaply.
	• **Construction date** probably after, but close to that of kitchen flanker (c.1765).
	• Evidence of a **fireplace** but its foundation does not exist.

cation purposes. A wonderful example was the day Rosemary Brandau[5] of Colonial Williamsburg, Charleston Museum archaeologist Martha Zeirden, and curator Chris Loeblein[6] led us through the requirements of several different table settings in the Manigault House dining room using period ceramic and silver collections the public rarely sees. The program continued in the museum's conference room, which was set up for a hands-on activity re-creating a typical eighteenth-century dinner service with real food, paper tablecloths, plastic dishes, and utensils. Despite modern materials, eating peas with a knife and wiping your mouth on the tablecloth provides unforgettable insights into the sensibilities of the past.

It is always very important to take the time to discuss how to apply new information to your current interpretation. (Drayton Hall's history of dining spans centuries of changing customs and involves several different rooms. How much do you include in a one-hour tour?) An effective way to do this is to ask specific interpreters to make a presentation about how they are using, or might use, the new material. This promotes great group discussion and recognizes individual abilities and interests. It also helps interpreters learn to discern the difference between developing their interpretation and simply padding it with fun facts—a mighty temptation for us all!

Tool #7—Support

As much as interpreters are drawn to the intellectual and aesthetic rewards of working with historic sites, they are also there because they like to teach or perform, preferably both! No doubt they have friendly, outgoing personalities and truly enjoy working with people. But excellent, engaging interpretation requires a lot of energy, and guests expect smiles and personal attention throughout their visit. No matter how they are feeling, interpreters must be "on" when they enter the public areas of the site. It is absolutely necessary to help your interpreters keep up their enthusiasm and professionalism with ongoing support and appreciation.

Drayton Hall provides daily support with friendship and camaraderie. The staff kitchen and attached conference room form the literal hearth of museum operations. They provide a centrally located place to meet, vent, commiserate, and celebrate while fueling up on coffee, sharing leftovers, or concocting "pantry surprise." Informal meetings regularly occur over boxes of chocolate or pans of brownies. This free flow throughout the day keeps communication open, and often nips potential crises in the bud. Staff members also celebrate birthdays with a monthly potluck lunch and go formal for landmark events such as weddings and new babies. In between there are thematic parties around the holidays, and "just because" get-togethers. In times of stress, such as the smothering humid summers, there is plenty of iced tea and sympathy. There is also a large staff cat lying around whose overfed contentment and thick orange fur calms the soul (unless you are a dog person).[7]

In addition to providing a space to convene, the conference room conveniently houses the staff lending library and baskets of the latest professional periodicals. The proximity of great reading materials to caffeine and desserts creates a bit of a coffeehouse atmosphere and encourages interesting discussions about history, interpretation, and preservation, as well as good old shop talk and grapevine news. This hub is instrumental in drawing staff members working all around the property together.

A weekly or biweekly (depending on the season) staff newsletter keeps everyone associated with the property advised on the latest happenings—from bird sightings to council meetings. Everyone who does something for Drayton Hall is mentioned in bold print. Modern technology has made it possible to turn this manual publication into an e-mail posting, which saves both time and postage. A real bulletin board in the office entry salutes individual accomplishments and features cards and letters from friends and visitors. Drayton Hall's fabulous volunteer photographer[8] records everyone at his or her best, and worst, for publication and office display. Though no one will ever earn a fortune working for the site, they are assured of fame. See, you are reading about them now.[9]

Construction Note

These seven tools are the basics. As Drayton Hall develops, the use of each tool will continue to evolve, specific techniques will be refined, and more tools may be added. In building a tool kit for your interpreters, look around at what you already have, ask your interpreters what they need, and use whatever else you can borrow. While it may take years to put your kit together, the guiding principle should stay the same: give your interpreters the opportunity to enjoy excelling in their work. Everyone will benefit.

Notes

This article is dedicated to all who have helped make Drayton Hall a home for so many since opening to the public in 1975, and to all of the educators and museum and preservation professionals who have shared their expertise and friendship with me over my eighteen-year career. I have never stopped learning.

1. For more information about Drayton Hall's actual methods of interpretation, see "Archaeological Preservation: Drayton Hall," in *Presenting Archaeology to the Public: Digging for Truths*, ed. John H. Jameson Jr. (Walnut Creek, Calif.: AltaMira Press, 1997).

2. Drayton Hall Performance Standards, 1991.

3. Termination is the last step if all else fails. The evaluation process will provide the documentation necessary to address the issues with the trainee.

4. *The Docent Educator, The Quarterly Journal for Dedicated Educators* (Alan Garten-

haus, publisher, P.O. Box 2080, Kamuela, Hawaii 96743); Alison L. Grinder and E. Sue McCoy, *The Good Guide* (Scottsdale, Ariz.: Ironwood Press, 1985); Freeman Tilden, *Interpreting Our Heritage* (Chapel Hill: University of North Carolina Press, 1984); *The Colonial Williamsburg Interpreter* (bimonthly publication of the Department of Interpretive Education, Colonial Williamsburg Foundation).

5. The late Rosemary Brandau was a renowned foodways interpretation specialist for Colonial Williamsburg. She is greatly missed.

6. Since this article was first written, the museum field lost another outstanding and beloved professional. Christopher True Loeblein died 12 September 2001, leaving a legacy of dedication, expertise, enthusiasm, and kindness.

7. Charlie the cat also welcomes visitors in the gift shop and serves as their pet away from home. Kitty Drayton was the first staff cat. He was on duty for seventeen years and often accompanied tours through the house.

8. Retired professional photographer Gene Heizer has been with Drayton Hall since 1986.

9. Photograph and program materials provided by Drayton Hall, a National Trust Historic Site. My tremendous thanks to Tracy Hayes, Cathy Jenkins, and LeeAnne Maher for their assistance in updating information for this chapter. All the best to all the rest of the Drayton Hall staff who help people enjoy Drayton Hall as much as they do.

CHAPTER THIRTEEN

ENDLESS POSSIBILITIES: HISTORIC HOUSE MUSEUM PROGRAMS THAT MAKE EDUCATORS SING

Jamie Credle

In the late 1990s, the American Association of Museums (AAM) initiated an effort to define standards for interpretation in museums. A clear understanding of what interpretation actually is was essential to the process. For a working definition of interpretation, the AAM's 1999 National Interpretation Project committee settled on the following:

- Interpretation is a dynamic process of communication between the museum and the audience.

- Interpretation is the means by which the museum delivers its content.

- Interpretation media/activities include but are not limited to: exhibits, tours, Web sites, classes, school programs, publications, and outreach.[1]

As this definition acknowledges, interpretation is not just a tour script or set of reports; instead, it is the malleable "people part" of a museum's function. It encompasses the content of historic sites and the methods of sharing it, as well as the manner in which the museum's message and values are conveyed to various audiences. It is how museums educate.

Ideally, everyone involved with a historic site considers himself or herself to be an educator, one who links the museum's story with its visitors. At museums, including historic house museums, however, an education department, interpretive team, or group of experienced volunteers concerned about educational activities usually directs the creating, implementing, and sustaining of interpretive presentation. The AAM's *Statement on Professional Standards for Museum Educa-*

tion refers to museum educators as "advocates for museum audiences"—facilitators of learning for those who come through the museum's doors, as well as for many who cannot participate in programming on-site.[2] Audience advocates want the people who visit museums to learn, understand, and retain the knowledge their institutions have to share.

Professional literature also asserts that, while the collection is the *heart* of a museum, what we have come to call education is the *spirit*.[3] If museum educators are audience advocates who hold the spirit of institutions in their hands, they must ask themselves: Are we meeting our potential with the resources available? What goals have we set? What goals have we met? Where have we fallen short? Identifying the most effective methods for conveying meaning about sites is critical to the educator's task, as is continuous program evaluation. In going about their work, historic house educators need to resist the tendency to be so site-focused that they isolate themselves from the numerous resources that are available. Among these valuable resources are other sites. One can look to any number of programs at historic house museums around the country to find helpful examples of programming success. While wide ranging in content and audience focus, they share common characteristics, which ensure that the spirits of their respective sites soar.[4]

Educating at Historic House Museums

No two house museums are alike. What will work at one place may fail at another, so each site has to discover what it can and cannot do. Aside from budgets, time periods, and the like, the management styles and personality dynamics, particularly between staff members and volunteers, differ widely. Most house museums do not have the resources of large history museums, science centers, and children's museums; instead, they rely on docents, interpreters, and museum teachers, most of whom are volunteers. Creating a positive educational environment while balancing the needs of all of the individuals involved in coordinating programming is essential.

Regardless of the circumstances of their sites, house museum educators share common problems. They do not have enough time, space, or money to do what needs to be done. Classroom teachers do not have time to make teaching site materials a priority. School administrators are often indifferent to the tremendous resources available to them through historic sites. Buses arrive late. Classes arrive unprepared. Everyone wants to visit at the same time. Sites have difficulty attracting and retaining committed volunteers to execute their programs. Education activities are often relegated to sheds, the outdoors, or spaces not designed for programs—or there simply may be no program space at all.

Although, in a broad sense, educators at historic house museums do essentially what their counterparts at other types of museums do, the historical settings and residential focus require a different approach to teaching and developing programs. Even though the historic house is by far the most prevalent museum type, little formal information is available about how visitors learn best at these sites specifically or about how to apply education theory to the historic house environment. Consequently, those performing the education role in house museums have developed workable learning strategies and techniques that might mystify classroom teachers accustomed to an ordered curriculum and ample work space. These "reflective practitioners" have through trial and error figured out for themselves what works best. However, the efforts of these historic house educators could benefit from knowledge of what classroom teachers do, from collaborating and brainstorming with colleagues at other sites, and from taking advantage of the resources and networking opportunities offered by the various museum associations. Because many of them are not trained teachers or trained museum educators, it is useful for them to investigate current pedagogic theory and audience research in hopes of creating useful and memorable experiences for visitors.

A significant advantage for historic house educators is that their sites offer the opportunity and the freedom to teach. Even with all of their quirks, house museums are usually blissfully nonbureaucratic. Most of the time, any idea can be accomplished if it conforms to the house's mission and period of interpretation, is not destructive to the site, and does not cost much money. When the McFaddin-Ward House in Beaumont, Texas, presented a day-camp program on popular dances from the 1930s, its education staff commandeered the site's in-home gymnasium for use as the classroom and shuffle-ball-changed, jitterbugged, and grand-marched its way through a terrific morning of history lessons, as well as needed exercise, with a group of enthusiastic children. Schools rarely provide this kind of fun teaching and learning, but, with a little imagination, house museum educators can offer highly entertaining, as well as poignant, experiences with history that make participants want to come back and be a part of the place.

School Groups

Isn't it remarkable that some people can remember what historic site field trip they took in the fourth grade but cannot remember any other thing they did that year? Museums possess the power to make lifelong memories. The universality of the daily life that house museums interpret allows them to tap into the emotional side of human nature. Living in a house or other residential structure is an experience common to most people, as are many of the rites of passage historic sites interpret. Capitalizing on this by connecting with the visitor's affective side can lead to successful programming. This means reaching people through emotion, such as triggering a memory of an item grandmother owned, creating a sense of the struggles of the pioneer experience, or stirring passions about liberty, freedom, equality, and justice.

Children especially need the connection with the past that house museums provide. As Beverly Sheppard explains in *Building Museum and School Partnerships*, "Our children live in a world with lots of information but little encounter. Few have much experience with how things work, how they were made, or how extraordinary it is to create something of value with their own hands. Museums remain one of the few environments where encounter is the basis of learning."[5]

When planning programming for schoolchildren, most house museum educators would agree that planning should be guided by certain fundamental assumptions. These include:

- All programs ought to be age appropriate and tied to the school curriculum, especially state curriculum mandates. Museum educators should be knowledgeable of state curriculum standards and be able to adapt site materials to meet curriculum needs.

- Children need to experience as well as see. Museum educators should design activities to allow for critical thinking and active learning.

- The museum becomes an extension of the classroom where learning objectives are accomplished and can be measured. Partnership and communication with classroom teachers is, therefore, essential.

- Creativity is the key to programming. The same old way of doing things, such as rote delivery of a house tour, is not going to work with twenty-first-century students.

Historic house museums are usually willing to share their education materials with colleagues. This is an excellent way to gather examples of successful school programs. Also, the National Register of Historic Places developed a useful formula for historic site lesson plans in its *Teaching with Historic Places* program. Lesson plans for a multitude of historic properties, ordering information for obtaining copies of *A Curriculum Framework for Professional Training and Development*, which explains the program and offers methods for putting together new lesson plans, along with a variety of articles on teaching about the built environment are available on the National Park Service Web site.[6]

Keys to Successful Programming

A museum director once noted that "an effective experience with the past goes beyond cognition—it's magic."[7] Though its impact cannot necessarily be explained, the experience can be transforming. House museums have the power through their resources and training to change someone's world view. Each of us can probably relate a magical time at a historic site when we were profoundly moved by an object or the idea of the place or were mesmerized by a living history presentation. Those lifelong memories are what museums seek in successful programming, but planning them can be hit or miss.

Good programming and program development require the coalescence of a variety of elements and activities. Among them are appropriate access to the site's historical resources, including object and archival collections; careful research and accurate application of scholarship; sincere and committed teachers and educators; an environment that fosters creativity; a well-conceived mission statement for guidance; and an openness to the use of new technologies. Other key steps, requiring a concentrated effort on the part of educators, are careful planning; awareness of audience needs and interests; communication with staff members and community advisory groups; training of program personnel; and continual evaluation of programs.

Planning

Ideally, all museum education programs provide historical context and stimulate learning. Effective programs, however, don't just happen; they result from careful planning. The interpretive planning process considers the site's historical collections and documentation and relates researched themes to the site's mission statements, programmatic goals, and strategies for achievement. Guided by a comprehensive interpretive strategy, museums can most efficiently plan programming that accomplishes the institution's established goals.

In developing education programs, museum personnel must consider a number of issues, taking care not to miss any of the steps that are essential to careful planning. The first of these is the idea, the point where program planning begins. Ideas should be brainstormed, culled, and refined. At historic house museums, the idea must relate to history. Important advocates of history and its lessons, historic sites need to be dynamic reminders of a shared past.

Another key consideration is the museum's budget for the educational program. Is money available to proceed with the desired program? If not, is cosponsorship an option? The staff must decide if it intends for the program to provide a free community service with the museum absorbing all the expenses; if it hopes simply to break even, expenses covered by the registration fees paid by a predetermined number of people; or if it expects the program to turn a profit, which could in turn be used to support other programs. In the case of the second option, staff members should determine in advance the number of registrations needed and acknowledge that cancellation may be necessary if the break-even point is not met.

A work plan is useful to program development, as it sets forth information about project leadership and workers and a timetable of the tasks to be done. One of the most important of these tasks is research. The content of education programs must be based on the very best scholarship possible. The work plan will be influenced, in part, by the program's curriculum. What is the subject matter and who is the audience? Curriculum considerations include the size of the group, the age range, and any special interests or characteristics its participants may have. For school programs, curriculum development will entail deciding on objectives, strategies, pre- and postvisit exercises, a description of how the program's focus correlates with state curriculum mandates, and evaluation methods. For other types of programming, the curriculum may not need to be as detailed. It should, however, include an agenda for the program with a breakdown of activities, times, and locations. Once the curriculum is established, the museum staff should then plan for training the personnel who will carry out the program.

Planners must also establish parameters for participant registration. At the most basic level, this means deciding how people can sign up for the program and choosing a cut-off date. Anticipating as many registration-related circumstances and problems as possible is time well spent. Will walk-ins be allowed? With regard to school programs, who at the school is in charge of scheduling? It is vital that steps be taken to ensure that both the school district and the museum communicate all necessary logistical details with regard to school program attendance.

Making decisions about supplies, purchasing, and printing leads to questions about who will do the purchasing, when the purchasing will be done, and how it will be paid for. Can the museum create the program media or does it need the assistance of a designer and other outside help? What is the turnaround time for media production and does it correspond to the program's implementation schedule?

The many other details that must be attended to often defy categorization, but understanding and being able to handle the minutiae of programs makes the difference between a positive and a frustrating experience for all involved. With school groups, for example, program personnel may need to supply the school district bus barn with maps to the site. And it will probably be necessary to call schools the day or week before the program to obtain final student counts and other last-minute information. Other details may include making name tags; placing directional signage; setting up the program space and rounding up tables and chairs; verifying accessibility provisions; sending out special notices to police, neighboring businesses, and emergency agencies that should be aware of what is taking place, especially for large programs; and taking care of all details with respect to the speakers, presenters, and performers.

Some sort of publicity will be necessary to ensure that potential participants know about the program. This could take many forms, from simple hand-distributed fliers to extensive media coverage, before and even after the event. Should the museum schedule a press conference, and should it prepare a press release or provide photo opportunities? Who will take pictures? The site's newsletter should include in a timely issue an article announcing the program, as well as a follow-up review.

Miscellaneous tasks on the day of the program must be identified and delegated in advance to reduce the chance that some necessary preparation is overlooked. Who will open the site? Will someone be stationed in the parking lot to provide information to arriving participants? Who will be in charge of setup, cleanup, and refreshment duties? Inevitably, program planners are confronted with something completely unexpected. It helps for everyone to be aware of this, even though you will not know exactly what might happen. Develop a general strategy for handling the unexpected. Who will make decisions? What are the emergency procedures? What will you do if it rains?

Last but not least, it is important to thank the parties who helped with the program. Throughout the program planning and preparation process, keep a list of individuals, groups, businesses, or other organizations that contributed resources, including time, to the project. Never fail to say thank you in writing or to give them some sort of special recognition.

Knowing the Audience

To develop successful programs, educators must know who the intended audiences are and target the programs specifically to them. House museums have external audiences—tourists, students, organized tour groups, special interest groups, and the general public—and internal audiences—staff members, particularly support and frontline people; interpreters and volunteers; board members; and member organizations. A museum should identify these people and determine what they need from the museum and its programs, as well as what the museum has to offer them.

275

Knowledge of community demographics, such as average household incomes, education levels, ethnicity, and age breakdowns, aids in planning programs for diverse audiences. Offering inclusive programming is one of the fundamental responsibilities of any historic house museum. Inclusion and diversity characterize the most successful educational efforts. Not only does demonstrating how a museum fulfills its commitment to the different sectors of its community go to the heart of the AAM's initiative, *Museums in Community*, but it can also be useful in obtaining federal grants.[8]

Short of contracting with outside consultants and audience research specialists, house museums can take simple steps to conduct basic research. Resources at public libraries reveal city, county, and community demographics. Current community issues may provide clues to areas in which the museum could play a role and fill a need, particularly if education is a concern. Museum guest registers and frontline personnel hold insights into who the visitors are. Training hosts and interpreters to take note, discreetly and respectfully, of their visitors' approximate ages, genders, ethnicity, and group sizes and types is time well spent. If guest registers are inadequate or nonexistent, regular surveys of license plates in the museum parking lot could be useful. And every site can benefit from a review of attendance figures, comparing those of various years, events, and programs. These suggestions are starting points for understanding the current museum user and the community in which the museum exists. Knowing who is visiting a site is the first step in learning how to serve those who are not.

Communicating and Consulting

Any aspect of interpretive planning must involve an ongoing dialogue about the dynamics of the message the site sends out through tours, media, programming, and special events. Clear and open communication is crucial to successful program development and delivery because it allows for everyone involved to be invested in a positive outcome. If one person or museum department is alone responsible for every aspect of education planning, that person or department will be the only staff with an intrinsic interest in the outcome of the plan. As Cary Carson, vice president of research at Colonial Williamsburg, has said, "Museums should not be lonely places to work."[9] Even museums with only one or two employees need to hold education planning discussions with other interested parties, such as board members, volunteers, and local school personnel.

In addition to a committed staff, many successful museums have education advisory groups as part of their program planning teams. Sometimes these are board driven, others are volunteer based, while still others are largely staff based. The type of advisory group a museum cultivates depends on who the targeted audiences are and how the institution operates. In general, these education advisors consider program content, delivery, and logistics. If a strong and active board governs the museum, then board members may lead the education advisory committee. Alternatively, if the staff at a site is charged with executing programming, then staff members will develop the committee and coordinate the agenda.

Education advisory groups used by historic house museums around the country exist in a variety of forms. One museum's advisory group is made up of teachers, administrators, staff, and board members who meet monthly. The museum receives input from a local children's museum staff, teachers, volunteers, experts in content and subject area, education professors, and visitors. A large house museum has formed an outreach task force that includes the director, curator, chief of interpretation, interpreters, culturally diverse community representatives, local teachers, and museum and education professionals. They work together to assess current programs, establish achievable goals, and develop a five-year plan that addresses future programming. At an internationally known house museum the education department does not consult only one advisory group, but instead uses teacher advisement on a project-by-project basis.[10]

When the McFaddin-Ward House initiated a task force to provide input on existing and future programs, staff members sent out a broad appeal to volunteers, teachers, and community resource people such as county extension personnel and local university professors. The group that actually gathered consisted primarily of teachers who already used museum resources. The museum staff realized after the initial meeting that the teachers were not interested in discussing the larger picture of educational offerings at the site. While they cared about the museum, high school teachers were not interested in coming back to the museum to discuss programs for preschoolers or in developing adult learning programs. The teachers were, however, interested in discussions related to their own work and areas of specialization. What began as a desire for an integrated committee of community educators resulted in several focused subcommittees. These committees worked toward concrete and clearly delineated goals—to improve existing programs or to create new ones. Seventh-grade teachers regularly critique and offer suggestions to improve an established district-wide program. A group of high school teachers worked with the staff to create two curriculum-related programs involving the museum's period of interpretation and wealth of documentation: "The Gilded Ages as Reflected at McFaddin-Ward House" and "The World War II Home Front in Beaumont."

Training

At many sites the only experience available to visitors is the "one size fits all" house tour. Many of us can name sites where docents give the same rote tour regardless of the visitor's learning level or interests. Uninspired delivery is not always the docent's fault. Interpreters and museum program personnel are only as good as their training, and, in today's short-staffed house museums, it is too often considered more important to have a warm, reliable body than a well-trained one.

Farsighted house museums, however, commit adequate time and resources to docent education, frequently using training models that already exist. The National Park Service and the National Association for Interpretation offer training, articles, and informative conferences. The National Docent Symposium gathers biannually to meet, discuss, and celebrate the work of docents. Minds In Motion publishes *The Docent Educator* six times a year as a practical guide to the docent's job. Each issue focuses on a particular theme with regard to hands-on museum education. Realizing the centrality of interpreters to the museum's purpose, Drayton Hall in Charleston, South Carolina, invests in continuing interpreter education—as it would in any other education program—by holding monthly meetings, workshops, and roundtable discussions; producing an in-house newsletter; hosting a yearly lecture series; and participating in cooperative training with other sites.

For those involved in the presentation of other types of museum programming, training is also desirable. If time allows, museum staff members should develop a job description for program personnel—paid staff or volunteer—noting the extent of training required. It is good practice to allow only those who have gone through interpreter training—who know the site's interpretation and the special nature of the museum's collection—to work with programs. It is also a good practice to be familiar with and to gear training to the characteristics of the ultimate audiences. If the program is for schoolchildren, presenters should be aware of the intellectual and social development level of the specific age or grade they are presenting to. The same goes for family groups, senior citizens, and others. Planners need to decide: What kind of training is needed? Will content training be sufficient or should it be supplemented with training on various logistical matters? When should the training take place?

Program Evaluation

Museums committed to interpretive planning know what successful programs are because they decide during the planning process how they will define success. They also implement assessment mechanisms that reveal whether goals have been met. Many people who work in education programming for an extended time get a feel for their work and know in their hearts when an activity or lesson is successful. In much the same way, an actor perceives whether the audience is grasping a performance; the actor knows when he hits the mark and when he misses. Institutions cannot, however, afford to rely on intuition. They must establish methods for tracking and assessing programs. Doing so not only allows for an accurate analysis of efforts, but also ensures that staff members not directly involved in a project understand its impact.

Evaluation, or the range of methods used to measure quality, is the generally accepted way of determining success in museum programming. Many house museums do a less-than-effective job of evaluating their programs. Any of a variety of factors may be to blame: museum staff members do not know how to evaluate their programs properly; they feel unqualified; they do not have enough time; their program/tour is already developed and change is unlikely; or they fail to see any value in evaluation.

Effective evaluation should be built into the program development process and utilized throughout—at the beginning, in the middle, and at the end. Ideally, planners need to know that a program or activity will meet objectives before they spend time and money to implement it. An effective way of doing this is to assemble a focus group early in the planning process to discuss the proposed tour, program, or concept. Another, less effective way to gauge how a general audience will receive a project is to use an internal audience—staff, volunteers, and the museum community—to analyze it. These people are, however, often too close to the subject to be objective. Focus groups and on-site interviews with guests in historic areas are among the methods the visitor research department at Colonial Williamsburg uses to obtain answers about how well visitors respond to the museum's interpretation. The staff believes that conducting evaluation interviews is not highly technical but requires objective questioning skills, patience in allowing visitors to respond completely, and the appearance of detachment. It also requires allowing adequate time to conduct site interviews and to compile the data.[11]

A basic form of general evaluation is the exit card or end-of-experience comment card. Data collected from these cards is usually intended more for marketing information than for measuring quality or revealing information. Market research or the selling of a product should not to be confused with evaluation and the need to understand the visitor experience.

Services to schoolchildren usually receive more evaluation attention than offerings to general audiences. Typically, school classes cannot visit a museum unless the experience meets certain curriculum goals or strategies. Many sites offer pilot programs that they hope will become standard offerings for school audiences. Planning committees review tested programs and revise them accordingly. Following a school program, house museum educators often have teachers complete written evaluation forms, which gauge content delivery as well as measure logistics and service satisfaction. Unfortunately, the program participants—the students—are often left out of the evaluation process, and rarely are parents asked how their children responded to an activity at a museum.

When thinking about developing an evaluation process, house museum staffs should remember that visitor studies is a discipline. Researching the subject through related books and professional journals may help generate ideas on the appropriate methods for evaluating a particular program.[12] The evaluation strategy should be planned well in advance of the event. Among other benefits, this will allow time for training volunteers to conduct visitor interviews, if this is a method chosen. If it is, someone should review the evaluation process while it is ongoing to see if it meets program specifications and, when it is completed, compile and analyze the data. Another approach might be to have docents conduct evaluations simply by asking visitors what they will remember about the site or program. The museum should keep a log of these responses and of any unsolicited comments. If a museum chooses to use comment cards, they should include questions about interpretive content by asking, for example, what visitors will remember most and how they would characterize what they experienced.

As a building block for continuing programs, education planners should prepare written internal evaluations after each activity, noting the program's characteristics and goals, supply costs, attendance, problems, volunteer and staff workers, and comments. Evaluating a program's educational worth, potential audience, benefits to the museum and to the existing audience, positive and negative impacts on the budget and on staff time expenditure, as well as positive and negative impact on the historic structure, is a valuable exercise for any historic site. It can use the results to make informed decisions on whether to retain, amend, or eliminate any educational offering. Institution-wide evaluation, which requires input from all departments affected or connected to the project in any way, will ensure the most accurate assessment.

Programs That Work

Historic house museums are developing new and exciting education programs every day. They can inspire and stimulate our imaginations as we strive to find relevant new applications for the stories our sites stand ready to tell. The programs described below make magic in big and small ways every time their sites offer them. They represent only a few of the many successful educational programs already in place, but they provide insight into what an effective program can be.

Extensive Calendar of Interpretive Exhibits

Following an ambitious strategy for a small-to-mid-size organization, Adsmore in Princeton, Kentucky, changes interpretive programming and tour presentation several times a year. A 1998 publicity flier for the museum lists the following changing room interpretations: a Wake, Winter at Home, Spring and Easter, Home from Washington, Selina's Engagement, Black Patch War, Selina's Wedding, and Christmas. The staff regards the museum's holdings as "a unique family collection," comprehensive enough for the presentation of eight different and significant events in the life of the family. Of those eight, the wedding and wake have been the most popular.[13]

Programs Inspired by Exhibits

The Manship House Museum in Jackson, Mississippi, has a small staff and limited funds. One of its interpretive successes stemmed from a temporary exhibit obtained from the Rogers Historical Museum in Rogers, Arkansas, and installed in the visitor center exhibit area. In conjunction with the exhibit, titled *Final Respects*, the staff dressed the museum house as if its residents were in mourning and developed a series of coincidental special events, including a tour of a historic cemetery, a talk on the Victorian use of cemeteries as gathering places for social and recreational activities, and a presentation on cemetery monument architecture. Building on the theme of a temporary exhibit, the Manship House Museum developed new interpretation providing relevant historical lessons and expanding its audience.[14]

Girl Scouts

The Orchard House, Home of the Alcotts, in Concord, Massachusetts, offers "Journey through Journals: The Alcotts in Their Own Words." This program is adapted to the Girl Scout "My Heritage" program, and Scouts who complete various components fulfill requirements for the "My Heritage" badge. Goals include exploring identity through words and possessions; decoding journals to learn about the past; and, through the Alcotts, who were passionate about their own journals, understanding the benefits of keeping a journal. To prepare for the site visit, which includes a living history experience, Scouts become familiar with *Little Women* (the novel or movie) and review previsit materials, such as biographical profiles of family members, an informational sketch of the home, and quotes from the Alcott family. Filling a need in the community, this program meets state-mandated curriculum requirements and allows the museum to tell its story to groups of eager participants. The museum schedules it to suit its own calendar, as well as the needs and wishes of the Girl Scout leaders, many of whom are working mothers. Troops visit after school, during the slow months of the museum's year, and on early release days.[15]

Filling a Need

The Fulton Mansion near Corpus Christi, Texas, utilizes in-house expertise to educate its audiences, which include tourists, locals, and "Winter Texans," the name given by locals to the retirees from the North and Midwest who take refuge on the warm Gulf Coast. The site presented a panel exhibit, developed by the curator and coordinated by the educator, on preserving one's family photographs. Once viewed at the site, this exhibit will travel throughout Texas, primarily to libraries, allowing the museum to teach correct preservation techniques to an eager audience of amateur genealogists and memento savers.[16]

Oral History and Community History

As part of its effort to interpret the period from 1906 to 1950, the McFaddin-Ward House collaborated with the Tyrrell Historical Library, in Beaumont, Texas, on a World War II home front panel discussion. The collaborating institutions assembled a group of longtime residents to talk, in a structured way, about what life on the home front was like and how the war years changed the community. The audience filled the Tyrrell Library, and the panelists' recollections, which were recorded on videotape, added to the town's collective memory. The program cost next to nothing.[17]

Educating K–3

The Kaminski House in Georgetown, South Carolina, offers a program called "Feet: A Look at Craftsmanship and Creativity." The museum developed this program when an observant staff member noticed the collection's numerous pieces of furniture with interesting carved feet and to try to overcome a perception of being unwelcoming to children. The experience allows early elementary schoolchildren (K–3) to examine the collection from their own viewpoint and learn about the anatomy and craftsmanship of furniture. The staff and volunteers of this small museum with limited resources regularly review the program's content and learning objectives as they present the program to approximately 450 students each year. Because of the program's usefulness in teaching about the site, the staff adapted it into a flexible outreach activity for multiple grade levels, thus reaching approximately a thousand schoolchildren annually who are not able to visit in person.[18]

Horticulture and History

Grumblethorpe, which is part of the Philadelphia Society for the Preservation of Landmarks, offers, free of charge, a series of year-round programs to local schoolchildren. One of these is a horticulture program that connects inner-city children with the original owner's interest in plants and their cultivation. Fifth-grade students plant pumpkins to learn how long it takes for a food source to grow. The students incorporate history, math, and biology in their observations of the pumpkins. In the fall, after the harvest, the students bake pies to discover what was involved in preparing part of a meal. They take the extra pies to a local soup kitchen.[19]

Curriculum-Based Programming

Brucemore in Cedar Rapids, Iowa, has had long-term success with its sixth-grade program, "Built Environment." It focuses on how people shape their environment and involves a two-hour visit to the museum. By linking the site to the community, the program conveys that historic neighborhoods contribute to the quality of life. In the greenhouse, museum educators and docents teach about earth science. Viewing the exterior of the house, they discuss math—angles, scale, and ratio. In all areas, the young people are encouraged to analyze and evaluate the function and aesthetics of what they see. Museum staff members describe the program as a "multi-unit extension of the classroom" and believe the students who participate in the program will benefit the preservation movement when they become adults.[20]

Evolving Fourth-Grade Program

The Homestead Museum in City of Industry, California, has a fourth-grade program called "A Journey through Time," which was first implemented in 1983 and updated in 1996. A binder of twenty lesson plans allows teachers to pick and choose according to their students' needs in exploring California history in three different time periods: the 1840s, 1870s, and 1920s. The lesson plans explain how activities meet state curriculum requirements and include references to text-book pages containing information that emphasizes the dovetailing of museum lessons with textbook content. After preparation through previsit materials, students visit the museum for a two-and-a-half hour, structured, activity-based experience. The museum's educator insists that following the state's curriculum framework and being familiar with the textbooks students are using have been essential to the success of this program. Notably, the program is continuously reviewed and adapted to meet current needs. Several of its lesson plans are on the museum's Web site, and the goal is to have the entire set of materials posted as portable document files (PDF), making lessons and graphics easily download-able.[21]

Collaborative Innovation

The Ellwood House in DeKalb, Illinois, has an imaginative fifth-grade program, "Under One Roof," that it uses as an alternative to the whole house tour. The program concentrates on the bedrooms of the owner's family, governess, and servants to contrast lifestyles within one household and to reveal how residents shared spaces while they remained separated by class.

The museum, the history and art departments at Northern Illinois University, and teachers at a local middle school developed the program jointly. Its forty-six-page manual includes previsit materials—slides, biographies, city maps, activities using primary documents including a want ad for household help, and discovery box techniques—and visit materials, such as a floor plan of bed-rooms, detective sheets with probing questions for each of the rooms to be visited, and inquiry sheets pertaining to the house's architecture. Postvisit materials include discussion topics on lifestyle, an assignment to write a letter from the point of view of an immigrant, a crossword puzzle, architectural bingo, a glossary, a list of local research facilities, and bibliographies for teachers and fifth-grade readers.[22]

Immigrant History

The Northern Indiana Center for History in South Bend, Indiana, uses three buildings on its ten-acre site to compare and contrast the lifestyle of a wealthy local family with that of a Polish immigrant family during the 1930s. The Work-er's House Museum, outfitted in the style of a Polish-American family, is an interactive history "lab" where visitors (especially students) get to open drawers and doors to discover household items used during the Great Depression. The museum uses an inquiry tour—a type of tour that uses question-asking and comparison strategies—to illustrate how ethnic groups held onto their traditions in the crossroads of America and how the ethnic working classes contributed to the growth and prosperity of the St. Joseph Valley region. Museum educators hope that through the tour experience and its hands-on components, "Kids see themselves somewhere in the museum when they visit."[23]

Interactive Techniques

The James J. Hill House in St. Paul, Minnesota, offers interactive, two-and-a-half-hour workshops for upper elementary students. Large groups split into three sections: parlor activities, social lessons, and the riddle tour. In the parlor activities area, students practice elocution with tongue twisters; act out sections of period stories and novels, including *Little Women*, *Alice in Wonderland*, and *The Tell-Tale Heart*; read letters by Hill family children; and play parlor games. They discuss art collecting, listen to the pipe organ, and participate in a sing-along. Social lessons teach bowing and curtseying, proper greetings, and good posture through book balancing. Students learn proper dress, such as how to wear a detachable collar, and dining etiquette, including silverware placement. The riddle tour area offers a discovery experience in which students focus on, identify, and extract meaning from various features in the house. The museum schedules the program on days the house is not normally open to the public and offers about a dozen of these workshops a year.[24]

Activity-Based Interaction

Of the approximately twenty thousand annual visitors to the Francis Land House in Virginia Beach, Virginia, eight thousand are schoolchildren, whose teachers choose from a menu of offerings suited to their grade levels. For the fifth-grade program, "Life in Colonial Virginia: The Plantation and Its People," classes receive detailed location-specific materials about mid-eighteenth-century Tidewater residents and their lifestyles, all having some relationship to the 1770 site. As part of the site experience, students travel through six interactive, hands-on stations. Students share their impressions as they explore the lives of the gentry, middle-class artisans, and slaves. They act out a lesson with a tutor, try colonial dancing with a dance master, explore the production of cloth, and study early trades. The museum's education specialist points out that, because the program adheres to the Virginia Standards of Learning, the "community considers the Francis Land House to be a parallel school." The museum assists teachers by making clear exactly which block of teaching a program at the museum will cover.[25]

Concentrated Pandemonium

Many house museums experience concentrated pandemonium: seeing large numbers of children for a specific program, scheduled during a specific time, usually during the slow season. Belle Meade in Nashville, Tennessee, does this with "Hands-on-Harvest," a curriculum-based program occurring one week in October. During this week, the museum sees a thousand students in grades K–6 from all types of schools (including home schools) and economic backgrounds, as well as Scouts from the middle Tennessee area. At twelve stations, professional craftsmen demonstrate period activities, such as candle dipping, natural dying, fireside cooking, quilting, spinning, and carding. The hands-on nature of the program teaches students about daily concerns of their ancestors in a fun manner, and, says one educator, "It also provides opportunities children don't normally enjoy, such as jumping in our haystack."[26]

Site-Specific Programming

Some programs are so unique and closely tied to a site that they are perfect vehicles for conveying the tangible nature of the past, as well as evoking the special character of the place and its people. The Froebel Block Workshops at the Frank Lloyd Wright Preservation Trust in Oak Park and Chicago, Illinois, are an example.

Wright's mother discovered Froebel toys, called "gifts," at the Philadelphia Centennial Exhibition of 1876. Developed in the 1830s in Germany by Friedrich Froebel to encourage abstract thinking in children, they include a sphere, cylinder, cube, oblong blocks, planes, squares, straight lines, curves, and points. These gifts inspired Wright's interest in design at an early age. At the Froebel Block Workshops, people of all ages can experience the expensive gifts during a single visit or over several sessions. Museum educators believe that allowing participants to delve into the type of abstract learning that Wright enjoyed encourages an understanding of the famous architect's design philosophy.[27]

Museum Theater and Romance

As a Valentine's Day event for the Cooper-Molera Adobe and three other historic adobes in Monterey, California, staff and volunteers present four vignettes written especially for the structures that dramatize the love story of someone in each of the houses. One ticket for the program, "Days of Romance," offers admission into the four houses along with a catered gourmet boxed lunch. For the tightly timed event, costumed guides lead visitors on a specific route to the homes where actors perform the vignettes ten times each day to no more than twenty people at a time. The event showcases and relies on the sites' docents, who act, interpret the sites, produce the event, decorate the adobes, and serve as costumed traffic coordinators. Period music and dancing entertain visitors while they dine in a designated area. As a Valentine's touch, each lady receives a red rose.[28]

Re-created Holiday Event

The staff at Decatur House in Washington, D.C., developed a Christmas event based on records of the home's last private owner, Marie Beale, who was instrumental in the effort to preserve her neighborhood, Lafayette Square, which includes the White House. The program, "Caviar, Carols, and Champagne," re-created the Christmas Eve party Beale hosted in 1952 as household records and detailed diary entries describe it. The museum replicated everything from the artificial tree sprayed white to the bacon and peanut butter appetizers to the singing of the same carols sung at the original party. (Note: Guests did not consume food or beverages inside the historic house.) In 1997, the museum held the hugely successful event three times with a limited number of people attending at fifteen dollars a person.[29]

Tapping into Technology

Even though house museums are rooted in the past, they must embrace advances in technology if they hope to be relevant. Magnolia Mound in Baton Rouge, Louisiana, heeded this advice by initiating a Web site called "Partners in Online Education at Magnolia Mound" (POEMM). It is sponsored by the Louisiana State University (LSU) Office of Community Preservation and located on the LSU School of Architecture's Web site. This Web site is separate from Magnolia Mound's informational home page. Its stated mission is "to extend Magnolia Mound's education impact beyond its actual location, using new technology to tell the story of Louisiana's heritage, culture, and people." Users can access primary documents including early recipes, table settings, gardening techniques, and a child's game called "*Parlez Vous* Magnolia Mound." Teachers are encouraged to use the Web site for pre- and postvisit materials when planning a visit. One of the site's more specific goals is to provide an accurate online depiction of colonial life at Magnolia Mound Plantation through student-generated work posted on the site. In 1998, the Web site featured its first student research project, a historical essay about the life of a typical student boarder at the Ursuline Academy in New Orleans, the convent school attended by the daughters of Magnolia Mound's eighteenth-century owner.[30]

Interaction Online

In the late 1990s, Monticello, Thomas Jefferson's home in Charlottesville, Virginia, took over the "Thomas Jefferson Online" interactive correspondence, which was previously managed by the Virginia Department of Education. Under the section "Plan a Trip," students and classes around the world write Mr. Jefferson and receive responses (written in first-person language) from the education staff. Children ask questions, such as "What's your middle name?" and "What's your favorite color?" as well as more challenging questions like "How can you own slaves if you wrote that all men are created equal?" Museum educators note that staff continuity is key to efficiency; people who have worked at the museum long enough generally know the answers to most of the questions or where to find them. In addition to online interaction, www.monticello.org also features lesson plans, an introductory quiz to test one's Thomas Jefferson knowledge, and a Web-based scavenger hunt.[31]

Touch-It Rooms

In the summer of 1998, Monticello opened, for the first time, a discovery room. The department received money to staff the facility but not very much to equip it. The staff soon realized that expensive hands-on items were not necessary for educational success. The room contains a "what's it?" table, an old-time games section, a coloring area and building blocks, and, most popular, the writing-with-a-quill-pen station.[32]

Teenage Connection

The McFaddin-Ward House cultivates the notion of students teaching students. Its Junior Guide program is composed of teenagers from a local high school that allows students to be away from campus on Fridays to perform community service. These student guides, mostly minorities, make it possible for all seventh-grade Texas history students in the local school district to tour the museum. This peer teaching approach has allowed the museum to reach middle school students on their level, providing new avenues of communication for tour giving, history lessons, and leadership. Junior Guides train and conduct tours on

Fridays throughout most of the school year. They are committed to the museum and are among its best ambassadors.

Junior Interpreters

The McFaddin-Ward House also trains Junior Interpreters. These young people range in age from thirteen to twenty-one. They learn the museum's interpretation in the summer and volunteer throughout the year in various capacities at the museum. Happily, they have also developed an important peer group among themselves. They appreciate the museum, they understand the importance of community service, and they enjoy being with each other. With its Junior Guide and Junior Interpreter programs, the museum is building its own history army.

Through creativity, appropriate resources, and the desire to do important things, the possibilities for successful educational programming are endless. The great differences in governance, management, financial capabilities, and manpower bases ensure that the historic house museum community will always feature a diverse array of programs and program potential. The common goal should be excellence. If a historic house is a museum, its staff must teach history and teach it well. Individual sites have to determine for their own situations the best ways to do so.

As the sites mentioned in the program descriptions demonstrate, house museums can connect with their communities in ways that will ensure their relevance not only in the present, but also for the future. Certainly they must be mindful of the enormous educational potential for integrating new technologies with current learning opportunities in appropriate situations. To further heighten the likelihood of success, museum educators should develop plans, know their audiences, continually evaluate, be guided by the museum's mission and by good scholarship, draw upon the site's collection and historical documentation, fill community needs, be inclusive, seek advice from and communicate with peers, and make their programs memorable. Following these steps will be rewarding to the site, to its visitors and program participants, and to its community, and will leave the museum educator with a song in his or her heart and the satisfaction of an important job well done.

Notes

1. *Standards and Best Practices for Interpretation, the National Interpretation Project: Report to the Mountain Plains Regional Study Group and Preliminary Analysis of All Regional*

Study Groups (Washington, D.C.: American Association of Museums, April 2000), cover. See also www.aam-us.org/NIPoverview.htm (visited 20 April 2002).

2. Standing Professional Committee on Museum Education, *Statement on Professional Standards for Museum Education* (Washington, D.C.: American Association of Museums, pamphlet), n.p. The standards first appeared in "Standards: A Hallmark in the Evolution of Museum Education," *Museum News* 69 (January/February 1990): 78–80.

3. *Excellence and Equity: Education and the Public Dimension of Museums, A Report from the American Association of Museums* (Washington, D.C.: American Association of Museums, 1992), 10. The statement first appeared in *Museums for a New Century* (Washington, D.C.: American Association of Museums, 1984), 55.

4. The basis for my research for this chapter, which began as a conference presentation, was a survey of the programs about which the thirty house museum educators I contacted were most enthusiastic. The museums included National Trust for Historic Preservation properties, as well as sites mentioned by Terry Zeller in his article "Re-interpreting the Whole House for School Tours," *Docent Educator* (Summer 1998): 8–11.

5. Beverly Sheppard, *Building Museum and School Partnerships* (Washington, D.C.: American Association of Museums, 1993), 3.

6. Information about the *Teaching with Historic Places* program along with the National Register for Historic Places (National Park Service, 1849 C Street, NW, Suite 400, Washington, D.C. 20240) is available at www.cr.nps.gov/nr/twhp (visited 1 April 2002).

7. Frank Jewell, conversation with author during a National Endowment for the Humanities-funded Interpretive Self-Study field trip for Shadows-on-the-Teche, 23 July 1991.

8. An example of a useful published statistical compilation is *The Sourcebook of County Demographics* 2000 (CACI Marketing Systems. The source of business information in the Sourcebook is *Info*USA, Inc., Omaha, Neb.). The *Museums in Community* initiative is "a national initiative to explore the potential for dynamic engagement between American communities and their museums." For information, see www.aam-us.org/m&c/index.htm (visited 20 April 2002).

9. Cary Carson, "Researching a Changing Past" (paper presented at the Seminar for Historical Administration, Williamsburg, Va., 10 November 1999).

10. Information about the three house museums discussed in this paragraph was obtained through grant application review. The agency sponsoring the grants asks that specifics about individual sites remain confidential.

11. Connie C. Graft and Randi Korn, "Good Job? Evaluating Your Programs" (lecture presented at the Seminar for Historical Administration, Williamsburg, Va., 11 November 1999).

12. A helpful resource is the Visitor Studies Association, headquartered at Colorado State University in Fort Collins. Their e-mail address is visitorstudies@qwest.net (visited 1 April 2002).

13. Ardell Jarratt (curator/director, Adsmore), telephone conversations with author, February 1998 and 21 February 2001.

14. Marilyn Jones (curator, Manship House), telephone conversation with author, February 1998, and faxed correspondence, 28 February 2001. The Manship House is administered by the Mississippi Department of Archives and History.

15. Cara Shapiro (director of education, Orchard House, Home of the Alcotts), telephone conversation with author, February 1998; Cheryl Peters (director of education, Orchard House, Home of the Alcotts), telephone conversation with author, 21 February 2001; Jan Turnquist (outreach specialist, Orchard House, Home of the Alcotts), e-mail to author, 29 March 2001.

16. Robin Gilliam (education coordinator, Fulton Mansion State Historical Park), telephone conversation with author, 21 February 2001.

17. "World War II in Beaumont: Remembering the Home Front," cosponsored by the McFaddin-Ward House and the Tyrrell Historical Library, 15 April 1997.

18. Ralph Calhoun (director, Kaminski House), telephone conversation with the author, February 1998; Cindy Pease (education coordinator, Kaminski House), telephone conversation with the author, 21 February 2001.

19. Katrina Mullins (education coordinator, Grumblethorpe), telephone conversation with the author, February 1998; Sophie Bernard (site manager, Grumblethorpe), telephone conversation with author, 5 March 2001. Grumblethorpe is one of four properties owned by the Philadelphia Society for the Preservation of Landmarks.

20. David Janssen (assistant director, Brucemore), telephone conversations with author, February 1998 and 21 February 2001. Brucemore is a property of the National Trust for Historic Preservation.

21. Mary A. Roberts (public programs manager, The Homestead Museum), telephone conversation with author, February 1998; Carol Henderson (education coordinator, The Homestead Museum), telephone conversation with author, 21 February 2001.

22. Fran Larson (educator, Ellwood House Museum), telephone conversation with author, February 1998 and 21 February 2001.

23. Kathy Deka (education coordinator, Northern Indiana Center for History), telephone conversation with author, February 1998; Travis Child (director of school programs, Northern Indiana Center for History), e-mail to author, 28 February 2001. Dom Robotnika, A Worker's House Museum is administered by the Northern Indiana Center for History operated by the Northern Indiana Historical Society, Inc.

24. Sue Fair (assistant site manager, James J. Hill House), telephone conversations with author, February 1998 and 21 February 2001. The James J. Hill House is a historic house museum owned and operated by the Minnesota Historical Society.

25. Vicki Harvey (museum education specialist, Francis Land Historic Site and Gardens), telephone conversations with author, February 1998 and 21 February 2001. The Francis Land Historic Site and Gardens is owned and operated by the city of Virginia Beach, Virginia.

26. Karen Crocker (education director, Belle Meade Plantation), telephone conversation with author, February 1998; Beth Cooper (education director, Belle Meade Plantation), telephone conversation with author, 21 February 2001.

27. Joseph Socki (education manager, Frank Lloyd Wright Home and Studio), telephone conversation with author, February 1998; Jan Kieckhefer (director of education, Frank Lloyd Wright Preservation Trust), 21 February 2001. The Frank Lloyd Wright Home and Studio is a property of the National Trust for Historic Preservation.

28. Linda Larson (lead state park guide/historian, Cooper-Molera Adobe), telephone conversations with author, February 1998 and 21 February 2001. The Cooper-Molera Adobe is a property of the National Trust for Historic Preservation and is operated by California State Parks.

29. Molly Neal (curator of education, Decatur House), telephone conversation with author, February 1998. The Decatur House is a property of the National Trust for Historic Preservation.

30. Connie Anderson (education coordinator, Magnolia Mound), telephone conversation with author, February 1998; Julia Rose (education coordinator, Magnolia Mound), telephone conversation with author, 21 February 2001.

31. Robin Gabriel (director of education, Monticello), telephone conversation with author, February 1998, and e-mail to author, 26 February 2001. Monticello is owned and operated by the Thomas Jefferson Memorial Foundation, Inc.

32. Ibid.

CHAPTER FOURTEEN

PROGRAMMING AT THE SHADOWS: EDUCATION WITH A MISSION

Patricia L. Kahle

The Shadows-on-the-Teche, situated in New Iberia, Louisiana, is a historic house museum owned and operated by the National Trust for Historic Preservation as one of their twenty-one historic sites. Like many historic house museums, it has a small staff, a small budget, and a big mission: to preserve the buildings, landscape, collections, and the historical integrity of the site; to research and interpret through education programs a nineteenth-century southern Louisiana plantation's economy and community and their evolution; and to encourage an appreciation of and interest in historic preservation.

For education programs, the audience is New Iberia and Iberia Parish (the equivalent of a county in Louisiana). New Iberia has a population of 32,000 and Iberia Parish approximately 68,000, thirty percent of whom are minorities, mostly African Americans. Louisiana is one of the poorest states in the nation and also has one of the lowest high school graduation rates. Even so, the Shadows, which in 2001 celebrated its fortieth anniversary since opening to the public, annually presents onsite education programs for more than 5,000 children from Iberia Parish schools and has had a strong working relationship with local educators since the 1970s.

Staff size and limited resources have not prevented the site from presenting a surprising variety of quality education programs. Rather, these challenges have encouraged an amazing level of support from the community in volunteers and funding, which makes it possible for the site to successfully fulfill its education mission.

The Site

"[T]he interest is entirely in seeing how the people in these houses lived. . . . To the public, the picture of the life is important."—William Weeks Hall, *An*

PATRICIA L. KAHLE

Account of the Restoration of An Old House, 1940, Shadows-on-the-Teche
Archives

Built in 1834 for sugar plantation owners David and Mary Conrad Weeks, the
Shadows was home to four generations of the Weeks family for 125 years until
the fourth-generation private owner died in 1958, leaving the house to the
National Trust, which opened the site in 1961. It was the last private owner, William
Weeks Hall, great-grandson of David and Mary C. Weeks, who very early
in his ownership of the property identified the importance of his family home as
an architectural survivor in a time when so many of the old plantation homes
were being destroyed through "neglect, termites, fire, or just bad restoration." In
the 1920s and 1930s, a great oil boom was taking place, and as Hall noted, "the
path of progress was every bit as destructive as the path of decay." While Hall
did not open the house to the public during his lifetime, he did occasionally open
the gardens to visitors. It was through his observation of these visitors that Hall
began to understand what people were looking for when they visited historic
sites. "[T]he interest is entirely in seeing how the people in these houses lived.
. . . Seeing old furniture in dozens of shops does not appease them in the least.
They want to see rooms intact and what they looked like when an older generation
lived in them. . . . To the public, the picture of the life is important."[1]

With this in mind, Hall left not only the house but also its contents to the
Trust, including family portraits from the 1840s, two extraordinary watercolors
depicting the Shadows in 1861, early photographs of the sugar plantation, clothing
worn by the planters and their enslaved labor force, and household furnishings.
Hall's bequest also included the Weeks family papers, consisting of more
than 17,000 documents: family letters, business correspondence, grocery receipts,
legal documents, inventories, and plantation papers. The papers had been collected
and stored in trunks on the third floor of the house, added to by each of
the four generations who called the Shadows home. These documents, recording
personal relationships and illustrating the concerns and activities of daily life on
the plantation, have been invaluable, as Hall recognized they could be, in providing
that "picture of the life" to the 25,000 people who visit the site every year.[2]

Presenting a "Picture of the Life"

"[T]o research and interpret through education programs a 19th century
southern Louisiana plantation economy and community and their evolution."
—Excerpt from the Shadows Missions Statement, 1992

294

From the earliest days of Trust ownership, the Shadows staff recognized the value of the collections, particularly the rich resource it had in the Weeks family papers. Over the almost forty years that the site has been open to the public, staff and volunteers have continually returned to that source, which serves as the basis for all site restoration and as the foundation for all of its education programs. These programs range from the site tour, experienced by daily visitors, to curriculum-based school programs in which more than 5,000 students participate annually.

All Shadows education programs emphasize the use of primary documentation in an attempt to present a myth-free "picture of the life." Response to the use of primary documentation and the interest it has created has been seen on all levels, from volunteer interpreters and members of the volunteer research team to area educators. The full-time staff consists of a director (who is also director of interpretation and collections), curator of education, administrative assistant, curatorial maintenance technician, and marketing director. The part-time paid staff includes eight interpreters and one maintenance assistant. Without the interest and support of volunteers and local teachers, the staff would be unable to present the quality and quantity of education programs that people have come to expect from Shadows-on-the-Teche. Their contributions are critical to the success of these programs.

For the first fifteen years that the site was open to the public, efforts were concentrated on completing the period room restorations, maintaining the gardens, cataloging the collections, and giving tours to an increasing number of visitors. During this period, the most fundamental education program, the public tour, was led daily by a small group of part-time staff guides. In the mid-1970s, the Trust hired the site's first museum professional as director, who, when faced with budget cutbacks, presented programs, highlighted by excerpts from the family papers, at local club meetings and attracted volunteers from the community to form the Shadows Service League in 1977. While these volunteers primarily helped with daily tours, it is no coincidence that the site's first school program, "Charley at the Shadows," was presented in December of that same year.

The Charley program was the beginning of a longtime partnership between the Shadows and the Iberia Parish schools. The participation of teachers and curriculum supervisors in program evaluation and development help ensure that site programs effectively meet curriculum goals. This relationship between teachers and staff resulted in a team of four teachers developing a five-day lesson plan in the early 1990s to strengthen the Charley program. Another outcome of the site/school partnership is that as they retire, an increasing number of these experienced educators are volunteers for museum education programs.

Five years after the Charley premiere, a second education program, "Dormers to Doorknobs," was created by a volunteer interested in architecture and concerned (much as Weeks Hall had been fifty years earlier) about the trend in the community to tear down older buildings in the name of progress. The Shadows first presented this program for fifth graders in 1983.

During the 1980s, the addition of a new staff member as programs coordinator allowed more time for research in the Weeks family papers, both by staff members and by a volunteer research team formed in 1989. Since that time, members of the research team have transcribed thousands of letters and read these same letters numerous times, each time pulling excerpts relating to a different topic including slavery, leisure, sickness and medicine, weather concerns, plantation operations, foodways, clothing, holiday celebrations, courtship and marriage, and transportation. This new research, combined with the enthusiasm of the new programs coordinator, resulted in stronger interpretive and education programs in the 1990s. The Shadows presented its first annual Civil War Encampment weekend (1988) and the first workshop for social studies teachers (1990, on slavery), and began offering special focus exhibit/tours such as "Expert at My Needle," about nineteenth-century ornamental and useful needlework (1991); "Coping with Climate" (1992); "Fear of the Sickly Season," about health and medicine (1993); "Weeks Hall Centennial Year" (1993–1994); and "Beautiful Sugar," about sugar plantation work and lifestyles (1995).

Throughout the 1980s, the site's education programs were essentially limited to the Charley program for first graders and the Dormers program for fifth graders. As at many house museums, efforts were concentrated on elementary students, but there were no organized programs at the middle or high school levels. In the late 1980s, the museum began a summer program for eighth and ninth graders, initially called Summer Interns, but now known as the Junior Interpreters program. Approximately fifteen students meet at the Shadows once a week for eight weeks during the summer to participate in different aspects of museum work and to learn how to give a site tour.

Another program for older students came about after a local educator became interested in a document display at the Shadows Community Day open house in 1991. Many of the documents are related to slavery on the Weeks sugar plantation. As she read the inventories and letters about enslaved persons who had lived and worked at the Shadows, she noted that very few African Americans were among the hundreds of people taking advantage of the highly publicized open house. Shortly thereafter, she contacted the Shadows staff to discuss the development of an education program utilizing the documents she had seen. The program she initially suggested was a mentor program involving retired teachers working after school at the Shadows with students from the Gifted and Talented Program to conduct research in the Weeks family papers.

A meeting between Shadows staff members and two educators from the Iberia Parish special education department to discuss development of the mentor program coincidentally took place just a few weeks prior to a National Endowment for the Humanities (NEH)-funded colloquium at the Shadows, which was attended by historians, museum educators, and interpretation specialists from across the United States. One of the participants was Dr. Rex Ellis, who suggested developing an education program centered on oral history and the study of the more recent past, rather than simply concentrating on slavery. "Even if programs which bring in minority audiences do not specifically fit into your period of interpretation," he said, "it is important to include them and to make these minority members of your community feel a part of the museum."[3] Based on his experiences at Colonial Williamsburg, he believed that the local African-American population's response to the education program would be more positive if a "whole story" approach was attempted, one that involved researching and presenting programs on the African-American experience in the community as it related to the more recent past, and across the 125 years of the site's history.

Now, twenty-five years after the site offered its first education program, Shadows annually presents three full-fledged education programs for school-children: "Charley at the Shadows" (first grade), "Building a Foundation" (fifth grade), and "Oral Traditions" (high school). All three of these programs are included in annual objectives for Iberia Parish teachers for the respective grade levels, and are evaluated by the curriculum supervisors to be sure the content of each program continues to support the objectives set by the state board of education.

In addition to these, the Shadows offers a variety of other programs for audiences of different ages. These include an annual storytelling event at Halloween, "Terror-on-the-Teche" (cosponsored with the parish library); the Civil War Encampment; Christmas Tour of Homes; and workshops and lectures on gardening, photography, and historic preservation.

The portion of the Shadows budget dedicated to education programs is approximately $50,000 (including portions of the salaries of all full-time staff, because they all are involved in programming efforts). This is roughly fourteen percent of the site's total operating budget. Additional funding comes from special project grants from organizations such as the Louisiana Endowment for the Humanities, and donations from local civic clubs and businesses. While all full-time staff members work on education programs to varying degrees, daily tours and presentations of the Charley or Foundations school programs depend on the help of many volunteers. In fact, the site's three school programs provide examples of the vital roles played by volunteers and the many other elements involved in bringing all programs to life and sustaining them with limited resources and staff, a condition common to many house museums throughout the United States.

Charley at the Shadows

"The Charley Program is a part of the Christmas season. Seeing the wonder in the children's faces as they tour the house is something I look forward to all year long."—Marie Steen, volunteer coordinator for the Charley Program, quoted in *Friends of the Shadows Newsletter*, Winter 1989

The initial idea for the Charley at the Shadows education program was borrowed from another house museum by one of its volunteers, who was also a member of the Shadows Advisory Council.[4] The original program was geared to first graders and was presented in December when the children visited the museum and heard about how Christmas was celebrated in earlier times. Shadows staff members and volunteers took this basic idea and made it Shadows-specific by turning to the family papers and building the program around young Charley Weeks (1831–1900). The resulting story discussed everyday life from Charley's point of view as a young boy in 1840. The story contrasts Charley's life by making comparisons with aspects of life that first graders understand and identify with: transportation (steamboats and carriages versus cars and buses), lighting (chandeliers and candles versus electric lights), heating (wood-burning fireplaces versus central heat or space heaters), school (schoolhouse and tutor in the backyard versus public and private elementary schools), and Christmas celebrations (candles in the tree versus strings of Christmas lights). The story focused on particular collections objects to support the storyline: mosquito netting on the beds, a tin bathtub, the dining room chandelier, horsehair upholstery on parlor furniture, a trundle bed, the plantation medicine chest, and period clothing.

Prior to visiting the Shadows, first-grade teachers read the Charley story to their class and the students made an old-time ornament for the Shadows Christmas tree with materials and patterns supplied by the Shadows Service League, the museum's volunteer organization. Over a five-day period, all parish first graders, approximately 1,500 students, visited the Shadows for a tour that emphasized collections objects and facts that supported the Charley story.

In the mid-1980s, as ongoing research continued to shed more light on individual family members and daily life on the plantation and in the Shadows household, the staff revised and updated the Charley story to reflect not only more in-depth information about Charley and his family, but also changes in the community that current first graders knew, such as the addition of a Wal-Mart store.

Adding a Living History Component

By the late 1980s, as the staff began to share more family papers with social studies teachers through teacher workshops and newsletters, evaluations from teachers for the Gifted and Talented (GT) Program and some of the first-grade teachers began to include suggestions that a living history component be added to the Charley program. The Shadows was fortunate to know a talented playwright in the community who volunteered his services in 1988 to write a script based on the site's primary documentation.[5] Discussions between teachers, staff, volunteers, and the playwright resulted in a script for two characters, Charley and his older sister Harriet, with four vignettes set at various points of the Shadows tour in which Charley or Harriet would describe aspects of their life in the 1840s. This new feature required planning meetings with the teachers of the GT Program, and additional time by staff members and volunteers constructing and caring for costumes and also scheduling and working with more than 100 GT student actors for rehearsals prior to the program.

By this time, the ten-year-old, familiar Charley program was a favorite with the many volunteer guides, some of whom had been helping with the program since it began. While the GT teachers and students were very excited and eager to add the living history elements to this established program, some of the volunteers found it difficult to adapt their "regular" tour to accommodate these changes. This is a natural development when changing what has become familiar to house museum interpreters and volunteers. In this case, however, the volunteers did not resist the changes because they did not like them, but just occasionally forgot the new routine, creating problems with tour flow and confusing the young actors. The Shadows staff notified volunteers well in advance that the program was changing and kept them abreast of new information via a monthly newsletter and training sessions, but a few years passed before everything worked smoothly. Ultimately though, as they became more familiar with the revised program, volunteers discovered they liked the changes and working with the costumed students, especially when they saw how much the first graders enjoyed meeting Charley.

Also, once the living history component was added, the direction of the program became more complex. It was now necessary to direct not only the first graders and the volunteer guides, but also several sets of actors. Due to the theatrical elements of the tour, timing became increasingly important. To ensure that each first-grade class only "met" one set of actors, only two classes could tour at one time. For the first ten or eleven years, the program had been almost entirely directed by a team of volunteer coordinators. The program changes required additional supervision, including two staff members monitoring the actors (one per set of actors performing simultaneously) and at least one volunteer supervising volunteer tour guides and directing group arrivals, tour flow, and departures.

On paper, classes are scheduled thirty minutes apart, but because of busing costs, lunch schedules, and driving distance from the school to the Shadows, it is usually necessary to have as many as four classes on site at the same time. At first, to occupy the classes not on tour, GT students not participating in the tour demonstrated period games in the side yard for the first graders. But not every GT teacher had extra students beyond the actors needed for the day, so eventually the staff developed an outdoor classroom with varying topics, depending on the staff member or volunteer doing the teaching: period games, plants, cemetery, or garden tour (avoiding areas where actors traveled). The only problem with this activity, which was originally meant to be a time killer for traffic control purposes, was that the outdoor classroom became so popular that first-grade teachers complained if their students didn't get to participate. In fact, after twenty-five years, the biggest complaint from teachers is still that they want more time on-site.

In 1992, the Charley and Harriet script was expanded to include Caroline and Riley, two enslaved children who were contemporaries of Charley and Harriet. As with Charley and Harriet, Caroline and Riley were taken directly out of the site's history, the Weeks family papers, and courthouse documents. Caroline and Riley were the children of Louisa, the head housekeeper, and her husband, Isaac. The script includes stories of bear hunts, Christmas frolics in the sugar house, and general observations about children's daily lives, taken for the most part directly from family letters of the pre–Civil War decades.

Collections Concerns

From the beginning of the Charley program, group size was frequently a problem, not so much because of the children, but because of the number of parents or grandparents who wanted to accompany the children on their visit to the Shadows. Large groups not only detracted from the quality of the overall experience for the first graders, but also greatly increased the risk of damage to the collections. After discussing this problem with school supervisors and the first-grade teachers, staff issued a letter restricting the number of chaperones per class. In addition to restricting the number of chaperones, the staff also made adjustments to the period room exhibits to allow more space for the first graders and to ensure the safety of the collections. For the duration of the Charley program, for instance, a daybed that normally is at the foot of the bed in the master bedroom is removed.

After GT students became involved, the parents of the actors wanted to come, not just to see the children perform but often to videotape the performances. This not only caused problems with group size, but also distracted the actors and the first graders. To make it possible for the parents to see and videotape their children without disrupting the program when the first graders were on tour, the staff began scheduling dress rehearsals for all GT classes the week before the actual program took place. Allowing more than one hundred actors to perform during these dress rehearsals occupies the time of at least one staff person for almost the full week between Thanksgiving and the Charley program, which begins on the first Monday in December.

Evaluation Process

The Shadows asks for written evaluations each year from the first-grade teachers, who, in turn, provide feedback from their students. Every teacher who visits the Shadows for Charley receives an evaluation form and return envelope to make participating in the evaluation process as easy as possible. Participating GT teachers and student performers also turn in written evaluations. The parish curriculum supervisor and the GT supervisor come to the site to experience at least one tour every year, and they too participate in the evaluation process by attending a meeting each January with the curator of education, other staff members, and volunteers to discuss the program and respond to the written evaluations received from the GT and first-grade teachers. Approximately twenty-five to thirty percent of the teachers return evaluations, with suggestions ranging from providing a simpler ornament pattern for the first graders to adding a living history component to having animals on the grounds. As stated earlier, evaluation recommendations led to the program being revised to include living history. Many simpler changes have also been made in response to suggestions by teachers, students, volunteers, and staff members.

It Takes a Community

The annual presentation of the Charley at the Shadows program is a collaborative effort for the whole New Iberia community: the site, the schools, local businesses, and volunteers. Schools take care of scheduling the first-grade classes, making bus arrangements, and distributing the schedule and previsit materials, with the elementary curriculum supervisor serving as coordinator. The museum's curator of education meets with GT teachers each fall to discuss the program, but the GT supervisor and the teachers themselves take responsibility for overseeing the auditions, ensuring that actors learn their lines, scheduling the GT performers, and distributing schedules and scripts.

The Shadows provides costumes, which are constructed and repaired by volunteers and laundered by staff members almost nightly to keep more than 100 actors in clean costumes over the eight-day period. For the four scenes performed both inside and outside the historic house, the museum also supplies props, including fishing poles, a bucket of goat's milk, a checkerboard, and even worms. Shadows staff and volunteers purchase, assemble, and distribute ornament kits to all first-grade classes. Staff and volunteers decorate the house with trees and greenery purchased and donated by local civic clubs and businesses. Two to three volunteer musicians donate their time to lead the first graders in singing carols. The museum's membership group, Friends of the Shadows, provides daily snacks for the actors and candy canes and Christmas cards for the first graders.

Every first grader in Iberia Parish participates in the Charley program, and depending on the number of first graders in the school system, anywhere from 1,300 to 1,800 students might visit the site over an eight-day period in December. In 2001, 141 GT students participated in the living history portion of the program.

Preparations for and presentation of the program require fifty volunteers, who give a total of 300 hours. Five full-time staff members manage scheduling, rehearsals, supervision of volunteers, and coordination of the daily program. They also give tours when needed, staff outdoor classroom activity, assist with costuming actors every morning, and do laundry, for a total of 250 hours.

During the program's first twenty-four years, 35,000 to 40,000 students experienced it. Since it became a multilayered program, more than 1,000 GT students have been involved. And of course, greater student participation increases the involvement of teachers and expands public awareness of the Shadows in the community, both by word of mouth (especially those of excited children) and by newspaper and television coverage.

Building a Foundation

> "Soon nothing will be left for the stranger to gaze upon to remind them of the deeds of our Ancestors."—Excerpt from "Building a Foundation" script

Although the Shadows is Greek Revival and Louisiana Colonial in style, the predominant architectural style represented in New Iberia is Victorian, most of the structures having been built in the late nineteenth century. The architecture of the Victorian period, therefore, is a natural focus for a program.

A First Attempt

For the site's first fifth-grade program, "Dormers to Doorknobs: The Outside Story," a volunteer wrote a script in which Queen Victoria and Alphé Charpentier, a Cajun carpenter-builder, discussed aspects of life in the Victorian age, and in particular reviewed building techniques in nineteenth-century Louisiana. A third person served as narrator for the program and introduced artistic concepts of line, shape, texture, color, and composition. The program was presented as a pilot to selected fifth-grade classes for one week in the fall of 1983, with volunteers and staff members portraying Alphé and Queen Victoria. The program was well received by the students and teachers. The next year the program was expanded to include all fifth graders in the parish, and professional actors were hired. To accommodate approximately 1,350 students, the one-hour program was presented three times a day for ten days. Prior to coming to the site, each student received a glossary of architectural terms that would be covered during the program.

Students spent approximately forty minutes in the museum's administrative/education facility interacting with the narrator in a brief overview of art and architecture, observing the play, and participating in a question and answer session directed by Alphé. Students were asked to point out architectural features (defined in their glossaries) using a Victorian dollhouse, parts of the stage set, and architectural elements in the room. For the final fifteen to twenty minutes, volunteers led the students one block down Main Street in the New Iberia Historic District, where, using checklists, the students identified Victorian architectural features on two houses. As a postvisit construction project, each student received a handout including pictures of different architectural features which could be cut out, colored, and glued together in any way each student chose when building their own Victorian house.

"Dormers to Doorknobs" was presented from 1983 through 1995, with only a few small changes based on annual evaluations by actors, teachers, volunteers, and staff. While it had some staunch supporters and got mostly positive feedback from teachers and students (except for a recurring complaint from both that the program didn't include a visit to the Shadows itself), actors and staff members (and later visiting evaluators during an NEH self-study) questioned the program's relationship to the site's mission, particularly the use of a Cajun carpenter and the presence of Queen Victoria, neither of whom had anything to do with the family who lived at the Shadows. The general consensus was that the Shadows wealth of documentation could support development of a stronger mission-based program, one more closely tied to the site's history as the home of a sugar planter's family that was an important part of the community's past for four generations.

Mission Accomplished

In 1995, the newly hired curator of education and a graduate intern began rethinking the fifth-grade program. Architecture and community history are subjects that tie directly into the Shadows mission of preservation and to the lives and interests of the four generations who lived there. The museum's staff hired the playwright who wrote the revised Charley scripts to write a script, covering the 1860s through the 1950s, that included one individual from each generation—two men and two women, with the four roles to be played by two actors. The result was a dramatic presentation giving an overview of community history from the perspectives of four Weeks family members representing four generations. Following this thirty-minute production, which begins the new program, students visit the site to conduct a survey of architectural and landscape features (fig. 14.1).

Selected fifth-grade teachers and the curriculum supervisor were involved in creating this education program, which not only more strongly supports the site's mission, but also is a better fit with fifth-grade curriculum requirements. Building a Foundation was first presented in the fall of 1996. Annual evaluations by staff, actors, volunteers, and teachers have resulted in several changes. Students wanted to go inside the Shadows, so the site survey now includes the dining room on the first floor where guides discuss architectural design in terms of function, specifically cross-ventilation.[6] Another change was the addition of benches so that the students no longer sit on the floor. The result is better attention, less fidgeting, and more control when the lights go down during the play.

Approximately 1,500 fifth-grade students participate in this program each fall when the program is presented three times a day over a ten-day period. The program requires two actors, two staff persons, and two volunteers per day (many fewer than the very labor intensive Charley program) and has been supported for several years by the local Optimists Club.

Oral Traditions

"Our history books tell us a few things about slaves and great leaders, but they don't get into the basics. What is the point of teaching history if you are only going to teach part of it?"—Entry in student journal, 1993

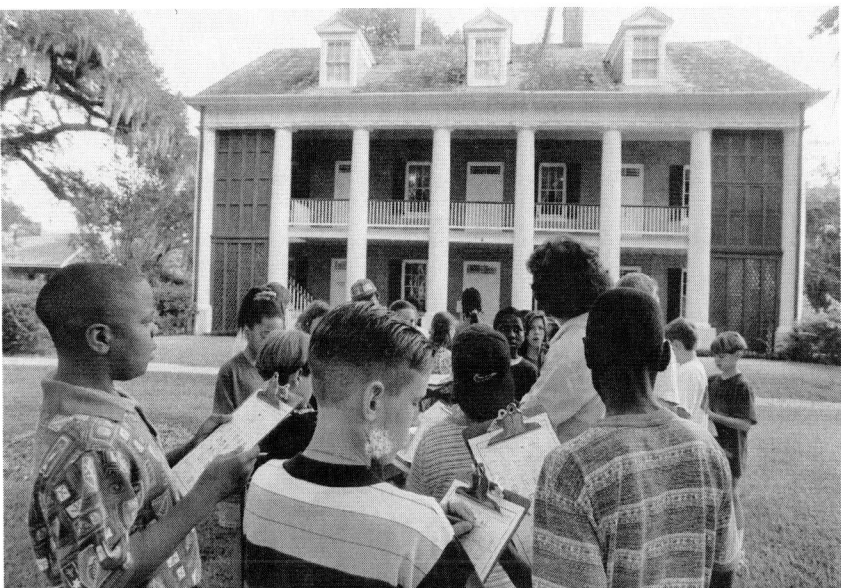

Figure 14.1. As part of the Building a Foundation program at the Shadows, fifth-graders survey the site's architectural and landscape features. Photograph by Lee Ball. Courtesy of the *Daily Iberian*.

In the spring of 1992, educators from the Iberia Parish Schools special education department met with the Shadows staff to produce a description of a program for high school students that would focus on African-American history in the community through the use of oral history. The class was to be presented at the high school level as an elective, and class size was to be limited to twelve students. Students would meet at New Iberia Senior High School three days a week, and two days at Shadows-on-the-Teche. The course objectives were: (1) to heighten student awareness of local African-American history through an oral history program in conjunction with a local museum, (2) to increase research skills through a variety of media, using oral historians, academic historians, museum professionals, and others, and (3) to investigate different avenues through which history can be studied and presented.

The Louisiana Board of Elementary and Secondary Education approved the class, and the museum first presented the pilot course, called "African-American Studies: Oral Traditions of the African-American Community in Iberia Parish," to students in the 1992–1993 school year. The students in this class study history in a nontraditional way. During the first several years there was no textbook for

305

the class, though staff members often asked students to compare standard history textbook accounts to the other sources used, such as period newspapers, oral histories, slave narratives, articles from periodicals, and videos. Each year the program features a series of speakers, including national and regional historians and community leaders, who meet with the class. The speakers of national note—such as Rex Ellis (then director of the Office of Museum Programs at the Smithsonian Institution), Dorothy Redford (director of Somerset Place and author of *Somerset Homecoming: Recovering a Lost Heritage*), and Lorraine Johnson Coleman (nationally acclaimed storyteller and author)—not only meet with the Oral Traditions class, but also present a teachers' workshop at the Shadows after school and a public program in the evening, which is frequently held off-site and hosted by a local, predominantly black congregation. Thirty-five to fifty teachers usually attend the in-service teachers' workshops, which last approximately one-and-a-half to two hours. The evening programs, which are offered free of charge, attract anywhere from fifty to a hundred or more people.

The teacher workshops and public programs have been a successful offshoot of the Oral Traditions class. The Shadows offers these workshops in partnership with the Iberia Parish school system, and the public programs are often collaborative efforts of the Shadows, the library, and the schools, which provide either space for the programs, funds, reception food, or audiovisual equipment. The Shadows rarely rents audiovisual equipment, as the library or the schools already have the necessary equipment and are more than willing to loan it to the Shadows for public programs.

As the title implies, a major component of this class involves learning the importance of oral history and learning how to conduct interviews. Many of the major speakers have talked with the students and their teachers about how to develop a list of questions, what equipment to use, and how best to ensure that the interview is a good productive experience for both interviewer and the interviewee. During the first year Oral Traditions was offered, the staff planned for each student to do two one-hour interviews. Students were then expected to transcribe the tapes, a painstaking process that can take as many as ten hours for a one-hour interview. This soon proved to be unrealistic, and the staff reduced the requirement to one one-hour interview. From the transcriptions, the students chose excerpts to be used as part of their final, which, rather than a traditional exam, was a public program presented by the class during National Preservation Week in May. Invitations were sent to everyone interviewed, students' families and friends, teachers, and community leaders.

The course introduces the students (often for the first time) to doing research with primary documents (such as the Weeks family papers), including plantation inventories of the 1830–1840s, business correspondence, family letters, and photographs. They also work with selected slave narratives from southern Louisiana, census records, courthouse records, and period newspapers. Using these materials, the students identify family groupings of up to three generations on the Weeks plantations. They also learn about the various skills and job assignments of specific African Americans who lived and worked on the site and who made the lifestyle portrayed in the period room exhibits possible.

On one of the first days that the class comes to the Shadows each year, students tour the site, often with one of the staff interpreters (with special behind-the-scenes tours to the cellar and the attic). At the end of the tour, one of the students in the 1994–1995 class declared that he thought he would make a good tour guide, so we decided to give the whole class a chance. Following the tour, we asked the students to think about what they had heard on tour, and asked if there was anything they wanted to know about the site's history that they had not heard. This discussion resulted in a list of questions, ranging from where the slaves were buried to whether or not they had pets. We then talked about how we might find answers to some of their questions, using the Weeks family papers or other sources. After identifying a series of tour stations, Shadows staff members worked with the students to develop tour information for each one and the students then selected their individual stations.

The resulting tour, called "The Living Foundation Tour," premiered the evening of May 6, 1995. The name of the tour comes from a quote from Weeks Hall, who said, "[T]he great houses followed the great crops: in Virginia tobacco, in South Carolina rice, in Mississippi cotton, in Louisiana sugar. Supporting it all, a living foundation, like a great column of blood, was the labor of the slaves."[7] The tour is not promoted as a public program; it is simply for the students' families and friends, and a small number of social studies teachers who evaluate the tour. Shadows interpretive staff and volunteers are also invited.[8]

Everyone who attended the tour on that first evening was asked to fill out an evaluation form. One of the questions asked guests to name four persons who had been important to the history of the Shadows. When the staff compiled the information, the names listed were evenly divided between the black and white persons associated with the site. Based on this, it was clear that the students' first attempt, though certainly not the definitive tour, truly presented a more "whole story" picture of life at the Shadows than museum interpreters had in the past.

With the implementation of the block system by the Iberia Parish Schools in 1999, the school programs now must cover in four-and-a-half months what they once covered in nine.[9] The Oral Traditions program had to be revised accordingly. Students now do just one thirty-minute interview and present a final program, which includes the Living Foundation tour and an exhibit highlighting what they studied during the semester. In the spring of 2001, the program included classes from two parish high schools, bringing to twelve the number of classes that have participated in the Oral Traditions program since it began. A third high school offered the class in the fall. The majority of students signing up for this elective class are African American. The Living Foundation tour and exhibit presented by the students as their final exam bring parents, grandparents, and other family members to the Shadows, many of them for the first time. The program not only has proven to be a strong education program, but also has served to increase public awareness of the site within the African-American community.[10]

However, the most important outcome of any education program is the impact it has on the students. Asked to reflect on what she had learned, one student wrote in her journal: "Since we read the letters and have now seen some of the artifacts which belonged to them [the slaves], I feel that I can relate to these people. Every time we learn something more of the slaves at the Shadows, I get a brighter picture of them. . . . I feel as if I know the people personally. To me it is like watching the soap operas or talking about what happened over the weekend."[11] Relating to people from the past. Getting to know them personally. In other words, for this student the Oral Traditions program had presented a brighter "picture of the life." This personalization of the past, which makes history not only interesting but also relevant, is the goal of all Shadows education programs.

People are interested in people. Education programs that successfully make history come alive for adults and children by using the house museum, primary documents, and collections objects to present a "picture of the life" will attract community participation and support. And for a historic house museum in a small community, with a small staff and a smaller budget, that is an important consideration. The hardworking staff at the Shadows could not develop, revise, and sustain its programs on its own. It is fortunate to have extensive primary documentation related directly to the site. It has also been inspired by program ideas at other sites. But the involvement of active and retired schoolteachers, dozens of eager volunteers, and various entities throughout the community (churches, libraries, businesses, and clubs—even the school system itself) has been and will continue to be central to the success and overall quality of educational efforts at the Shadows-on-the-Teche.

Notes

1. William Weeks Hall, "An Account of the Restoration of an Old House," 1940, Shadows-on-the-Teche Archives.

2. Documents in this collection—officially titled the "David Weeks and Family Papers"—date from 1782 through 1958. William Weeks Hall loaned the collection to Louisiana State University (LSU) in the 1930s, and the National Trust formally gave it to the university in 1984. It is part of the Louisiana and Lower Mississippi Valley Collections of the LSU libraries.

3. Rex M. Ellis, *Friends of the Shadows* newsletter (Spring 1993).

4. The house museum referred to is the Grevemberg House in Franklin, Louisiana, administered by the St. Mary Chapter of the Louisiana Landmarks Society.

5. The playwright was Raleigh Marcell who later joined the staff from 1989 through 1995, and who has been instrumental in expanding Shadows existing programming and developing new education programs.

6. The student evaluation for Building a Foundation is in the form of a report card allowing participants to grade and comment on various aspects of the program.

7. Weeks Hall, quoted in Henry Miller, *The Air-Conditioned Nightmare* (New York: New Directions Books, 1945), 97.

8. An interesting aside is that staff and volunteers truly found the tour to be a good learning experience and almost immediately began using information they heard on the Living Foundation tour in their own tours, which is certainly not always the immediate response to a more formal interpreter training session.

9. In the block system, the year is broken into two blocks or semesters, allowing students to take more credits in one school year. Class sessions are ninety minutes long compared with the sixty-minute classes of the old system, in which subjects were taught over the course of the entire nine-month school year.

10. As a direct result of the Oral Traditions program, Shadows staff was asked to participate in the organization of a Bunk Johnson Jazz Festival in 1997. In fact, the BunkFest board still meets at the Shadows.

11. Journal entry by Oral Traditions student, Jamilla, 1994.

INDEX

ABOUT THE AUTHORS

Bradley C. Brooks is director of Lilly House programs and operations at the Indianapolis Museum of Art. Previously, he served as director of the McFaddin-Ward House in Beaumont, Texas, and as curator, then museum director at the Moody Mansion and Museum in Galveston. He received a B.A. in communication arts from Elizabethtown College in Elizabethtown, Pennsylvania, and an M.A. in early American culture from the Winterthur Program of the University of Delaware.

Nancy E. Villa Bryk is curator of domestic life at Henry Ford Museum & Greenfield Village. She has directed the installation of more than a dozen historic buildings, including Noah Webster's 1835 home, the ca. 1882 Firestone Farmhouse, Amos Mattox's 1930 rural Georgia farmhouse, and Berry Gordy's ca. 1960 Motown Recording Studio and apartment. An adjunct professor in the historic preservation program at Eastern Michigan University, she also consults with museums on collecting strategies, program development, and historic house installation. She earned a B.A. in history and art history, an M.A. in American culture, and a graduate certificate in museum practice from the University of Michigan.

Patrick H. Butler III is a trustee of the Historic Alexandria Foundation in Alexandria, Virginia, and an independent consultant in museum and historical services. He has held various positions at Texas Tech University and Museum; the Office of American Studies at the Smithsonian Institution; the Institute for Museums, History, and Secondary Education at North Texas State University; the Harris County Heritage Society in Houston, Texas; and the Moody Mansion and Museum. He earned master's degrees from the Winterthur Museum, the University of Delaware, and Johns Hopkins University, where he also earned a Ph.D. in early American history.

Jamie Credle is director of museum education at the Stan Hywet Hall and Gardens, Inc., in Akron, Ohio. She previously served as education coordinator at the McFaddin-Ward House and as programs coordinator for the National Trust property Shadows-on-the-Teche in New Iberia, Louisiana. She has also held positions at the Cape Fear Museum, the Virginia Museum of Transportation, the Jekyll Island Museum, and the Museums at Stony Brook. She earned a B.A. in history and English literature from Salem College in Winston-Salem, North Carolina, and a master's degree in American history and public history from the University of North Carolina at Greensboro.

Jessica Foy Donnelly currently works with house museums and historic sites on collections and interpretation projects. Previously, she served as curator of collections at the McFaddin-Ward House, during which time she coedited *American Home Life, 1880–1930: A Social History of Spaces and Services* and *The Arts and the American Home, 1890–1930*. She also worked for Old Salem, Inc., in Winston-Salem, North Carolina. She received a B.A. in American studies and English from Salem College and an M.A. in history museum studies from the Cooperstown Graduate Program of the State University of New York at Oneonta.

Rex M. Ellis is vice president for the historic area at Colonial Williamsburg. He previously held positions at the Smithsonian Institution, first as director of the Center for Museum Studies and then as chair/curator of the division of cultural history at the National Museum of American History. Prior to that, he served Colonial Williamsburg for several years in various capacities, finally as director of the department of African-American interpretation and presentations. He received a B.F.A. from Virginia Commonwealth University, a master's degree in fine arts from Wayne State University, and a doctorate in higher education from the College of William and Mary.

Catherine Howett is professor emerita of landscape architecture and historic preservation in the School of Environmental Design at the University of Georgia. She served as a senior fellow in the studies in landscape architecture program of Dumbarton Oaks, a facility of Harvard University in Washington, D.C., from 1995 to 2001, and was the recipient of the 1998 Outstanding Educator Award from the Council of Educators in Landscape Architecture. She earned a B.A. degree at the College of New Rochelle (New York), an M.A. in English language and literature at the University of Chicago, and a Master of Landscape Architecture degree at the University of Georgia.

Patricia L. Kahle is director of Shadows-on-the-Teche, a National Trust for Historic Preservation property in New Iberia, Louisiana. She has also served the

Shadows as assistant director and as director of interpretation and collections. Previously, she was the assistant to the director at the Lycoming County Historical Society & Museum in Williamsport, Pennsylvania. She earned a B.A. in anthropology at Pennsylvania State University and did graduate work in history and museum administration at the College of William and Mary in Williamsburg, Virginia.

Meggett B. Lavin is retired curator of education and research for Drayton Hall, a National Historic Landmark and property of the National Trust for Historic Preservation in Charleston, South Carolina. The programs and materials she and the education, research, and interpretation staff created at Drayton Hall continue to inform best practices in the field and are featured in a number of publications, including *Great Tours! Thematic Tours and Guide Training for Historic Sites*. She earned a bachelor's degree in writing and literature from Wheaton College in Norton, Massachusetts.

Barbara Abramoff Levy is president of Barbara Levy Associates, providing interpretation planning and education consulting services to historic sites, history museums, and other history-related organizations. Coauthor of *Great Tours! Thematic Tours and Guide Training for Historic Sites*, she has held positions in interpretive planning with the Massachusetts Department of Environmental Management and was director of education and interpretation for the Society for the Preservation of New England Antiquities from 1989 to 1992. She earned a B.M. degree from the University of Michigan and M.M. and M.A. degrees from Boston University.

Sandra Mackenzie Lloyd is a museum consultant based in Philadelphia and coauthor of *Great Tours! Thematic Tours and Guide Training for Historic Sites*. She served previously as curator of education at Cliveden, a National Trust property, and as administrator and curator of Wyck, a historic house museum in Philadelphia. A graduate of Smith College with a degree in American studies, she also earned a master's degree from the University of Delaware's Winterthur Program in early American culture.

Valerie Coons McAllister worked at Old Sturbridge Village in Sturbridge, Massachusetts, where she managed all aspects of disability access for the site as assistant director of interpretation and as manager of visitor services and access. Previously, she was associate curator of education and access coordinator at the Winterthur Museum; she also held various staff positions at Colonial Williamsburg. She earned a B.A. in history at the State University of New York at Albany and an M.A. in history museum studies from the Cooperstown Graduate Program.

Margaret Piatt is president of Piatt Castles Co., Inc., in West Liberty, Ohio, where she is maintaining two 1860s limestone mansions as a private family history museum. She is also a museum education consultant currently working as living heritage artistic director at Carillon Historic Park in Dayton, Ohio. Previously, she served as assistant director of interpretation at Old Sturbridge Village and, in the education department, as museum teacher, assistant director, and associate director. She also taught in the education department and the museum studies certificate program at Tufts University. She earned a B.A. in secondary education from the University of Dayton and an M.A.T. in museum education from George Washington University.

Debra A. Reid is assistant professor in the history department at Eastern Illinois University. She has held other teaching positions at Texas A&M University, Baylor University, and the Cooperstown Graduate Program, and museum positions at the Governor Bill and Vara Daniel Historic Village, the Farmers' Museum Inc., the Patterson Homestead, Old World Wisconsin, the Washburn-Norlands Living History Center, and Henry Ford Museum & Greenfield Village. She earned a B.S. in historic preservation from Southeast Missouri State University, master's degrees from the Cooperstown Graduate Program and Baylor University, and a Ph.D. in history from Texas A&M University.